In No Uncertain Terms

HELEN SUZMAN

———

In No Uncertain Terms

———

MEMOIRS

Jonathan Ball Publishers
Johannesburg

Originally published in Great Britain in 1993 by
Sinclair-Stevenson an imprint of Reed Consumer Books Ltd

This edition published in 1993 by
Jonathan Ball Publishers (Pty) Ltd
PO Box 2105
Parklands 2121

ISBN 1 86842 001 9

Typeset by Deltatype Ltd, England
Printed and bound by Clays Ltd, St Ives Plc

Editor's note: in this book, upper case has been used for
Blacks and Whites, as well as Coloureds and Indians,
to conform with the publishers' house style.

To all the Progs
who over so many despairing years helped
to keep democratic values alive

Contents

List of Illustrations

John ('I am smiling') Vorster in Cape Town.
Same-size reproduction of a letter about Neil Aggett smuggled out of prison.
With the parents of Neil Aggett (*The* Star).

Between Pages 182 and 183

1983: celebration of the 30th anniversary of my becoming an MP (*I. Markman*, Cape Times).
1984: Mosie's 80th birthday.
1985: With my grandchildren.
Addressing the crowd at a mass funeral (*Times Media Ltd*).
Molly Blackburn, MPC.
With Black Sash observers.
Talking to residents of Oukasie (*Paul Weinberg, Afrapix*).
China, 1987.
Israel, 1988.
With Winnie Mandela at my home.
With Robin and Annie Renwick and Max Borkum.
With Colin Eglin.
With Zach de Beer.
With Ray Swart.
With Chief Buthelezi (*The* Argus, *Cape Town*).
With Alan Paton at a book launch in Johannesburg (*Times Media Ltd*).
With Harry Oppenheimer (*Times Media Ltd*).
With Margaret Thatcher outside No. 10 Downing Street (*Associated Press*).
Oxford University: with Harold Macmillan and Sir John Maud.
Warwick University: with Janet Suzman.
Outside Buckingham Palace, after the conferment of the DBE, 1989 (*The Press Association Ltd*).
Visiting Nelson Mandela shortly after his release from 27 years in prison (*Associated Press*).

Foreword

by Nelson Mandela,
President of the African National Congress

Helen Suzman's autobiography is not only a journey through a remarkable political life, but has provided us with a unique insight into the struggles that have taken place in White politics.

The book also depicts the powerful political presence that Helen Suzman is and as I read through each chapter I was reminded of my first encounter with her. I was having a consultation in Pretoria Prison with Bram Fischer QC, the leader of the South African Communist Party, in 1963. We were preparing for the Rivonia Trial.[1] Bram got up and whispered almost in reverence as a woman passed in the corridor, 'Helen Suzman' – significant coming from a man whose political views would not normally lead him to respect a liberal.

Over the years that I spent on Robben Island and in Pollsmoor Prison as a political prisoner I came to know Helen Suzman very well and to understand her forthrightness and political astuteness.

This book relives a magnificent battle against apartheid. Without apologising for her using the South African parliamentary process, Helen's participation in opposing the complete absence of democracy in South Africa under Nationalist Party rule must be applauded.

This book provides extraordinary historical facts and a succinct account of the political processes contained within the apartheid machinery. I recall that on one of her many visits to Robben Island I engaged Helen on the subject of beginning a process for the early release of all the political prisoners. In 1915, Afrikaner rebel leader Christiaan de Wet had been released before he had served his full sentence for having committed high treason. I told her that his crimes had been more serious than the collective crimes of any individual serving a life sentence after the Rivonia Trial. He had been responsible for the deaths of 300 people and the military occupation of several areas in the Orange Free State. He had also caused damage to government property amounting to more than half a million pounds. I felt that the Rivonia trialists had been sentenced to life for struggling against apartheid rule without the benefit of any privilege of access to the machine of government, as had de Wet.

She replied in the tone that this book suggests of her strength and her complete understanding of the strategies of the Nationalist Party government. She said to me, 'There is a vast difference between your case and that of de Wet. The government could afford to release de Wet because his rebellion had been crushed. Yours is in the future.'

I believe that this book should be read by all interested in South Africa as a political history and as an account of the political courage of a remarkable South African woman.

Nelson Mandela,
South Africa,
1993

Prologue

Race discrimination and exploitation, in the style of all colonial countries, was accepted custom in South Africa for decades before the National Party came to power in 1948. Thereafter, the traditional practice was codified and extended under the title *apartheid*.

When I became a Member of Parliament in 1953, the National Party government had already laid the foundations of what was to become the most racially defined society in the world, in which Whites and Blacks were segregated by laws covering every aspect of their lives. The Race Classification Act of 1950 determined the status in life of each person born in South Africa; children of different races were forced to attend separate schools; certain jobs were reserved for Whites only. The rights of ownership and occupation of South Africa's land and property were defined on racial lines, as was the use of all public amenities – separate but unequal. Sex and marriage across the colour line were forbidden. The right to vote was virtually a White privilege. By and large, the relationship between White and Black was that between master and servant.

This book describes my part in opposing the evolution of this bizarre system and its manifestly drastic and unjust consequences. I used Parliament to expose the tragic effects of these laws on millions of South Africans. I tried to keep alive the democratic values which were systematically eroded by apartheid. Parliament offered me almost unlimited opportunities to play this role, despite the fact that I never belonged to a party in power. Indeed for thirteen years I was the sole representative in Parliament of the only party espousing a policy which rejected race discrimination.

It is perhaps ironic that a government as authoritarian as that of the National Party had a deeply rooted respect for the parliamentary system which provided me with a forum to challenge their policies and elicit information. This ensured that I had many opportunities as an elected MP to highlight the evils of the apartheid system, to present alternative policies and to disseminate them through the parliamentary press gallery.

I took advantage of my status as an MP to gain access to many places out of bounds to the general public, such as prisons, Black townships and 'resettlement areas' in the Black rural homelands (or 'Bantustans' as they were called). I put into practice my conviction that, to speak with authority, one must see for oneself.

I do not claim any credit for the remarkable changes that have been introduced in South Africa over the last few years. I can only say, to paraphrase Theodore Roosevelt, that I did what I could, where I was, with what I had.

1

The Background and Beyond

As I write these memoirs, South Africa is enduring an unprecedented wave of violence which started in 1984. It is the violence caused by political organisations vying for power in the run-up to a new government; it is the violence promoted by members of the security forces and of a suspected right-wing 'third force' strongly opposed to change; and it is also criminal violence unrelated to political unrest, caused by mounting joblessness and poverty. Together, these forms of violence have accounted for the deaths of more than 100,000 people over the past eight years.

Another form of violence, however, ravaged South Africa long before the present trauma of political transition. During the 1969 session of the South African Parliament, I listened with disbelief to boasts from the government benches that our country was enjoying peace and quiet [rus en vrede] while other countries were gripped by violence. I did not agree, as I said in a debate in the House of Assembly:

> There is another interpretation to violence, apart from the violence against the state, riots or attempts to overthrow the state. In its broader sense, violence can also mean the unfettered use of power by the state against a citizen, so as to deprive him of his normal civil rights. In this sense we have a great deal of violence in South Africa. Mass removals of African people from their homes is a violence . . . the thousands upon thousands of Africans in resettlement areas, leading hopeless and helpless lives of poverty and unemployment, is a violence; the very way in which those removals have taken place is a violence – these people were removed without any proper planning having been done for housing, health, education, medical services. The destruction of the

Coloured community [South African term for people of mixed race] in District Six is a violence. The uprooting of Indians from cities and dorps [small towns] is a violence. The Pass Laws[1] are a violence . . . I say that the pass raids are a violence. I say that uprooting people at dawn or on a wintry evening in a shanty town, and bundling women and children into police vans is a violence . . . I say that the fact that we are turning something like a half a million people per year into statutory criminals in this country is a violence. The malnutrition and infant mortality rate in a rich country like South Africa are a violence. The denial of collective bargaining rights and the low wages that result are a violence. No strikes, says the government proudly, ignoring the fact that African trade unions are not recognised and that strikes are a criminal offence. I say that all the powers that circumvent the normal civil liberties are a violence. Banning, house arrests, detention without trial, banishment, are all a violence.[2]

The Minister of Bantu Administration, M. C. Botha, interjected: 'You are violating your liberty' and another Nationalist MP, J. K. Henning, commented bitterly: 'You want to sell us on a tray'. This was mild comment compared to the verbal abuse and threats that usually came my way during my thirty-six years in Parliament – especially during my thirteen years as the lone Progressive Party MP.

'Mau Mau', bleated one MP every time I rose to speak. Dubbed a 'sickly humanist' or a dangerous subversive, I was frequently urged to 'go back' to Moscow, or to Ghana, or to Israel.

In fact, I came from none of those places.

I was born in Germiston, a little mining town just outside Johannesburg, on the day of the Russian Revolution of 7 November 1917.

The Gavronsky brothers, my father Samuel and his brother Oscar, emigrated from Klykoliai, a *shtetl* [small Jewish village] on the border of Lithuania and Latvia at the turn of the century. They left for the usual reasons: to avoid the draft of twenty-five years' service in the tsar's army, to escape the pogroms and to seek a better life than that of restricted opportunities which Russia offered to Jews. They were very poor on arrival and knew neither English nor Dutch, the two main languages spoken by Whites in South Africa at that time. The country was still recovering from the drastic effects of the Anglo-Boer War. The 'Native question' was far less significant than the continuing hostility between British and Boers. The Gavronsky brothers went to the Witwatersrand, the burgeoning area to which a large number of immigrants had been attracted after the discovery of gold in 1886. The South African economy was almost entirely based on the primary sectors of agriculture and mining, and Johannesburg, the largest town on the Witwatersrand, was still only a mining camp.

The brothers were enterprising men and soon established themselves in business, originally buying cattle then setting up as wholesale meat dealers and using every part of the animal: the skins, the hides, the bones, the hooves, the tallow, the lot. Oscar, the elder brother, attended to the cattle buying and acquired the reputation of being able to estimate the total weight of a pen of animals to the nearest ten pounds. Sam was the financial brain of the partnership, which prospered. Like many Jews who emigrated to South Africa, they eventually invested in land and property; they also acquired a soap factory. My father harboured an ambition to put Lever Brothers out of business – in vain.

The two brothers married two sisters, my mother Frieda and Hansa David, also emigrants from villages in Eastern Europe, who had settled in Kimberley, the town on the border of the Cape Province which had also attracted many fortune seekers from overseas after the discovery of diamonds in 1868.

I never knew my mother. She died after I was born; she was twenty-eight years old.

My father, my sister Gertrude, who was then nearly five years old, and I, lived with Oscar and Hansa, who were childless. Nobody in the family ever spoke to me about my mother. I think it was too painful a subject for my father, and my aunt was too reserved to broach it. I first saw a photograph of my mother when I was fifty-five years old. My aunt Hansa died in 1972 and while sorting through her belongings, I came across a photograph of my father as a young man seated on a chair: next to him with her hand on his shoulder was a young woman – Frieda, my mother.

When I was about five the family moved to Berea, then a lower-middle-class suburb of Johannesburg. The household also included the two teenage orphaned daughters of another David sister. Auntie Hansa was a very introverted woman, probably deeply affected by her own childlessness in a household consisting of other people's children. Each afternoon she retired with a bandage soaked in vinegar over her forehead to relieve her headaches, apparently brought on by her domestic responsibilities. Nevertheless, she resented our leaving her when my father eventually remarried.

My abiding memory of that period of my childhood is of the absence of books in the Berea house. The minute I was functionally literate, which was probably at the age of six or seven, I longed to read. I would run around the house looking for something to read, but found nothing other than newspapers and the *Zionist Record*. Those years were not marked by any physical deprivation, but there was an obvious absence of maternal affection. Perhaps that engendered in me the strong spirit of independence which persists to this day.

When I was nine and my sister was thirteen, my father remarried. His second wife was Debbie, an English-born divorcee. Debbie was an expansive hostess and she and Sam lived a full social life. He enjoyed his poker and bridge (three no trumps was his favourite bid, partner notwithstanding). They were a gregarious pair and loved entertaining. Debbie's enthusiasm for beautiful possessions introduced a new dimension into my life. We moved into a sprawling old stone house in the suburb of Parktown, built by the famous English architect Sir Herbert Baker, with a large garden shaded by huge oak trees, and a tennis court. I loved the house, though it was freezing in winter, as it faced south (Had Sir Herbert forgotten he had crossed the equator?).

Family life had more than its fair share of tensions, with Pa, himself no model of equanimity, trying to cope with warring females. Debbie and Gertrude never got on together. Gertrude married at eighteen and left home, but she subsequently joined our father in running his different enterprises and became a competent businesswoman.

Like Jewish immigrants the world over, my father believed a good education for his children was essential. Private schools in South Africa were thought to be the best. As Anglican schools in those days were reluctant to take Jewish children, and Catholic schools more willing, Gertrude and I were sent to Parktown

Convent in Johannesburg, where to my great joy I found a well-stocked library.

After I matriculated at sixteen, I went to the University of the Witwatersrand where I began studying for the degree of Bachelor of Commerce, with the intention of taking a post-graduate law degree. My time at university was carefree and wholly enjoyable. I was a keen participant in innumerable faculty dances, which may have been one of the contributory factors to my failure in the exams at the end of the third year. I also went on two student tours overseas. Each jaunt cost my father only £100, for the return voyages from Cape Town to Southampton on Union Castle liners and for accommodation in London, Paris, Zermatt, Rome and Venice. Bliss for a young South African who had never before left her native shores. I longed to remain in London after the second tour ended and finish my degree there. But Pa said 'No'.

So back I came to Wits, dropped out before I graduated, and married.

What did my school, home and early university education contribute to my subsequent career? At the convent, teaching by rote was the main method used by the nuns, and I have a very good memory as a result. We were taught to be punctual ('other people's time is as valuable as your own') and conscientious. To this day, when I shirk something I know I ought to do, the ghost of Sister Columba, the head nun, whispers in my ear 'Do it, child', and I do. We also learned to be bad losers because, unless we won at games, we would be severely chastised by Sister Columba. And that probably was very good training for me in politics. There is no point in losing an election in South Africa, for there is no second prize in our 'first past the post' electoral system.

One day in 1966, more than thirty years after I had left school, I received a phone call. A soft Irish voice said, 'May I speak to Helen, please?' I replied, 'Hello Sister Columba,' and she exclaimed, 'Lord love us, child – you recognised my voice!' She told me the nuns were all praying for me as the next election was about to take place.

I doubt whether the nuns had any influence on my subsequent interest in race relations or concern for simple justice. We were taught manners and to be polite to everybody, irrespective of colour, but I had the typical South African upbringing of a White child in the city, having no contact whatsoever with Black people other than the Black domestic staff at home and at the convent. (It was only years later that I was struck by the incongruity of my writing 'specials' night after night authorising our domestic adult male employee to be away from our house after the nine o'clock curfew. The permit would read, 'Please pass bearer Jim to town and suburbs to return at eleven p.m.', and it would be signed by me, aged twelve.) There were no Black children at Parktown Convent, and certainly there was no socialising across the colour line (today the school is co-educational, the head teacher is a man and the vast majority of the scholars are Black).

My later concentration on race relations has been confidently ascribed by several rabbis to the influence of the 'Jewish ethos'. If so, it was subconscious, for there was not much emphasis on Jewish philosophy or religion at home, although we lit candles on Friday nights and had large gatherings for the Jewish festivals. My father and stepmother attended synagogue on the High Holy days. I did not. Nevertheless, there can be no doubt that the Jewish experience of persecution heightened my awareness of the evils of race discrimination.

Neither Debbie nor my father was imbued with liberal ideas. If anything, my father had a rather contemptuous attitude towards anyone who didn't succeed, irrespective of colour, since he was a self-made man. He had worked very hard, and made his own way in the world, and he couldn't understand why other people couldn't do the same. To his mind, they had to be lazy or stupid. I tried in later years, when we had many political arguments, to point out that the Blacks in South Africa were subjected to many of the restrictions which he, as a Jew, had suffered in Russia, such as those on mobility and other discriminatory laws. But this argument didn't impress him. He could never really understand why I bothered about the condition of Blacks in South Africa. But to his credit, apart from saying 'What do you want it for?' when I stood for nomination for Parliament, he never tried to dissuade me from entering politics, and indeed in 1958, when I was hesitating about standing for re-election, his comment was, 'Why not? you are doing well', though he was uneasy about my voicing liberal opinions.

On one occasion, when I was overseas, I received a letter from a friend in South Africa telling me there had been an article in the local press saying that 'Mrs Suzman's father had given £500 to Dr Verwoerd's Scholarship Fund'. On my return, I was met at the airport by Debbie. 'Where's the old boy?' I asked grimly. 'Too scared to come,' she replied. When I saw him at home I congratulated him on his generosity to my arch enemy, the Prime Minister, and suggested he write out a cheque for the same amount for the Progressive Party to which I belonged. Meek as a lamb, he complied. My stepmother said later, 'You were very hard on him. He did it only because he thought it would protect you.' Since he did not support Verwoerd's Nationalist government, that may well have been the case.

However, my father was no admirer of General Smuts either; he never forgave him for supporting the Aliens Act introduced by General Hertzog in the 1930s, which severely limited the entry into South Africa of German Jews anxious to escape from Nazi persecution. But then, he regarded the entire political spectrum in South Africa with disdain: Nationalists, United Party and Progressive Party. I often wondered if he voted for the Progressive Party at elections, or simply spoiled his ballots. His lack of regard for its politicians was not, however, reflected in his intense patriotic feeling for South Africa. Whenever I asked him, in moments of despair, why he had not emigrated to America when he left Lithuania, he firmly proclaimed South Africa was the best country in the world.

On another occasion I addressed a public meeting in the Parktown constituency where Debbie and my father lived, and she took him to the meeting. A resolution was put pledging the audience to work for the end of racial discrimination and for South Africa's return to the Commonwealth, which it had left under Verwoerd when it became a republic in 1961. The resolution was passed unanimously, but old Sam Gavronsky said that was only because he was too tired to lift his arm to vote against it!

Although my father and I had many an argument about politics and race relations, he had a wonderful sense of humour and when I made him laugh, the battle was won. He was, however, a most litigious man. After his death his lawyers sent for Gertrude and me, who were his executors. They informed us that our father had several law suits on the go, every one most unlikely to succeed. When told this by his lawyers Gavronsky had roared, 'Sue the bastards!' Gertrude and I promptly settled the cases out of court.

Perhaps one of his most endearing characteristics was his love of animals. He used to set off for work each morning, sitting on the front seat of the car next to his Black driver, and on the back seat were his two dogs who spent the day with him at his office. When he returned home, he lavished affection on his cats.

I inherited three things from my father: his stamina, his love of animals, and his enjoyment of a Scotch and soda in the evening – that is, apart from the generous bequests in his will. He died of a heart attack in 1965, aged eighty; Debbie, indefatigable to the end, was eighty-seven when she died suddenly in 1987, elegantly dressed for a bridge party.

I was nineteen when I married Mosie Suzman in 1937. He was thirty-three, an eminent physician from a well-known Jewish family in Johannesburg.

I was now part of a big family, because Mosie had four brothers and three sisters. We lived first with his eldest sister, younger brother and two nephews in a big house, also in Parktown, to which people repaired at all hours of the day and night. Mosie and I had a great time, both being fond of dancing and horse-riding. Once I jocularly said I had married Mosie because he had a horse I coveted. A surprising number of people took this remark seriously.

Later we built our own home at Northcliff – on a high ridge with a superb view of the distant Magaliesburg mountains – and moved in there. I led the life of a privileged young White South African housewife during that period – the only time I ever reverted to type!

I had my first child in September 1939, a few weeks after the start of the Second World War. The arrival of my daughter, Frances, put a brake on my keen desire to participate in the war effort. The popular and much respected Professor Hansi Pollak, who had been my Economic History lecturer at the university, was then second in command of the Women's Auxiliary Force in South Africa. I rushed off to her and said, 'I want to join up.' She asked, 'Haven't you just had a baby?' 'Yes, I have.' She said, 'Well, go home and look after it.'

I was most upset about being excluded from war service and decided that if I couldn't get into the army, I was at least going to complete my degree. So I went back to Witwatersrand University, combined my unfinished subjects into one year, studied hard and passed them all, receiving two first classes in my major subjects.

The knowledge of 'Native Law and Administration' I gained from Professor Julius Lewin during that year was to stand me in good stead in the future. I now had a qualification, Bachelor of Commerce, and I made another attempt to join up. This time I was accepted in a special capacity, not in the army proper but at the War Supplies Board, which tried to track down war profiteers, a boring but essential job, at which I worked for the duration of the war.

Meantime Mosie had joined the South African Medical Corps. I was pregnant with our second child, Patricia, who was born on 1 January 1943, after Mosie went 'Up North' to Egypt, where he was the second in command of the medical section of 106 South African General Hospital at Qassasin for about two years. He was posted to a military hospital just outside Johannesburg when he returned from Egypt, and after he was demobilised, he went back to private practice, later becoming senior physician at the Johannesburg General Hospital. (Many expatriate doctors have accosted me on overseas visits and told me they had learned all their medicine while working in Ward 11 at the General under Mosie.)

At the end of the war I sold the Northcliff house and bought some land just north of Johannesburg. It was an agricultural holding, off an untarred road. After Mosie was demobilised we built a house there. It was much closer to the school the girls were to attend, and also more accessible to the hospitals Mosie visited and to the suburbs where most of our friends lived. We called the house 'Blue Haze', as, in those unbuilt-up days, the valley we overlooked always had a beautiful morning mist. We have lived at 'Blue Haze' ever since, but today the property is very much part of the urban spread of Johannesburg. I never actually resided within the nearby constituency of Houghton which I represented in Parliament for so many years.

★

In 1945 I was offered and accepted a tutorship in Economic History at Wits University by the erudite and brilliant Professor Herbert Frankel, who in my final year taught me everything I know about economics and the art of analysing cause and effect. After he left Wits, Herbert Frankel had a most distinguished career at Oxford University, where he occupied the Chair of Economics of Underdeveloped Countries at Nuffield College. My tutorship job expanded into a lectureship which I held until I stood for nomination for Parliament in 1952. Those years of teaching the economic history of South Africa were to prove enormously useful to me when I became an MP, for they provided a solid background on which to base my speeches and developed my skills in researching source material.

An interesting assortment of students attended my lectures at Wits, many of whom have since had distinguished careers in South Africa and abroad: John Maree, chairman of South Africa's huge parastatal power company Eskom, and chairman of Nedbank, one of the country's leading banks; Derek Keys, former chairman of Genkor and now Minister of Finance and of Trade and Industry; Advocate Arthur Chaskalson, head of the Legal Resources Centre; Sir Mark Weinberg, founder of Abbey Life Insurance in the UK; Sir Sydney Lipworth, head of the Monopolies and Mergers Commission, also in the UK; and Charles Feinstein, Professor of Economic History and Fellow of All Souls, Oxford.

Two of my ex-students pursued spectacular careers in their different fields of endeavour: Joe Slovo, once exiled, who later returned as leader of the South African Communist Party, and Eduardo Mondlane, who became head of Frelimo, the Mozambique Liberation Army.

In 1962 when I was in the United States as a guest of the State Department, I addressed a seminar at the Columbia University School of International Studies. In the group, I noticed a Black man who smiled whenever I caught his eye. I thought, I know him. He is an African, not an American – where have I met him before?

After my talk he approached me: 'You don't remember me, do you? I am Eduardo Mondlane and I was in your Economic History class at Wits.'

I said, 'Now I remember you – you wrote the best essay on the "poor White problem" I ever marked.'

'You gave me an A,' he reminded me with a grin.

'What are you doing here?' I asked.

'I've been teaching at Syracuse University, but now I am going back to Mozambique to drive the Portuguese out of there. And then,' he added with another grin, 'I will go to South Africa to drive the Whites out of there too.'

'Not so easy,' I replied.

Frelimo did eventually drive the Portuguese out of Mozambique, but Mondlane did not live to see it because he was blown up by a letter bomb while on a visit to Tanzania.

During the eight years I spent teaching at Wits, I became interested in politics. I joined the South African Institute of Race Relations and became a member of its Executive Council. It was there that I got a broader background about the disabilities of South African Blacks. At the committee meetings the main subject of discussion was always the treatment of Blacks under South Africa's discriminatory laws, and I learned a great deal there from others who had been working in this field for several years. But before and during the Second World War, I was much more concerned about the defeat of Nazism than about the disabilities of Black South Africans. Thus I was a late starter in the field of race relations, but once I got going, I became utterly preoccupied with it.

In 1933, General Jan Smuts's South African Party and General J. B. M. Hertzog's National Party fused to become the United South African National Party (later known as the United Party). In 1939, the Fusion government broke up, because Hertzog opposed Smuts's motion to take South Africa into the war on the side of the Allies. Smuts's motion was carried by thirteen votes; Hertzog resigned from the cabinet, joined the Reformed National Party and went into opposition. Soon afterwards, much disillusioned, he left politics, and the more militant Dr D. F. Malan replaced him as leader of the official opposition. In 1943, the United Party under Prime Minister Smuts won a general election with a handsome majority.

In 1946 Smuts appointed a commission under Judge Henry Fagan to examine the laws applying to Blacks in the urban areas. Smuts was no liberal, but he was a man of great intellect, and he recognised that the restrictions imposed on Blacks before the war were unlikely to endure now that the war had ended. Pass Laws and Influx Control, which severely restricted the mobility of Blacks and especially their entry into urban areas, had been suspended for the duration to obtain Black labour to sustain the war effort. The South African ports of Cape Town and Durban were important places of supply for the troop ships on their way from Britain to the Middle East, and secondary industry expanded greatly during the war years as the demands of the South African Defence Force had to be met. Local products were substituted for scarce imported goods. All this required the increased use of Black labour.

The hundreds of thousands of Blacks who flocked into the cities during the war, therefore, were not only migrant workers who had came from the so-called Native Reserves, leaving their families behind in the rural areas; now the families came as well to reside permanently in the urban areas, despite the appalling lack of proper accommodation. The existing Influx Control Laws were based on the principle laid down by the Stallard Commission of 1922 – that Natives (as they were then called) could come into the urban areas to serve the Whites, but should depart when their services were no longer required and return to the Native Reserves, the rural areas set aside for their exclusive occupation and ownership by the Land Act of 1913 (later extended in 1936). The entire structure and use of labour had therefore been based on a migratory system.

Smuts saw the necessity of holding a judicial enquiry into the changes to the laws which the post-war situation demanded.

The Institute of Race Relations asked me, together with Ellison Kahn, also a lecturer at Wits and later Professor of Law, to prepare evidence to submit to the Fagan Commission. It took us about six months, and during that time I learned a great deal more about the severe restrictions on the mobility of South African Blacks and the difficulties they had in leading family lives and earning a living. I was appalled. It was this experience that brought me into politics.

The Fagan Commission, reporting early in 1948, conceded that conditions had altered fundamentally and that the laws had to be changed. Its recommendations, however, did not go so far as the repeal of the Pass Laws advocated by the Institute of Race Relations. Perhaps the essence of the Fagan Commission Report was its simple phrase, 'We need them and they need us.' The Commission concluded that the flow of Blacks to the urban areas could be regulated, but not stopped, and it acknowledged the 'push factor' of rural poverty among Blacks and the 'pull factor' of job opportunities in the urban areas. It accordingly recommended that the pervaded urbanisation of Black people be recognised and catered for in law – an important change in principle.

General Smuts accepted the recommendations of the Fagan Commission, but then came disaster: the May 1948 general election.

On the night of the election I was attending a play in the Great Hall at Wits University when the news broke: Smuts had lost his seat. The hall emptied instantly and we streamed downtown to watch the election barometer which had been erected there. It soon became evident that Smuts's United Party government was defeated and that the National Party was in. Utter gloom pervaded our group. I thought despairingly: We will never get the Nats out.

That prediction held good for more than forty years.

As I have already said, race discrimination and segregation were practised in South Africa as part and parcel of the colonial system in Africa and everywhere else where White rule prevailed. But from 1948, when the National Party government came to power (with a majority of five seats, thanks to a coalition with 'Klasie' Havenga's small Afrikaner Party, which had won nine seats in addition), legal enforcement of race segregation dominated every aspect of life in South Africa – political, economic, educational and social. The new government promptly rejected the recommendations of the Fagan Commission and returned to the old Stallard dictum based on the migratory labour system, a policy which the National Party implemented relentlessly from then on.

Smuts lost the election largely because he was misled by his lieutenants, who told him only what they believed he wanted to hear. He was therefore under the impression that his support was undiminished. Although he had won the 1943 election during the war with a big majority, in 1948 he lost even his own parliamentary seat. Substantial sections of the White electorate were thoroughly dissatisfied with many aspects of government after the war ended, and decided they would 'teach Smuts a lesson' by voting against United Party candidates. They did not, however, envisage putting him out of power. What Smuts did not appreciate was the degree of discontent among the returned soldiers as well as in the country as a whole, and that the National Party had gained considerably in organisational strength and unity. Moreover – a most important factor contributing to his defeat – Smuts stubbornly refused to amend the law that loaded the urban seats (where the United Party had most support) with disproportionately more voters than the rural seats.

The election upset brought in a radically different government. The Nationalists had backed Germany during the war, proclaiming that they were anti-British rather than pro-Nazi, but none could doubt the support for Nazism among Afrikaners throughout that period. Many had been interned for belonging to subversive, anti-war organisations, and one such, John Vorster, later became the Prime Minister of South Africa.

I was extremely uneasy at the prospect of such a government taking power, and wondered whether we should leave South Africa. I was sure that Mosie, with his qualifications and post-graduate experience, would find a good job or could open private practice in either Britain or the United States. But he was very attached to his family in South Africa and well established in his profession. I had other reservations about leaving: I enjoyed my job at Wits, and we had two young children who were settled at school. Also I had excellent domestic help who attended to all the chores I hated. And I couldn't cook! I envisaged a chaotic household and a starving family. The natural beauty of the country was another compelling reason for staying in South Africa – its wonderful climate, the opportunities for playing golf and tennis, the magnificent beaches and its incomparable game parks. In short, the sunny comforts of South Africa proved too good to leave. And within a short time after the election, politics had ensnared me and I was firmly committed to remain, despite my misgivings and some occasional second thoughts over the years.

Many other South Africans, however, left for foreign parts during the next four decades, often after crises such as the Sharpeville massacre of 1960 and the Soweto riots of 1976. As I told the Nationalists in Parliament, one of the greatest indictments against the government was that its oppressive race policy had driven thousands of South Africans out of the country, among whom were some of our best educated and most talented young people, including 'Coloured' (mixed race) professionals, teachers and nurses, whose expertise was being used elsewhere than in South Africa. The reply was a concerted 'Good riddance, they are not patriotic South Africans.'

Although apartheid is now on its way out, not many emigrants are likely to return permanently to South Africa. They have put down roots elsewhere, and their children have settled in the countries of their adoption. They return on visits only, and more and more often, sadly enough, to attend the funerals of their parents.

The small Jewish population in South Africa (approximately 106,000 people) has felt this emigration most keenly. It is not uncommon to find a Jewish family with one child in the USA, one in Australia, one in the UK and one in Israel. However, they usually maintain contact with their South African relatives. Those of my parents' generation, who arrived in South Africa as refugees at the turn of the century, were rarely able to revisit the families they left in Eastern Europe, and any remaining links were wiped out by the Holocaust.

Political exile of thousands of Black people has also taken a heavy toll on their family life. After the Sharpeville massacre, the Soweto uprising and the subsequent escalation of state violence and draconian measures which severely curtailed civil liberties, many Black activists went to other African states for education and military training and some ended up behind the Iron Curtain. Their parents often had no knowledge of their subsequent fate. After amnesty for political exiles was declared in 1990, many thousands returned to South Africa, but their re-integration has not been easy, owing to lack of jobs and accommodation.

Ironically, when one hears talk these days about leaving South Africa, it is not from people who hate apartheid, but from people who fear Black majority rule. The appalling violence in the Black townships and elsewhere does not inspire confidence in a stable democratic future for South Africa. And the alarming increase in serious crime which has accompanied widespread unemployment has led to further misgivings among some Whites, including some liberals who steadfastly opposed the apartheid regime throughout four decades.

But, happily, these pessimists are outnumbered by the hundreds of thousands of white South Africans who have no intention of leaving the country, and who are determined to remain and to play their part in a new South Africa.

2

Introduction to
Politics and Parliament

After the defeat of the United Party in 1948, I became more active in politics. I left the Milner Park branch of the United Party which I had formed off-campus at Wits in a vain attempt to interest the students. I joined the Hyde Park branch in the Johannesburg North constituency where we now lived, hoping to keep alive within the party the views of Jan Hofmeyr, its former MP and brilliant Cabinet Minister in the Smuts government. Hofmeyr had died in December 1948, deeply distressed that his liberal views on race relations were considered the reason for the election defeat. I became the secretary of the branch and also the senior vice-chairman of the constituency committee. My political life had now commenced in earnest, what with fund-raising, canvassing for members and attending meetings and party congresses. I was appointed the honorary Information Officer of the Witwatersrand Women's Council of the United Party where I gave a talk on current politics at the monthly meetings. It was in this capacity that I first became well known as a speaker. But the idea of becoming a public representative, even at local government level, had not entered my mind. I had my family responsibilities and I was enjoying my job at the university.

The general election of 1953 was approaching. Many people were still under the impression that the 1948 election result had been a slip up, that poor organisation had caused Smuts's downfall. We felt it needed only a major effort to win back power. At the end of 1952, nominations for the parliamentary seats were called for by the United Party. I was phoned by Dr Reggie Sidelsky, the chairman of a branch in the Houghton constituency, which was, as Americans would say, 'a silk stocking district', with quite a large number of Jews on the voters' roll.

He said, 'Look here, the MP we've got doesn't represent our views. We are a liberal constituency and we would like you to stand for Parliament in Houghton.'

I said, 'No, no. I can't possibly do that. It's ludicrous. I've got two young children. I've got my job. It's just not on.'

Mosie, who overheard this conversation, asked, 'What are you saying "no" to?'

'It's crazy. They want me to stand for Parliament.'

To which he replied, 'They're not crazy. You're crazy. Of course you should stand for Parliament. It's the natural outcome of the work that you've been doing all these years.'

I said, 'How can I do it? It means going to Cape Town to sit in Parliament for nearly six months of the year, leaving the kids.'

When I thought about it, I felt I was not likely to win the contest anyway, because the sitting MP had been there for fourteen years. I couldn't see myself displacing him.

So I agreed.

It turned out to be a three-cornered nomination contest between Joyce Waring (a United Party city councillor who subsequently joined the National Party, though she presented herself as a liberal at the time of the contest), Eric Bell, the sitting Member, and me. I wrote to each member of the candidates' committee and to each chairperson of the United Party branches in the Houghton constituency setting out my qualifications and offering to meet them. Each candidate was asked to give a fifteen-minute speech in front of the nomination committee and then had to answer questions. My speech made it clear that I was concerned mainly with improving race relations, eliminating poverty, and ensuring equal opportunity. Yet I got the warmest applause when I replied very simply 'I don't know' to one of the questions. The committee was evidently impressed by this unusual display of honesty in a would-be politician.

If one of the candidates obtained an overall majority on the first vote, that was it; if not, the candidate with the lowest number of votes dropped out, and it became a straight fight between the remaining two. But it didn't come to that. I won the nomination on the first count, and it was clear that I would become the MP for Houghton at the forthcoming election as Houghton was a safe United Party seat.

My career nearly ended before it began. In 1953, during the short session before the election, the United Party voted for a vicious Bill, which included the penalty of whipping, to combat the widespread defiance campaign against apartheid laws. The campaign was mild enough – totally non-violent, defiance taking the form of Blacks and Whites sitting on benches or using public entrances marked 'Whites only' or 'Non-Whites only'. About 8500 people were arrested, including Patrick Duncan, son of a former Governor-General of South Africa. But the fearsome prospect of physical punishment ended the campaign.

The liberal element in the United Party on the Witwatersrand was shocked by the action of the caucus in supporting the Whipping Bill, and there was a serious threat that some of us would leave the party. One of the most influential and senior MPs, Marais Steyn, was sent from Cape Town to explain the United Party's reason for supporting the Bill. He told us that there was genuine fear of widespread violence. Pre-election panic was probably a more valid reason, but our threatened rebellion was averted.

I was not opposed at the election proper and on 14 March 1953 I became MP for Houghton. Both Smuts and Hofmeyr were dead, and the United Party leader was J. G. N. Strauss, a decent man, but not very popular.

The National Party increased its majority, to the disappointment of all the hopeful folk who had worked so hard for the United Party, and I found myself faced with the prospect of going to Parliament as a member of the official opposition. I offered my seat to another United Party candidate, who had lost his, and whom I thought able. He had been one of the class of 1948, one of Smuts's young men: Albert Robinson. He held liberal views, was a good speaker and fluent in both English and Afrikaans. (I understand Afrikaans perfectly, but do not speak it well. I certainly had to learn to understand it properly, because about seventy per cent of the debates in Parliament are conducted in that language.)

Of course the Houghton seat was not mine to hand over, but I knew that if I resigned he would get both the nomination and the seat unopposed. Albert was very nice about it. He met me the day after I'd made the offer, and said he'd thought about it, but 'No, thank you very much'. He thought I ought to go to Parliament, and in any case he was thinking of moving to Rhodesia, which he subsequently did. He became head of Central African Airways, and was later appointed High Commissioner for Rhodesia in Britain and knighted. He returned to South Africa to head a Johannesburg mining firm, and has now more or less retired. Whenever I meet Albert, we speculate about what would have happened if he'd gone back to Parliament and I hadn't begun my career there.

So off I went to Cape Town in July 1953 for a short post-election session of Parliament – shaking in my boots, I might add. I had met most of the United Party MPs only at party congresses, and they were not friendly to me because of my liberal views. However, we new boys and girls were given a reasonable reception by some of the older members. Harry Oppenheimer, the son of the mining magnate, shared our basic values, as did Harry Lawrence, a Cabinet Minister during the Smuts regime. Both gave the newcomers much support and encouragement.

Harry Oppenheimer had been in Parliament for five years. He and his wife Bridget were extremely hospitable to the back-benchers who arrived in 1953, and I was often invited to supper at the house they lived in during the sessions. It was near the Malay quarter, within walking distance of Parliament, and just beyond the garden wall was a mosque from which one saw and heard the muezzin calling the faithful to prayer. Having us as guests was a courteous gesture, but it was more than that. Harry was interested in getting the so-called 'liberal wing' of the United Party activated, because he found us positive in our views and shared many of them. We were immediately attacked by the reactionaries in the United Party, so it was comforting to know we had support from so influential a quarter.

Harry must be one of the most modest and self-effacing millionaires in the world. At times when I was engaged in fierce caucus rows, his diffidence upset me. I knew that one word from him would reduce the angry voices of the United Party protagonists of social and political segregation to a surly mutter. But Harry was reluctant to throw his weight about; he probably exerted more influence behind the scenes than he did in caucus. He spoke in Parliament rarely but always well, and mostly on financial subjects. I was amused at the rapt attention he received from Nationalist MPs when he spoke in the House. Were the mesmerised Nats hoping for a tip on the Stock Exchange?

Harry gave me much encouragement over the years, and his appearance on my platforms at future elections was invaluable. Bridget shared his views on race relations. When Soweto erupted years later and the unrest persisted, she formed an organisation, Women for Peace, which cut across the colour and political divides of South Africa, to foster better understanding between Black and White, and between English- and Afrikaans-speaking South Africans.

The irrepressible Harry Lawrence, the other great supporter of the liberal backbench both in and out of Parliament, had frequent sharp exchanges with Speaker Conradie (a highly irritable gent) which often resulted in his expulsion from the House, to the accompaniment of loud guffaws from Harry. His witty repartee, especially after wining and dining, remains a warm memory of our years together in politics. He had great fortitude, suffering constant pain and ill health as a result of being manhandled by Nationalist ruffians at a political meeting during an election campaign. He and his feisty, good-looking wife, Jean, sacrificed more than any of the other MPs who left the United Party in 1958 and risked their political futures by joining the Progressive Party. They had limited financial resources, he was ill and getting on in years, and it was too late for him to go back to his law practice.

I was amazed that no effort was made by the Chief Whip of the United Party, big brusque Jack Higgerty, and his cohorts in Cape Town to call the new Members together, and to say to us, 'These are the written rules, and these are the unwritten rules of Parliament. Let me introduce you to Mr Speaker.'

I never got on with Higgerty. He would walk around the Lobby smoking a large cigar, gazing into the distance. Some years later, when I underwent emergency surgery a few days before the parliamentary session was due to begin, I said to Mosie as I was being wheeled into the operating theatre, 'Please tell Higgerty'. When I recovered, I thought to myself, Fancy those being my last words if I hadn't made it!

As a new MP I sat there slogging away, a little backbench Member of Parliament, very conscientious, very interested, watching and listening and learning all the time. I joined several of the parliamentary groups within the United Party to study Bills on specific subjects, mainly concerned with racial affairs and with labour, because I recognised that the connection between labour and the racial set-up was very close indeed.

From the beginning of my parliamentary career I decided I would deliver a Report-Back speech to my constituents at the end of each session. This, I felt, was the least I could do in the interests of accountability. In my first Report-Back in 1953, I told them that the work was much harder than I had realised, that I had always thought that MPs lolled around on their green benches as an easy way of extracting £700 per annum from the Treasury. I said that, if taken conscientiously, the hours were very long, what with committee work, afternoon and evening sittings, the studying of bills, the preparation of speeches (many of which were never delivered) and of course the interminable caucus meetings. I found the work completely absorbing. I also found that one had to guard against becoming cloistered in the atmosphere of the House, forgetting the outside world altogether and losing contact with party supporters and branch workers. For that reason, I began sending newsletters every month to members of my constituency branch committees.

In my first newsletter I said I had been surprised at the remarkable uniformity among National Party members, although really one shouldn't be surprised, because a large number of the rank and file MPs were employed by the National Party as organisers, all of whom had been spilling out the same old propaganda for many years. They were thoroughly regimented, accepted without question the Cabinet's proposals on Bills, and often stood up to speak merely to thank the minister concerned. I noted that one Nationalist Member thanked the Finance Minister no fewer than seventeen times in the course of a twenty-minute speech.

Throughout the thirty-six years that I was an MP, I took a special interest in all issues relating to discrimination, the rule of law and the administration of justice. But, although my maiden speech in 1953 dealt with the subject of women's rights (or their lack), gender discrimination was not my main preoccupation during my career in the House. My overriding concern as a South African was with race discrimination. Nevertheless, because I was a woman engaged in what was pre-eminently a male occupation in chauvinist South Africa, there were inevitably two questions I was often asked: How did you manage to combine motherhood and your political career? and Was being a woman a disadvantage in Parliament?

I did not have the feelings of guilt that I am told often plague working mothers. However it wasn't easy, mainly because being an MP entailed living in a variety of rented accommodation in Cape Town (1000 miles from Johannesburg) for nearly six months each year and my daughters were thirteen and ten years of age when I entered Parliament. In the early years, the journey took four hours in a non-pressurised plane and the airport serving Johannesburg was several miles south of the city, whereas we lived six miles to the north. I tried to fly home at least every second weekend to be with the family and to deal with whatever domestic crises cropped up. The girls flatly refused to go to boarding school and as I had adequate domestic staff to look after the household, it somehow worked. Mosie was a resident doctor, so to speak, and my father and stepmother were very attentive and loving grandparents. The children were fully occupied with school, sport and their friends.

Both my daughters attended university in Johannesburg and then went abroad for further studies. Frances continued with Art History at the Courtauld Institute in London. She later married Jeffrey Jowell, a Law graduate from Cape Town and Oxford, and they went to Harvard where they both obtained doctorates – she in Art History and he in Jurisprudence. Their daughter, Joanna, was born in Cambridge, Massachusetts, and their son, Daniel, in Toronto, where they taught before returning to London, where they now live. Jeffrey is Professor of Public Law at University College, London and a practising barrister, and Frances works as a freelance art historian.

Patty qualified at Wits Medical School, and lived in Paris for a year while awaiting admission for permanent residence in the United States. She lives in Boston where she is a nephrologist, practising at the Harvard Community Plan and the Brigham and Women's Hospital.

Although both my daughters have lived abroad for most of their adult lives, we have remained closely in touch by mail, telephone and, more recently, fax. We have been fortunate in being able to spend regular family holidays together, both in South Africa and abroad. In recent years, a bonus of my honorary doctorates and overseas lectures has been the opportunity to drop into London or Boston to be with them.

The second (more straightforward) question was: Has being a woman put you at a disadvantage in Parliament? Not at all. I concentrated on making well-prepared and factually accurate speeches, and gradually won the respect of the House, albeit on occasion with unsolicited effects. Once, after a speech on economics, I was accosted by an MP who said to me in the Lobby, 'Helen – you've got a man's brain!' His was not a brain I admired.

The South African Parliament had more than its fair share of male chauvinists, with traditional attitudes about 'a woman's place'. Such views were, of course, reflected in the long-standing political and legal status of women in South Africa.

Act 18 of 1930 extended the vote to White women in South Africa. This enfranchisement was not unopposed – it was accompanied by squeals of protest from the Members of the House of Assembly. Empty cradles would result, prophesied one Member; 'ruined men', warned another bleakly. A third Member told Parliament that 'suffrage would mean dragging woman down from the pedestal where she stands remote and revered as a symbol of good influence, into the muddy arena of party politics.' Those Members need not have upset themselves, because if there are empty cradles and ruined men and muddied females, it is not because women have stampeded into the arena of parliamentary politics in South Africa. There have never been more than five or six in the House of Assembly at any one time and indeed for six years I was the only woman Member of Parliament. It is only since 1989 that there has been a woman Cabinet Minister, Dr Rina Venter.

Enfranchisement of women had to do with the maintenance of White political power. They were given the vote in 1930 not only because men had realised, albeit reluctantly, that there could be no valid justification for denying adult females the vote, since women were playing their part in the community in every facet of life. More important, extending the franchise to White women, but not to Coloured or Black women, effectively diminished the vote of Coloured and Black men in the Cape Province. (This was reinforced a year later when the literacy and property qualifications for the vote were scrapped for White voters, but were retained for Black and Coloured men.)

Despite obtaining the right to vote, the legal disabilities of women persisted for many years. It was not until 1953 that any improvement in their status was effected and it took another thirty-one years for further significant changes to be accepted. I did not make gender discrimination a major priority, but I participated in every debate that affected women and women's rights during my years in Parliament.

In 1953, there were four women MPs: Bertha Solomon, Sannie van Niekerk and me in the United Party, and Mrs Margaret Ballinger, one of three Whites elected in the Cape Province as Native Representatives. Bertha was the champion of women's rights and spent many years arguing for the removal of their legal disabilities. Bertha, Sannie and I shared an office. The two women disliked each other and I often acted as peacemaker, but my relationship with Bertha depended on whether I was being difficult in caucus – if so she disowned me; if not, she referred to me as her 'protégée'. Sannie was a confirmed right-winger, so our relationship was distinctly cool.

Margaret Ballinger was a leading member of the Liberal Party, which had only two MPs, herself and Walter Stanford, also a Native Representative. She was a brilliant woman, who made just the kind of speeches I felt ought to be made in Parliament. She, too, had been a lecturer in History at the University of Witwatersrand. She was not a friendly person, rather self-centred and cold to all except admired and admiring friends. She gave little praise to the liberal wing of the United Party, which I felt she should have encouraged, because we shared her philosophy. In fact, she rarely gave us any credit for anything. But she was an excellent MP, there was no question about that, and she was a role model for me. Every speech she made was first class – crisp, well-prepared, full of relevant facts.

My maiden speech was on the Matrimonial Affairs Bill in 1953, known as Bertha's Bill, since it was initiated by Bertha Solomon. Based on British parliamentary tradition, maiden speeches in the South African House of Assembly were not interrupted by interjections from other Members, and were therefore expected not to be provocative. The Bill was taken over by the government and thus became non-controversial. It alleviated to some extent the position of women who were married in community of property (the normal matrimonial regime in South Africa, under which the husband exercised the marital power). This meant that such women were under the total jurisdiction of their husbands, as they had no contractual capacity and indeed were subjected, as Bertha put it, to the predatory demands of husbands who used to go to the factory doors, collect their wives' wages and proceed to the nearest pub.

Nevertheless the 1953 Bill went only part of the way towards eliminating the disabilities of women and a great deal had still to be done in the years after Bertha Solomon left Parliament in 1958. My speech was well reported in the press although, to Bertha's distress, the Bill was presented on the same afternoon as the budget, which obviously had a prior claim on available newsprint.

During my thirty-six years in Parliament, I went through, so to speak, five Prime Ministers, dozens of ministers and hundreds of MPs. As a United Party MP I served under three Nationalist Prime Ministers, Dr D. F. Malan, J. G. Strijdom and Dr H. F. Verwoerd. In these fledgling years, however, I had very little contact with Prime Ministers. There I sat, on my backbench in the ranks of the United Party, most of whose members were much subdued by its electoral defeats of 1948 and 1953. As a backbencher I had only occasional opportunities to speak in the House of Assembly and was certainly without a mandate to tackle Prime Ministers.

I had only two sessions while Malan was Prime Minister. He could be described as a dour old dominee [clergyman] who commanded more respect than affection within his own party; he was not the sort of man on whom one could lavish affection. He had rigid views and his mind was set not only on implementing apartheid, under which slogan his government had come to power in 1948, but on the transformation of South Africa into a republic. He was also intent on obtaining the transfer of the three British protectorates of Basutoland, Bechuanaland and Swaziland to the Union of South Africa. I remember comparing Malan to Humpty Dumpty, whom he physically resembled, as I listened to him presenting a motion on the transfer of the protectorates. He conceded that at the time of Union the British government had laid down that 'the wishes of the Natives will be carefully considered' before such transfer could take place. However, he said firmly, this did not mean that the consent of the Natives had to be obtained – just like Humpty Dumpty, who said equally firmly, 'When I use a word it means just what I choose it to mean, neither more nor less.'

Dr Malan was replaced by 'The Lion of the North', J. G. Strijdom, a grim, forbidding man who was Prime Minister for just over three years, from 1954 to 1958. He was much exercised in planning the removal of the Coloured voters from the Common Roll in the Cape Province. His successor, Dr Verwoerd, was the mastermind behind the social engineering of the apartheid policy.

3

Opposition Politics
– United Party Style

It soon became apparent in the United Party caucus that a small group of us shared the same basic liberal ideals. We had all come to Parliament with one objective: to do something about the racial situation, to give the United Party a sharp prod in this regard.

The party was equivocal on racial issues, although not on the most important issue at that time: the removal of the Coloured people from the Common Voters' Roll in the Cape Province. This was the great constitutional crisis of the 1950s, an echo of an earlier betrayal, the Representation of Natives Act of 1936, which deprived Black males in the Cape Province of the voting rights they had enjoyed with the same qualifications as Whites and Coloureds.

In 1910 when the Union of South Africa was formed out of the four territories – the two former Boer republics of the Orange Free State and the Transvaal, and the two British colonies of the Cape Province and Natal – one of the conditions was that the existing franchise for Black, Coloured and Indian people would be retained in the Cape Province. Absolutely no provision was made, however, for an extension of the franchise to the Coloured, Indian or Black people in the other three territories. The omission of any provision in the Act of Union for the extension of the franchise to all adult citizens, irrespective of race, was a serious dereliction of responsibility by the British government, and was perpetuated by successive South African governments.

However the Constitution of the Union contained an entrenched clause which laid down that a two-thirds majority of

Members of the House of Assembly (the Lower House) and of the Senate (the Upper House), voting together in a joint sitting, was required before the existing franchise could be removed from Black, Coloured or Indian voters. The two-thirds majority to disenfranchise Blacks in 1936 was obtained because Smuts, then Deputy Prime Minister in the Fusion government with General Hertzog, agreed to support the 1936 Act. To their everlasting credit, eleven Members of Parliament, including Jan Hofmeyr, voted against that bill. To replace their lost Common Roll voting rights, Blacks in the Cape Province were allowed to elect three White representatives for the House of Assembly and four White senators. The area which had been set aside for exclusive occupation by Blacks in the Land Act of 1913, was to be increased by a further 7.75 million morgen (1 morgen = 2.2 acres), bringing the Native Reserves up to 13 per cent of the land area of the Union (for 72 per cent of the population). An elected Natives' Representative Council was also set up, a purely advisory body soon dubbed 'the toy telephone' by Black leaders who rejected the 1936 Act *in toto* as compensation for the loss of their franchise.

Now, twenty years later, it was the turn of Coloured men in the Cape Province to lose their Common Roll franchise rights. As I have said, these rights had already been devalued in 1930 by the extension of the franchise to White women, but not to Coloured women, and a year later by the removal of the property and literacy qualifications for White men, but their retention for Coloured men. Despite this, the Coloured voters, although a minority on the voters' roll, were beginning to play a significant and decisive role in elections in certain constituencies. The National Party, with their relatively small majority in Parliament, could not tolerate this. They set out to destroy the Coloured franchise, although this meant flouting the Constitution since they could not muster the required two-thirds majority. The government tried to ignore the entrenched clause by passing an Act in 1951, with both Houses sitting separately, to disenfranchise the Coloured voters. The Separate Representation of Voters Act was challenged in the courts and declared invalid by the Appeal Court. Next, the government tried to establish a High Court of Parliament to rule on constitutional issues of a political nature – 'to place the sovereignty of

Parliament beyond all doubt'. This too was declared invalid by the
Appeal Court.

The machinations of the government led to considerable public
outrage. The Torch Commando, consisting of ex-servicemen
headed by a South African war hero, 'Sailor' Malan, was formed,
and held vociferous protest meetings. Together with two United
Party stalwarts, Marjory Juta and Ellen Hellmann, we formed
Women's Action, a female counterpart to the Torch Commando,
in an effort to galvanise women into political activity. The first of
several mass meetings was held in Pretoria and about 2000 women
were present. This was my first appearance as a speaker at a public
protest meeting and I was extremely nervous. Neither the Torch
Commando nor Women's Action was destined to last beyond a
couple of years. Both dissolved because the United Party leadership disapproved of separate and possibly competitive organisations in opposition.

The constitutional crisis also led to the emergence of the
Women's Defence of the Constitution League – commonly known
as the Black Sash, from the adornment they wore when standing in
silent protests. It was originally the symbol of mourning for the
destruction of the Constitution. The Black Sash proved more
durable. It converted itself into an extremely active and useful
organisation, advising and assisting victims of apartheid as well as
being a vigilant protest group. Two of its founders, Jean Sinclair
and Ruth Foley, were long-standing friends of mine from the
Women's Council of the United Party.

During this period the United Party caucus went through its
own crisis. The majority were strongly opposed to tampering with
the Coloured franchise. However, a small group wanted to offer a
compromise, by doing a deal with the National Party through the
relatively moderate 'Klasie' Havenga, Minister of Finance. The
group suggested that existing Coloured voters should remain on
the Common Voters' Roll, but that no new voters should be
enrolled. Eventually, after it was known that members of the
group were conducting unauthorised negotiations ('coffee drinking') with Mr Havenga, and with Prime Minister Malan, they were
expelled from the caucus; they formed a splinter party and sat as a
separate group of five MPs, ignoring the loud cries from those of us

on the United Party backbench who demanded that they resign their seats.

One of the five was a thoroughly objectionable man, Arthur Barlow. He was an evil old liar who, to support his arguments, constantly quoted outrageous statements allegedly made by important, deceased people (such as Smuts). After being expelled from the United Party caucus, he frequently remarked if I interjected while he was speaking, 'It's the lady from Lithuania again'. I didn't particularly mind this anti-semitic sideswipe (most of the Jewish emigrants to South Africa had come from Eastern Europe), though I was in fact one generation removed from Lithuania. What I did mind was that he always erased these words from the Hansard parliamentary records (which MPs may see and correct for grammatical errors or repetition before publication, but to which they may not make any material alterations). I observed this stratagem of Barlow's a few times, then accosted him in the Lobby and informed him that if he continued to do so, I would see that the press highlighted his comment, which would offend his Jewish constituents, and I would also report him to the Speaker for altering the Hansard record. He never did so again. I got my own back on this nasty old man when he made a speech complaining about the high murder rate in his constituency. I spoke immediately after him and told the House that if he dared put his head into his constituency, the murder rate would go up by one – a remark received with hearty 'hear-hears' from many Members.

The device the Nationalists finally used to deprive the Coloured voters of their Common Roll franchise was the Senate Act of 1955, which provided for an increase in the number of nominated senators. The Senate was packed with the number required to manufacture the two-thirds majority as laid down by the Constitution. This device was declared valid by the Appeal Court, ten to one – Judge O. D. Schreiner voting against. The South Africa Act Amendment Act was passed with both Houses voting together. The Coloured people were instead given four White representatives in the Cape Province who would be elected on a Separate Roll for the House of Assembly, two Provincial Councillors whose race was not specified – all elected by Coloured voters, male and female, and one nominated White senator.

★

Although the right wing had been ousted from the United Party on the Coloured vote issue, we liberals in the caucus were still in trouble. Bills were introduced by the government which the majority in the United Party caucus did not want to oppose, because they believed that by so doing they would antagonise their own reactionary supporters throughout the country. They were always hoping to win back some of the rural seats, which they never had a snowball's chance of doing. We backbenchers kept saying, 'Why don't you concentrate on the urban seats, where you've got people with more progressive ideas? It's no good trying to be all things to all men.' But other Members argued in favour of supporting Bills we thought should be opposed by the United Party as the official opposition.

Thus the group of United Party MPs who shared the same liberal philosophy seemed always to be on the wrong side in the caucus discussions on the different racist bills being tabled. We became known as the 'liberal wing' of the United Party. Of course the National Party press (the Afrikaans press) attacked us mercilessly, trying to undermine any influence we might have among Afrikaner voters and among more conservative English-speakers in South Africa, by saying that we were influencing the United Party towards 'leftist' views. (In South Africa, a 'leftist' was anyone who wanted to give Blacks the vote and was against race discrimination. The term was unrelated to economic policy.) During my first six years in Parliament, we liberals conducted a constant battle within the United Party caucus. We wanted to oppose every law which was racially discriminatory, but we were told that while the United Party's policy was economic integration, it supported political and social segregation.

However, the United Party did oppose the measure that probably caused the greatest harm to future generations of Black South Africans: the Bantu Education Act, introduced by Dr Verwoerd as Minister of Native Affairs in 1953, which deliberately condemned Black children to an inferior education.

In opening the debate in Parliament Verwoerd said,

Racial relations cannot improve if the wrong type of education is given to Natives. They cannot improve if the result of Native Education is the creation of frustrated people who as a result of the education they receive have expectations in life which circumstances in South Africa do not allow to be fulfilled immediately, when it creates people who are trained for professions not open to them, when there are people who have received a form of cultural training which strengthens their desire for the white-collar occupations to such an extent that there are more such people than openings available. Therefore, good racial relations are spoiled when the correct education is not given.[1]

Bantu Education was henceforth under state control and grants were removed from the mission schools which had provided a good education for many Blacks. Future generations of Black children were to be relegated to the status of drawers of water and hewers of wood. Verwoerd went on to say,

> What is the use of teaching the Bantu child mathematics when it cannot use it in practice? What is the use of subjecting a Native child to a curriculum which in the first instance is traditionally European? I just want to remind Honourable Members that if the Native inside South Africa today in any kind of school in existence is being taught to expect that he will live his adult life under a policy of equal rights, he is making a big mistake.[2]

The United Party opposed the Bantu Education Bill mainly because it deprived the provinces of a function entrusted to them by the South Africa Act. But it did oppose.

There were also exceptions to the United Party's equivocation on social integration. It opposed the first mass removal in the urban areas of a large number of Black people – the so-called Western Areas Removal Scheme of 1954 which affected some 60,000 residents in Sophiatown and adjoining areas where White suburbs had encroached. Sophiatown, close to the city centre, was one of the few freehold areas of Johannesburg owned or occupied by Black or Coloured people. The unfortunate residents were forcibly moved by police action to a place fifteen miles away named Meadowlands, now in Soweto. Their houses were razed to the ground and a new all-White suburb emerged: Triomf. Father Trevor Huddleston's Anglican Church of Christ the King was converted into the Afrikaans Pinkster Protestante Kerk – hardly an example of Christian brotherly love. The government called the

removal scheme a 'Black spot' removal and slum clearance. Slum it
may have been but it was a vibrant, lively community, and it could
have been improved *in situ*.

The Sophiatown removal was my first encounter with the mad
obsession of Verwoerd, then Minister of Native Affairs, about
'Black spots'. He said that while he recognised the presence of
Natives in urban areas, he did not recognise the permanency of the
individual. Sophiatown had to go because Blacks had freehold
rights to the land and that could not be tolerated in a White area.
This was the forerunner of many forced removals, part of the social
engineering inherent in the apartheid system, and one with the
most disastrous consequences.

During those early days the United Party also opposed an
extraordinary Bill dubbed by the press 'the Locations in the Sky
Bill' (Black townships were then known as 'locations'). The Bill
prohibited the occupants of flats from allowing their Black
domestic servants to live in rooms set aside for them on the roof
tops of the apartment buildings. It allowed one or two Black
cleaners employed by the owners of the blocks to live on the
premises, but otherwise the domestic servants were supposed to go
back and forth to the townships each day. This was both
impractical and unpopular: neither the transport nor the accommodation was available in the townships, and it meant additional expense
for domestic servants, most of whom were poorly paid. It also
resulted in many complaints from their employers, who were used to
having their domestic employees available to make the early morning
tea and to serve dinner in the evening. It all went counter to a long-
established practice among residents in the White suburbs. One heard
much sanctimonious talk from National Party MPs who said that
Whites had to make the supreme sacrifice in the interests of White
civilisation and brew their own early morning cups of tea.
Newspapers published an absurd photograph of two large male
National Party MPs wearing aprons and doing their own domestic
work. I correctly anticipated that I would be much occupied trying to
obtain permits for domestics to stay on the premises of my many
constituents who lived in flats. Only those employers who were ill or
aged qualified for this privilege.

The 1954 Job Reservation Bill marked a further welcome display of opposition by the United Party. As the secretary of the labour group in the party, I took a prominent part in that debate which extended the legislative colour bar to industry by reserving skilled jobs for Whites only. There had long been a colour bar in the mining industry, through the Mines and Works Act of 1911, passed many years before the coming of the National Party government. I emphasised the stupidity of introducing further restrictions on the economy, and how impossible it was to develop a country with South Africa's resources with only the skills of the minority White population; and that we had to use all our manpower to the best advantage. I talked about the expansion of the labour market leading to the expansion of consumer markets, which would benefit both agriculture and industry, with everybody's services in greater demand. It was really a speech on elementary economics.

A Nationalist MP angrily accused me of 'trying to grind the Afrikaner worker into the dust'. I countered that I was convinced that the majority of White workers, including Afrikaners, were perfectly capable of competing with other races without the artificial protection of job reservation. Those who required assistance should be helped by social welfare, not by putting industry into a straitjacket. The Minister of Labour, B. J. Schoeman, asked, 'What is our first consideration? Is it to maintain the economic laws or is it to ensure the continued existence of the European [meaning White] race in this country?'[3] He did not explain why he saw the two aims as mutually exclusive.

Ironically, when the Nationalist government abolished job reservation in industry in 1979 because of the sheer pressure of economic forces – which included the fact that there were more skilled jobs available than the White workers could fill, I listened to a speech by an MP from the right wing of the National Party supporting the removal of job reservation. He used almost the same arguments I had put forward twenty-five years earlier. He was talking to his blue-collar constituents in the iron and steel industry in the working-class area he represented, people who were fearful of competition from Black workers, and he used my arguments to try to convince his voters that their jobs were not endangered.

One of the apartheid Bills which the United Party decided to support was the Separate Amenities Bill of 1953. This measure allowed separate but unequal amenities, to be provided by local authorities, for Blacks, Coloureds, Indians and Whites. After considerable argument in caucus the United Party decided to vote for the second reading of the Bill, thus supporting its principle. Despite the caucus decision, I refused to vote for it – my first act of defiance – and I walked out of the House with Owen Townley-Williams, a Natal MP belonging to our special little group in the caucus.

I was summoned by the Chief Whip, the same Master Higgerty, who told me that I would be putting my political career on the line if I continued to defy caucus decisions. In somewhat unladylike language I told him what he could do with my political career, for nothing in the world would make me vote for a Bill of that kind. The United Party later changed its mind and opposed the third reading. Interestingly enough, the Separate Amenities Act was the first law the government scrapped in 1990 when State President F. W. de Klerk introduced reforms for the 'new South Africa'.

We continued to have many arguments in the United Party caucus. One major bone of contention was the refusal of the Party leader, J. G. N. Strauss, to reply unequivocally to the persistent challenge by the 1953 defectors to commit the United Party to restoring the Common Roll franchise to the Coloured people in the Cape, should his party be returned to power. Strauss was the type of political leader who chose to placate his enemies at the expense of his friends, and he evaded the question. We backbenchers were most unhappy at this equivocation.

A further major split in the party, this time from the 'left', was narrowly averted by the intervention of the two Harrys – Oppenheimer and Lawrence – who persuaded us that we had to remain as a pressure group within the United Party to advance liberal values. But one of the party's most brilliant debaters, a senior MP, Dr Bernard Friedman, resigned in 1955 on this issue, fought a by-election and lost his Hillbrow seat. I earned further bad marks from the party hierarchy by flatly refusing to speak in support of its candidate opposing Dr Friedman; instead, I took off on a visit to the Rhodesian Federation and to the Belgian Congo with my former Economic History lecturer at Wits, Professor Hansi Pollak and Dr Ellen Hellmann, my constituency chairperson. Our somewhat optimistic predictions of future events in those regions were way off the mark. We did not foresee Ian Smith's Unilateral Declaration of Independence (UDI) in Rhodesia in 1965 and the ensuing civil war there over fifteen years, nor the violent turmoil in the Congo after 1960 when the Belgians left.

In 1957, the government introduced the State Aided Institutions Bill which permitted authorities in charge of museums and art galleries, libraries and other public amenities to set aside certain hours or days of admission for different racial groups. During the discussion in caucus over this piece of legislation, I had a heated row with Sannie van Niekerk. She was an old dragon from Natal who represented one of the few rural seats held by the party. During our argument, Sannie drew herself up to her full height, which wasn't very high, and flung out her bosom, which was very large, and said, 'Well, I don't know about Mrs Suzman, but when I go to a museum, I don't like it if some strange Black man rubs himself up against me.' I said quietly, 'Don't you mind if some strange White man rubs himself up against you?' Of course, there was a lot of laughter, and Sannie didn't talk to me for the rest of that session.

Then came the 1958 election. I was dubious whether to stand again, because I was unhappy in the United Party, having endured many crises over racist laws and especially over the resignation of Dr Friedman. But in the end I did stand, and was unopposed for nomination and unopposed at the election.

Again, the United Party lost seats and the government was returned to power with a much bigger majority, winning 103 seats to the United Party's fifty-three. Back we went to Parliament, where the hostility towards our liberal group was now reaching its peak. In place of Hofmeyr, who had been blamed for the loss of the election in 1948, we, the 'liberal wing' of the party, were blamed by our colleagues for the loss of the 1958 election. Outside Parliament, some party supporters and organisers started a campaign to oust us at the earliest opportunity.

In the meantime the United Party had changed leadership, replacing Strauss with Sir de Villiers Graaff, an Afrikaner by birth who was more or less anglicised. He was an Oxford University graduate with a Law degree, and a man of considerable independent means. He had been a prisoner of war during the Second World War and could claim a devoted following among many ex-servicemen. Everybody assumed he would be an outstanding leader, but he proved a grave disappointment to us liberals. In no time at all he had thrown in his lot with the conservative majority in caucus, and was expressing views which we felt were totally inappropriate to the requirements of the times. Now we had to combat this new and popular leader, who commanded much greater loyalty from the rest of the caucus and from the public than Strauss had done. Graaff made some good legalistic speeches in parliament and he was strong on the Coloured vote issue. But on the discriminatory laws applying to Blacks, he was weak and ambivalent. His favourite piece of advice to the caucus on contentious issues was 'when in doubt, leave out'.

In June 1959 I received, anonymously, a leaked document issued by the Department of Bantu Administration. The circular gave instructions to the police that Blacks arrested under the Pass Laws should be induced to volunteer to work on farms in lieu of prosecution.

Shocking cases of ill-treatment of Black farm labourers had been exposed by the magazine *Drum*, one of whose reporters had got himself employed as a farm labourer. I was contacted by a lawyer who had given affidavits to Dr Boris Wilson, another United Party MP, and we launched a full-scale attack on the Minister and Deputy Minister of the Department of Bantu Administration and Development. The latter gave me a totally incorrect reply in the House to a question I had put about the 'in lieu of prosecution scheme'.[4] I wanted to know how many Blacks had been employed under this scheme; the Minister replied 'not one'. In fact, he denied that such a scheme existed, not knowing that I had the departmental circular in my possession. I called his bluff and denounced the scheme as forced labour. We exposed the appalling conditions such as poor and inadequate food, sacks for bedding, labourers locked up every night and beaten by the foreman in the fields. The Blacks arrested for Pass Law infringements had been told that if they did not go to work on the farms, they would be sent to the notorious Baviaanspoort Prison. They were not told, of course, that if they appeared in court they would simply have to pay a fine or go to jail for a short time. The entire scheme was obviously illegal.

We kept up a constant barrage throughout the Bantu Administration Vote, while the Nationalists bayed like hounds at a meet, accusing us of attacking the entire farming community. They called me the mouthpiece of the Black Sash, and got in some anti-semitic remarks by referring to some Jewish farmers who had been among those taken to court for abusing farm labour. The Nationalists did their best to gain political capital out of the debate and indeed one or two United Party MPs were distinctly uneasy about our speeches, but to Graaff's credit he backed us on this issue. The Minister announced that he would appoint a commission of inquiry. One of the weapons an opposition MP has in the South African Parliament is to move for a reduction in the salary of ministers in order to express disapproval of the way they had managed their portfolios. I moved the reduction of the salary of the Deputy Minister, which would have left him with £50. I said I hoped he would use it to improve his knowledge of how his department functioned.

Dr Verwoerd became Prime Minister in September 1958. As I told my constituents at my Report-Back meeting, South Africa had now embarked on a course of extremism with a fanatic at the helm. Verwoerd believed himself a man of destiny.

Two very contentious Bills were introduced during the 1959 session at Verwoerd's insistence. The first was the cynically named Extension of the University Education Bill, which restructured the 'open' White universities which had admitted students of all races. Instead, the government proposed to set up ethnic tribal colleges – three for the Blacks, one for the Indians and one for the Coloureds, controlled by the government insofar as staff, students and curricula were concerned. In short, the Bill introduced a serious degree of state interference in tertiary education in South

Africa, and replaced the existing facilities with inferior tribal colleges. Furthermore the 'Conscience Clause', which prohibited the admission of students or the appointment of staff on the basis of religious belief, was omitted from the Bill. The United Party opposed it mainly on the grounds that it interfered with the autonomy of the universities and academic freedom. I agreed, but also emphasised the inestimable value of contact between Black and White students at the open universities. The protests from hundreds of educational institutions throughout the world, the meetings and marches held by the staff and students from the open universities were simply ignored. The government steamrollered the measure through both Houses with virtually no amendments accepted. The University College of Fort Hare in the Eastern Cape, highly regarded throughout the continent, received the same rough treatment. It was producing, under missionary influence, the 'Black Englishmen' so hated by Verwoerd. It was transferred to the Department of Bantu Education and became an ethnic institution for Xhosa students only. This was the college at which many future African leaders – Robert Mugabe of Zimbabwe for one – had been educated. Also in attendance were three students who were to be expelled from Fort Hare for political activities – Oliver Tambo, Mandela and Buthelezi.

Unlike his predecessor, Strijdom, who had spoken unreservedly about White baasskap [domination], Verwoerd realised that it was not possible in the second half of the twentieth century to present a policy brazenly based on race discrimination; so he conceived the 'ethical' concept of Bantustans – independent Black rural home-lands – thus justifying his ever-increasing emphasis on the system of migrant labour and the deprivation of any franchise rights or claims to permanency by Blacks in the rest of South Africa. South African citizenship would thus be withdrawn from Blacks ethnically connected with the Bantustans, ultimately leaving a White majority in South Africa: the 'numbers game' of Dr Verwoerd.

That was the final aim of the policy of Grand Apartheid, as first translated into legislative form by the passing of the second highly contentious measure, the Promotion of Bantu Self-Government Act of 1959. Territorial authorities were to be set up to serve the so-called 'national units', or Bantustans, which were to be consolidated into eight areas. White commissioners-general would be appointed to the various national units to advise and represent the government. Since Blacks in the urban areas were considered by the National Party to be temporary sojourners, they would have tribal representatives as ethnic ambassadors. No consideration was given to the three million Blacks on White farms. But, in any case, the entire Bill was full of inconsistencies. The government ignored the fact that a large proportion of the Black population lived outside the Reserves, either in the urban areas or on White farms. The plan excluded the elective principle, except for the election of one-third of the tribal authority, but with the right of veto reserved by the government. For the rest, everybody was to be nominated by the Governor-General and subject to dismissal if government instructions were not carried out.

The government undertook to consolidate some 264 widely separated Bantu areas. From the Prime Minister downwards, everyone was evasive about the future boundaries of these national units. Nor did anybody have any idea of the cost of this grandiose scheme to partition South Africa. Two of the basic recommendations of the Tomlinson Commission, which had been set up soon after Verwoerd came to power to investigate the socio-economic development of the Bantu areas, were ignored by the government: the need to inject White capital into the Black rural areas and to abandon the inefficient system of tribal agriculture. Nor was the incompatibility of attempting to develop a modern industrial economy while maintaining tribal institutions taken into consideration.

I believe Verwoerd convinced himself and a number of Nationalist Party intellectuals and churchmen of the feasibility of this policy, ignoring its obvious and fatal weaknesses: the economic interdependence of White and Black in South Africa; the non-viability of the Bantustans; and the existence of a second and third generation of urban-born Blacks, many of whom had absorbed Western ideas and forsaken tribal customs and cultures.

The claims of the displaced minority groups of Coloured people and Indians, who had no separate national homelands in South Africa, were also ignored by the Grand Apartheid concept, although they were not threatened with the loss of South African citizenship; they remained second-class citizens. Their right to own or occupy land or property was severely circumscribed by the Group Areas Act of 1950, which set aside specific areas on a racial basis, heavily biased in favour of the White population. Indeed, people of Indian descent were prohibited from entering and remaining in the Orange Free State. Their franchise rights, moreover, were non-existent.

The *quid pro quo* for this so-called ethnic and ethical partition scheme and the future promise of political independence was the abolition of the seats of the three Native Representatives in the Lower House and of the four senators in the Upper House, who were elected under the 1936 Act. 'For as long as they are there,' said Verwoerd (who spoke for one and a half hours in the debate), 'Natives will be in continuous confusion as to where their future really lies.' He added, 'They also cannot be retained because they are the declared enemies of emancipation . . . and the principle of the safeguarding of the White man.'[5]

So at the end of their term of office in 1960, the three Native Representatives in the House of Assembly, excellent MPs such as Margaret Ballinger and Walter Stanford, and the four White senators, of whom Dr Edgar Brookes was the greatest loss, disappeared.

Parliament spent a great many hours debating the Promotion of Bantu Self-Government Bill and the entire United Party caucus was unanimously against it. But this display of solidarity did nothing to combat the inherent deep disagreement on many basic principles, including the differing reasons for opposing the Bill. Indeed, this Bill, fought with such common purpose in the House, was to prove the catalyst that split the United Party.

Matters came to a head in 1959, when a United Party congress was held in Bloemfontein. The conflict arose out of a resolution that no further land was to be given to the Blacks for their occupation and use. This referred specifically to the additional land scheduled to be added under the 1936 Land Act, over and above that allocated by the original 1913 Act. For some reason there were ever-recurring delays about handing over this extra land, and even in 1991 some two million hectares remained to be transferred.

Although the 1936 Land Act had been passed by the Fusion

government, with the concurrence of General Smuts, this did not deter Douglas Mitchell, one of the most reactionary English-speaking members of the United Party, and leader of the party in Natal. He moved that because Verwoerd, in the debate on the Promotion of Bantu Self-Government Act, had suggested that the Native Reserves would eventually become independent, and thus would no longer be part of the Union of South Africa, no further land should be handed over to the Blacks. The previous year, Mitchell had declared he did not think any further land should go to the Blacks 'because they ruined the land'; this time his rationale was that the land was going to belong to independent Black homelands in a carved-up South Africa. Mitchell hoped to win votes in the rural areas, especially in northern Natal, where much of the unallocated land was situated.

Mitchell's resolution was accepted at the United Party congress in Bloemfontein, despite strong opposition from the liberal wing – parliamentary and extra-parliamentary. It became obvious that a great deal of lobbying had taken place within United Party ranks to marshal the forces against us. Graaff voted against the resolution, but said he would not treat it as a mark of no confidence in his leadership if congress accepted it. That ensured that he stayed as leader, although he disagreed with the step taken by congress.

It also ensured a major split in the United Party.

4

The Birth of the Progressive Party
and Keeping It Alive

When the congress ended, I went to my car with Kathleen Mitchell, city councillor for Houghton and my great chum in politics. (She died of cancer in 1968.)

'Well Katie,' I said, 'this is it. I'm going home and I'm resigning. I'm not staying in a party with this disgusting attitude, with this totally expedient attitude to Blacks.'

'I'm with you,' she replied.

My friend Bunny Neame, the *Rand Daily Mail* parliamentary correspondent, had asked for a lift to Johannesburg. As well as the ride, he was to get a scoop as the first journalist to break the story of the United Party split.

As we were about to drive off, I noticed in the rear-view mirror of my car that three of my colleagues and close friends, Zach de Beer, Colin Eglin and Ray Swart, were in earnest conversation on the steps of the City Hall.

'Hang on a minute,' I said to Kate, 'something's happening.'

We jumped out of the car, and joined them. 'Come on chaps, what's going on?' I asked.

One of them replied, 'We're going to resign from the United Party.'

'Oh great,' I said, 'that's fine. We can all do it together.'

I parked my car again, and we went upstairs to a room in the Maitland Hotel in Bloemfontein. We sat talking far into the night, deciding how we were going to do it. In the end we composed a letter to Graaff. Several Members of Parliament and a number of other party supporters, including provincial councillors, signed it, and it was delivered personally to Graaff at the Bloemfontein airport.

He simply said, 'Oh well, some people will always try these things at congresses.' And off he went back to Cape Town, evidently unconcerned, and there we were, having announced our intention to resign from the United Party, but having no further plans for the moment.

Our immediate requirement was to make contact with Harry Lawrence, who was on holiday in Italy with his wife. It was extremely important that we be given respectability by having this man with us, for he was a brilliant frontbencher, and had been a Cabinet Minister in the Smuts regime. The rest of us were backbenchers. So we sent frantic cables to Italy, and to our great relief and joy Lawrence eventually cabled back that he was with us.

Fortunately, we also had a high-profile member of our group in the person of the former leader of the United Party in the Cape Province, Dr Jannie Steytler, an Afrikaner with a great sense of justice. Jannie was not a specially good parliamentary debater, but he was extremely popular and was an excellent speaker on public platforms, with much emotional appeal. Of great importance also was the backing we were given from the outset by Harry Oppenheimer, who had left Parliament in 1957 to run the Anglo American Corporation, the empire founded by his late father, but had retained his interest in politics. His continuing support, financial and otherwise, over future years helped our fledgling party to be viable and encouraged its acceptance by members of the business community.

We decided that we would each meet Graaff personally and tell him the reason for our resignation from the United Party, which we did. Two MP signatories, after speaking to Graaff, subsequently changed their minds about resigning. One of them, Clive van Ryneveld, who felt he owed his parliamentary nomination to Graaff, later withdrew his retraction and came back to us. The other, frontbencher Sidney Waterson, remained in the United Party.

Graaff made no effort to dissuade me from leaving the party, though he tried hard with some of the other dissidents. He

considered me a troublemaker, which I was, though I was not, as
he believed, the instigator of the rebellion.

We had to decide whether we would resign our seats. On this
question there was a difference of opinion: John Cope, MP for
Parktown, and I felt we should resign and fight by-elections. As
Transvaal candidates for the United Party, we had been required to
sign an undertaking drafted by Max Borkum, chairman of the
candidates' committee, that should we leave the United Party we
would resign our seats. Ironically, the liberal wing had initiated
this undertaking as a result of the defections in 1953 of the five
United Party MPs. Little did we realise that this would redound on
us. But Cope and I held the only two seats where there was a chance
of success because of the more liberal attitude in our two 'silk-
stocking' districts. In any event, we did not have the structure to
fight by-elections. Nor did we have an official policy, and the
electorate was not really aware of what had happened at
Bloomfontein. We needed time until the next general election, due
in 1963, to formulate policy and put our show on the road.

So, by a majority decision taken at my home in August 1959,
about a month after the United Party congress, we decided to call
our own congress, which we did. It was well attended by
enthusiastic supporters and very successful. We formed ourselves
into the Progressive Party, which was launched with Steytler as
leader and Lawrence as chairman. We adopted a policy rejecting
race discrimination and proposed a franchise which enabled adult
citizens who qualified on an educational standard or economic
achievement to have the vote. We also proposed a federal system of
government, a Bill of Rights and an independent judiciary.

We fanned out to spread the word, speaking at house meetings and
public meetings. I addressed dozens over the next few months.
Getting the support of the youth was especially important, so the
universities received a great deal of attention. I addressed a meeting at
Wits University, where the lecture hall was crammed with interested
students, including a few Blacks. At question time one of them asked,
'What would Mrs Suzman say if I asked her if I could marry her
daughter?' My younger daughter Patty (then a medical student) was
in the audience and she said loudly, 'Why don't you ask me – I *am* her
daughter!' Much laughter and an end to that old South African bogey.

There were many consultations with Black leaders. At one meeting at my house, Oliver Tambo, later president of the African National Congress-in-Exile, and other prominent members of the organisation, were present. Nelson Mandela was underground at the time. Ray Swart, Jannie Steytler and I went to Groutville in Zululand to see Chief Albert Lutuli, then a banned person (later awarded the Nobel Peace Prize), to discuss the emergence of the new party. Although none of the Blacks agreed with the policy of a qualified franchise, all expressed pleasure at the birth of a new political party committed to the principle of equal opportunity and to the eradication of race discrimination. (In 1978 the party's franchise policy was changed to universal adult franchise on a Common Voters' Roll.)

We were given enthusiastic support by many who had been dedicated workers for the United Party. The whole of my constituency committee, bar two people, joined the Progressive Party. Their work eventually proved in 1961 that 'elections are won between elections' as my campaign manager Max Borkum would emphasise, exhorting our supporters to enrol members and to raise funds.

Unfortunately I missed the opening of the 1960 session of Parliament through illness. I was packing for Cape Town and kept falling into my suitcase. Patty, who was with me said, 'Ma, whatever is the matter with you?' I said, 'I feel as if I'm dying' and she replied, 'You look as if you're dying – go to bed.' 'I can't – I have to catch a plane tomorrow.' Said the aspirant doctor, 'You won't be going anywhere tomorrow.' She was right. I had infectious hepatitis which kept me in bed for a few weeks.

I was therefore not present in January 1960 to hear Harold Macmillan deliver his historic 'Wind of Change' speech in the parliamentary dining room to a joint meeting of both Houses. It was on this occasion that he so brilliantly anticipated the growth of Black nationalism and the movement to independence on the continent of Africa. Years later, in 1973, when I was awarded an Honorary Doctorate of Law by Oxford University, of which he was Chancellor, I sat next to him at lunch in the Codrington Library at All Souls. When I admired the beautiful interior he said,

'Yes yes my dear, all built on sugar and the slave trade.' He also told me that Verwoerd was the most granite-like man he had ever met.

With Steytler as our leader, we twelve Progressive Party MPs took our seats at the far end of the opposition ranks in Parliament, amid screams of rage from United Party MPs who kept shouting at us to resign and fight our seats under our own banner. We ignored them, because to us the basic issue of unequivocal opposition to apartheid was more important than the fact that we had been elected as United Party representatives. We felt we had been sent to Parliament to fight the racist policy of the National Party, and that the United Party wasn't doing the job properly.

We had a truly rewarding time in Parliament between 1960 and 1961. The twelve Progs were relegated to basement offices underneath the Senate block, but the bonhomie and team spirit more than compensated for the physical discomfort. The twelfth member was Walter Stanford, one of the three Natives' Representatives. An excellent MP, he had been a member of the small opposition Liberal Party and decided to join us, and a valuable addition he proved to be. Margaret Ballinger, the only other Liberal Party MP, and also a Natives' Representative, whom we thought would join us, did not do so. Apparently she hoped the United Party would nominate her as a senator after the seats of the Native Representatives were abolished. It did not happen.

We did not have the benefit of the expected period of grace to build up support for the Progressive Party before the next general election, due in 1963. Startling events precipitated an earlier election in 1961, two years ahead of schedule.

On 21 March 1960, Robert Sobukwe, leader of the Pan-Africanist Congress, called for a pass-burning protest, which took place in many parts of South Africa, including Langa, a Black township near Cape Town, where Blacks and police were involved in violent confrontations. At Sharpeville, south of Johannesburg, a large crowd of unarmed Blacks converged on the police station with the intention of handing in their passbooks. A policeman lost his head and although no order was given to shoot, as the subsequent inquiry revealed, fired into the crowd; others followed suit. The casualty list was sixty-nine Blacks killed and 180 injured. The Sharpeville massacre sent shock waves around the world, particularly when the horrific photographs of the dead and wounded were published.

In South Africa tension ran very high and rioting occurred in many areas. In Cape Town a hitherto unknown young Black man, Philip Kgosana, clad in khaki shorts, led a huge procession of some 30,000 people from Langa along the beautiful De Waal Drive towards Parliament, to protest against the tragic events of the previous few days. I well remember looking out of the below-ground-level window of my small office and seeing the trembling, booted feet of a soldier, part of the military detail sent to guard Parliament.

The remarkable thing about that march was that it took place in total silence and was absolutely orderly.

When the procession reached the police station, a few blocks short of Parliament, Kgosana was promised an interview with the Minister of Justice, F. C. Erasmus. In return, he was to instruct the huge procession to turn round and go back to the township. And that is what he did. The crowd wheeled around and marched back to Langa. But the Minister (whose main claim to fame was that he had once shot a rhinoceros from an army helicopter) did not keep his word. Instead Kgosana was arrested when he turned up for his appointment, a deplorable act of treachery. He escaped and fled the country, yet another Black exile whose leadership qualities were lost to South Africa.

On 29 March 1960 I wrote to my daughter Francie, who was studying in Aix-en-Provence at the time:

I have had about eight meetings with all sorts of people from the bishop down in an effort to find out the real truth of the ghastly happenings at Sharpeville. All the evidence so far points to quite needless and hysterical shootings by the police. I've got a sworn statement from one of the two White eye-witnesses – the only two who were there other than the police. This was from a reporter from *Drum* named Humphrey Tyler, who said the crowd was quite good humoured and even when the actual shooting started, he didn't quite believe it was in deadly earnest. Only when the bodies started dropping, did panic set in. All terrifying and people are at last waking up.

The government's reaction has varied from one defying the world to

a sudden change of attitude in that the Chief of Police announced over
the weekend that no more arrests would be made under the Pass Laws
for the time being. Verwoerd has to attend the Prime Ministers'
Conference in London in May. He couldn't have fancied any more riots
either, so they called off the police pro tem, though I don't see how they
will ever reinstate the old order.

    Over the weekend there have been organised pass burnings through-
out the whole country, with Lutuli setting the lead. The ANC is
horrified at the success of the PAC campaign and is rushing around
calling for a one-day strike at home. Yesterday was declared a day of
mourning by the ANC and Johannesburg was like a dead city. Many
business places closed at midday, as the African staff hadn't turned up.
During the night, vast crowds assembled at Orlando and beat up
anyone who had gone to work and was returning on the trains.
Fortunately the police restrained themselves and there were no
widespread burnings of buildings or rioting. Just how successful the
pass-burning campaign will be, I don't know, but I imagine the
government will have to modify the pass system linking no jobs or
accommodation in the urban areas to permission to be in the area. [My
prediction was incorrect. The Pass Laws were soon reinstated, an
action encouraged by a United Party frontbencher who jeered at the
government for displaying weakness.]

After the Sharpeville massacre, the ANC and the PAC were banned,
all meetings were prohibited, and a state of emergency was declared.
Sixteen hundred people were imprisoned without trial.

    Never had South Africa been more unpopular abroad, and
unprecedented actions were taken against her. The United Nations
Security Council condemned South Africa (Britain and France
abstained, but did not use their veto). A motion of condemnation
of South Africa's racial policies in the British House of Commons
was not opposed, and trade boycotts were threatened. Bitter
comments appeared in influential papers like the London *Times*,
and the *Economist* wrote, 'Only a madman would buy South
African shares'. As *Die Burger* sadly commented, 'South Africa has
become the polecat [die muishond] of the world'.

    During all this turmoil, there was a deathly hush from the official
opposition. Under the cloak of the emergency regulations, Parliament was the only open forum from which the country could be
kept informed of what was happening. However, not one speech
of condemnation, not one question, not one protest issued from
the United Party ranks.

During that tragic period we Progs were able to show our worth as a true opposition. We opposed the declaration of the state of emergency, which gave the Minister of Justice power to detain people without trial; and we opposed the banning of the ANC and of the PAC. We worked well together as a dedicated group; there was never any difference of opinion in our caucus as to how we should handle these issues.

I readily accepted the offer made by Minister of Justice, F. C. Erasmus, that any Member of Parliament who wanted to visit the detainees in jail could do so. I flew to Johannesburg and collected my friend Kathleen Mitchell, and we drove to Pretoria to see the detainees at the Central Prison. I said to her, 'Katie, if I don't come out within an hour, start screaming.'

I've never forgotten that first entry into a jail. The awful clang as the iron door closes behind you and you're left in this grey-walled corridor with its cement floor, with only a series of barred doors ahead of you.

During the 1960 state of emergency the authorities did not keep detainees in solitary confinement. In Pretoria jail, the White detainees were all kept together in the prison hospital. They were lined up in a semi-circle in a courtyard to which I was escorted by an enormous commanding officer. All prison officers have military titles in South Africa – it's General this and Colonel that – and they wear uniforms, not identical with those of the army, but with military emblems on their shoulders.

As we walked in, a smile ran around the semi-circle from one face to the other, almost as though it had been passed from one man to the next. The detainees crowded around me, and the commanding officer said, 'Well, this is Mrs Suzman, the Member of Parliament for Houghton, and she's come to see you people, but I must warn you, you're not allowed to talk about any of the conditions inside this place. You can talk to her and give her messages for your family and so on, but no discussion about anything that's happening inside.'

A young lawyer I knew well, Ernie Wentzel, a member of the Liberal Party, immediately said, 'Commandant, you mean I can't tell Mrs Suzman we're on a hunger strike?'

The Commandant said, 'No man, you can't tell her that.'

Ernie then said, 'And I can't tell Mrs Suzman that we haven't had any extra food in here from our relatives?'

'No man, you can't tell her that either.'

'Can't I tell her we are not allowed any visitors?'

'No man, you can't.'

This went on for about fifteen minutes with Ernie spilling the beans, while I remained absolutely deadpan.

When I came out of the men's section I went across to the women's prison, and my opening gambit, out of the corner of my mouth, to the first detainee I met there was, 'Are you women on a hunger strike too?' She said, 'No, but we're thinking of it.'

So when I got back to Cape Town I was able to make a speech in Parliament in which I reported that detainees in Pretoria were on a hunger strike. Of course it was headline news, because anything one said in Parliament could be published in the newspapers, despite the strict censorship imposed on the press by the emergency regulations. Balthazar John Vorster, who had become the Minister of Justice, was asked by the press whether they could print what was said in Parliament despite the emergency regulations and he replied, 'Yes – anything said here in Parliament is protected – it is Royal Game' – a good comment from a sturdy republican.

An early election was precipitated not only by the trauma of Sharpeville but by a referendum held in 1960 by Dr Verwoerd among the White electorate on whether South Africa should become a republic. The Progressive Party, valuing South Africa's close links with the Commonwealth, campaigned against this, as did the United Party. This fudged the difference between the two parties, which later told against us Progs. We also lost one of our valuable MPs, Professor Sakkies Fourie, who differed with us on the republican issue and became an Independent.

Verwoerd won the referendum by some 74,000 votes and went to London to attend the conference of Commonwealth Prime Ministers. His intention was to keep South Africa a republic within the Commonwealth, but there were such strong objections from the rest of the members of that august body that he withdrew South Africa from the Commonwealth. He returned to a rapturous welcome from his supporters, and called for an early election in October 1961.

'Splitting the opposition' became a major issue wherever the Progressive Party contested a seat against a United Party candidate. We were also attacked because we had not resigned our seats in 1959. I received very angry letters from some of my constituents. Just prior to the election in 1961 I had an especially bitter letter:

Dear Mrs Suzman

I have received your circular letter of 7th inst: and have noted carefully your reason as to why you and your colleagues did not give up your seats in Parliament when you resigned from the UP. You say that '*We* thought about this very carefully' and that *we* decided etc. etc.

May I ask you what on earth gave you and your colleagues the right to make such a decision or do you, like Dr Verwoerd, claim a divine right for your actions?

Let us be honest with one another. In view of the undertaking which you personally gave to the UP, it was completely immoral for you to take a decision which instead was clearly one for *me* and *my fellow voters* in the Houghton constituency to take. As a businessman, I know what would happen to me if I were to act as irresponsibly as you have done.

Let us be yet more honest with one another. It was known, although perhaps not generally so, before you attended the UP Congress at which you took your decision, that there was every likelihood that you personally would 'cook up' a cause for resigning. In the event, you and your colleagues were bitterly disappointed that so few UP members 'ratted'. Some of you realised that if you did resign and failed to obtain re-election, you would then lose your parliamentary salaries and I think it was this fact more than any other that caused you, as a group, not to resign. I do not think that such a consideration would apply to you personally but for some to resign and others not to do so would have 'rocked the boat'.

Your letter finishes by asking me to vote for you on 18th October. In view of your past record, what guarantee can you give me that would mean anything, that if I vote for you as a Progressive you will not become a Liberal or anything else, perhaps even a UP or a Nationalist the next day?

Politics is at best a dirty game, made so unfortunately by the people who play in it, but a person such as you can at least 'try' to keep it clean.

Yours sincerely
J. W. A. W.

PS. Please excuse this paper and my writing but I am at present propped
up in a hospital bed.

I replied:

15 September 1961

Dear Mr J. W. A. W.
I have received your letter dated 12 September, and must thank you
for affording me the opportunity of replying to the questions you
have raised.

Firstly, may I point out that I did not 'simply decide' (by divine or
any other right) not to resign my seat. I met my Constituency
Divisional Committee at a special meeting, to which Mr Henry
Tucker was invited and where he was given an opportunity of
putting the UP case. Thereafter, having heard my side of the story
too, the entire Committee of forty, with two exceptions, resigned
with me from the UP. I then held a public meeting, which was
widely advertised in the press, and to which all Houghton voters,
including yourself, were invited in order to hear my reasons for
resigning. I received an overwhelming vote of confidence.

I deny emphatically your completely unfounded accusation that I
personally went to the 1959 UP Congress determined to 'cook up' a
cause for resigning. Quite the contrary. Certain UP 'right-wingers',
including a paid youth organiser, openly boasted that they were
going to get rid of the so-called 'liberals' in the UP. The press
reported this prior to the Congress. It is ironical that for years we
were told that our presence in the Party was the reason why the UP
lost election after election. Now we are told that our leaving the UP
has weakened it.

Let me deal with your very unfair allegation that we did not resign
our seats because we did not want to lose our Parliamentary salaries.
(I must say, in passing, that your exclusion of me personally from
this accusation does not help, for we all accepted joint responsibility
for our actions at that time.) Does it not occur to you that if
mercenary considerations motivated us, we could all have stayed
snugly in the bosom of the UP forever, and so ensured our
continued financial security? After all, at best we had only 3½ years
before we would have to face the electorate after the split. Surely,
then, if we were concerned about the financial implications, we
would have been taking a very short-sighted line of action by leaving
the UP when we did.

May I remind you that although I was elected to Parliament when
I was a member of the UP, I was primarily sent to Parliament to
fight the Nationalist Government? Can you or any other voter in
Houghton claim with justification that I have not fulfilled my
obligations in this regard?

As for 'guarantees', I can give you none except that I shall continue to fight racial discrimination and injustice. In the words of Edmund Burke, on being elected MP for the City of Bristol, 'It ought to be the happiness and glory of a representative to live in the strictest union, the closest correspondence, and the most unreserved communication with his constituents. But his unbiased opinion, his mature judgement, his enlightened conscience, he ought not to sacrifice to you, to any man or to any set of men living.'

I hope that you will soon recover from your present illness.

Yours sincerely
Helen Suzman

After the 1961 session of Parliament and before the general election, I tried to persuade my constituents at my Report-Back meeting that splitting the opposition and maybe the loss of a couple of United Party seats were irrelevant. I asked: 'What does the country stand to lose by keeping a few fearless people in Parliament? Does the country not in fact stand to gain a great deal if it can prove to the outside world that we have people prepared to fight racial discrimination in South Africa and prove to the millions of watching non-Whites in this country that all of White South Africa is not ganging up inexorably against them?'

I read out a statement of support from Chief Albert Lutuli, and I continued,

> You may well ask – if the United Party has no hope of taking over reins of government, what hope has the Progressive Party? The answer is that while we cannot at this stage hope to take over government, can you imagine the electrifying effect on the world and on South African thinking if the Progressives are returned in the seats in which they stand? And I'll go further – the government would never dare carry on the way they have done if they knew that Progressive policies had the backing of 100,000 voters in the country. And let me tell you, the contrary is also true: if the Progressives fail to win support there will be no stopping this government, we will be a fully fledged military dictatorship within two years, and with Mr Vorster as Minister of Justice, there will be no visiting of detainees in Pretoria Central. Nothing will convince the government more effectively that it has the White electorate solidly behind it on colour policy than the wholesale elimination of the Progressives.

And indeed the wholesale elimination of the Progressives was only narrowly averted. For ten of the eleven MPs who left the United

Party to form the Progressive Party in 1959, the premature election of 1961 was a disaster. Despite the considerable effort we put into the election campaign with twenty-six candidates, I was the only sitting MP to retain a seat and all our other candidates were defeated. Even our leader Jannie Steytler lost his seat, as did the brilliant Harry Lawrence. It was a sad reflection on the South African electorate that it rejected so many first-class candidates and replaced them with third-raters, many of whom barely uttered a word in Parliament during future sessions.

Why was Houghton the exception? My opponent was Hymie Miller, an ex-mayor of Johannesburg, and the United Party MP for Bezuidenhout Valley. The hierarchy of the United Party, keen to get rid of me in the House, enticed Hymie to leave his safe seat and beard the dragoness in her den. They felt that as he too was Jewish, well known and popular, he would have an excellent chance of defeating me. But they misjudged the situation in two respects: first, I had the support of the *Rand Daily Mail*, Johannesburg's influential morning newspaper, with its stirring leading articles by its liberal editor, Laurence Gandar; and second, my opponents did not take into consideration the vastly superior organisational skills of my campaign manager, Max Borkum.

The story of the 1961 Houghton election campaign deserves to be put on record. It was run with military precision by Max – Second World War veteran, leading stockbroker and political animal par excellence. He had drive, determination and imagination, and was a brilliant organiser. His forces on the ground consisted of a number of enthusiastic amateurs, many of whom had never worked in an election campaign before, as I had been returned unopposed in the two previous elections in Houghton. Several of the volunteers were elderly ladies more familiar with bridge parties than political parties, but there were also many young Progs imbued with missionary zeal. Max set about the daunting task of winning the Houghton seat for the Progressive Party with ruthless determination. He soon had his motley team of workers organised into specialist groups: canvass-card writers, envelope addressers, envelope stuffers, canvass-card batchers, foot canvassers, telephone canvassers and daily canvass tally-keepers.

The absentee vote section received special attention, as it always accounted for a considerable percentage of the total votes in any election in South Africa and gave a psychological advantage to the party that was ahead when the absentee vote balloting closed a few days before the election and estimated results were made public. Expert tracers in the Houghton office were sent to all parts of the republic to flush out voters still registered in Houghton but no longer living there. Information on their whereabouts was obtained from the current residents, from estate agents and from travel agents: the absentee voter agents pursued their prey like Bushmen trackers.

Personal contact with the voters was essential, as South Africa had no television in those days. (Indeed it was not introduced until 1976, after the departure of the then Minister of Posts and Telegraphs, Dr Albert Hertzog, who referred to television as the 'devil's box'. He made his opposition clear by telling Parliament, 'I want to emphasise that it would be absolutely fatal to the intellectual future of our country if a television service such as that which exists in most other countries was simply to be introduced into our country.'[1] Even after television finally arrived in South Africa – the National Party having realised its enormous propaganda value – it was not readily available to the opposition parties as it was government controlled.)

Effective publicity by way of placards, posters and manifestos was an important part of the campaign. Every second tree in the constituency was adorned with posters of my smiling face, above the simple slogan 'Helen Suzman for Houghton'. Three enormous billboards bearing the same slogan were erected at strategic corners in the constituency, where they could be seen by the voters driving in and out of the city centre every day.

The daily tally extracted from the information on the canvass cards was the barometer of progress towards the ideal of contacting every available voter on the roll. A new system of personalised canvassing was put into operation. Canvassers were classified by occupation or religion, and doctors, nurses, lawyers, teachers and accountants on the campaign team were roped in to approach their colleagues and were allocated special voters as their targets. Prominent members of the Anglican, Catholic, Methodist and Jewish communities were similarly recruited to contact voters belonging to their respective religious faiths. The old age homes in the constituency received special attention. We arranged postal votes for the infirm and used volunteers to canvass them in their home language if necessary: for example, German in Our Parents Home, which had been established by the German-Jewish community. (Many of the old folk stated emphatically that they intended to vote for General Smuts, who had been dead for ten years.)

My manifesto, which reached every voter, stressed my past record as their parliamentary representative. It quoted favourable comments made by the press, and it stressed my commitment to liberal values and to sound economic policies. The carefully spaced election meetings featured prominent people selected to speak in my support. Saturday morning committee meetings were held throughout the campaign and were used by Max to identify weak spots in the organisation and to exhort the workers to greater efforts. 'Let's capture the high ground and hold it' was his favourite phrase. During the last few days before the election, the preparation of transport sheets was the main preoccupation, to ensure that every supporter would be taken to the polls.

A special feature of the campaign was election day organisation. Every polling booth was decorated with Prog colours and posters and attractive young women welcomed the voters. Up-to-the-minute statistics were available at each polling station and forces deployed accordingly by the campaign manager. Max's presence at the count, and his expert knowledge of the procedures involved there, proved an invaluable asset and source of confidence to me. As election day wore on and the hour at which the polls closed drew near, desperate efforts were made to persuade errant supporters to come and do their civic duty. The effectiveness of the system was demonstrated by the final count. More than eighty per cent of supporters had recorded their votes by the time the polls closed, well above the average elsewhere.

To both candidate and campaign manager, the ultimate rewards of weeks of unremitting work were the wild cheers and tears of joy that greeted us from the huge crowd awaiting the result when we finally emerged from the count at 2 a.m., and the electoral officer announced that I had won.

The 1961 Houghton election campaign was an outstanding example of superb organisation which overcame the hostile climate towards the Progressive Party for having 'split the opposition'. Two days before the election, Hymie Miller confidently informed Graaff that he would win Houghton with a 2000 majority. My friend Tony Delius, the *Cape Times* parliamentary correspondent, phoned me to ask if this dismal prediction could possibly be true. Acting on Max's advice, relayed by me, Tony took all the bets going against the Progs winning Houghton. He was well supplied with whisky the day after the election. Max had predicted the result with uncanny accuracy – only twelve votes less than the 564 majority I obtained.

In the early hours of the next morning, when all the results had been announced over the radio, it became apparent that I was the only Prog who would return to Parliament.

My elder daughter, Frances, who had interrupted her studies at the Courtauld Institute in London to help in the campaign, turned to me and said in a despairing voice, 'Ma, what are you going to do?'

'I don't know,' was my quavering reply.

Little did I know that I would face that situation for thirteen years. In 1966 and in 1970, I was again the only Progressive Party candidate to win a seat, with Max as my campaign manager, using the same tactics and with even greater support from the English-language press, which had observed with approval my stand on contentious issues during the five years as the lone Prog. Joel Mervis, the editor of the *Sunday Times*, the newspaper with the largest circulation in South Africa and at that time a staunch supporter of Graaff and the United Party, wrote a leading article in 1966 entitled 'A Special Case'. In it he said:

> United Party supporters in Houghton are faced with a difficult decision on election day. Normally, there would be no problem – they would vote for the United Party candidate, Dr Bensusan. But this is not a normal situation. It is what the lawyers might call a special case. Mrs Suzman, after all, has carved a special place for herself in South African public life. Adherents of every party admire her for her courageous and intelligent showing in Parliament; and she is precisely the kind of person who deserves to be returned to Parliament. Indeed, if one takes

the great traditions of Parliament as a yardstick, it could probably be said that no other candidate, not even the Prime Minister himself, has a better claim to go back.

Max had the leading article blown up to billboard size and displayed outside every polling booth in the constituency. I increased my majority, albeit by only 147 votes.

All in all, I fought six elections during my parliamentary career; in three others I was unopposed.

Campaigns had their amusing side, particularly when canvassing voters. Some were very hostile to the Progressive Party, especially those who said 'We staunch UP – we non-political', and slammed the door in one's face. (That lot never seemed to have any use either for verbs or for us Progs.) To them our treachery in leaving the old party and thus 'splitting the opposition' was unforgivable and remained so until the United Party disappeared from the political scene.

Then there were those whose knowledge of the law was somewhat sketchy. One woman I canvassed on behalf of a candidate fighting a by-election in 1963 for the Progressive Party complained that she objected to the Progressive Party's mixed marriages policy. 'You want to get rid of the prohibition of mixed marriages,' she said coldly. (The Mixed Marriages Act prohibited marriage across the colour line.) I told her we had no fixed policy regarding mixed marriages, except that as far as we were concerned marriage was essentially a matter of personal choice and the state, we felt, should play no part in it. 'That's all very well for you,' she said. 'It's my daughter – she wants to marry a Jew.'

The Friedmans were an elderly couple living in a flat in my constituency. He was nearly blind and she was infirm and both required absentee voter ballots. Off I trotted with the application forms for them to sign. I obtained admission after giving repeated reassurances through the door that I was who I claimed to be, the MP for the area. The old lady was in a very bad mood. 'Blacks are ungrateful,' she said. She had given her maid a weekend off to attend a wedding and had even presented her with a dress to wear. Yet on her return the maid had objected when asked to make a cup of tea for Mrs Friedman, complaining that 'all day long she was on her feet'. 'Where else should she be?' asked the old lady. 'On her hands?' I soothed the old girl, and persuaded her and her husband to sign the forms. A few days later I went back with the ballots, acting as Commissioner of Oaths as required by law to validate them. This time the old man was irritable. 'Medical costs are far too high,' he grumbled. His wife needed to have 'her water tested' and the account from the Medical Research Institute was R65. I thought this charge extremely unlikely and asked to see the account. 'Good news, Mr Friedman,' I said, 'the account is six rands fifty cents, not sixty-five rands.' 'Oi darlink,' said Mr Friedman, 'have you earned your vote!'

I canvassed one constituent recently released from prison, after serving several years for committing fraud. I told him I was the Progressive Party candidate. He glared at me and said, 'With your views, you are a disgrace to the Jewish people.'

I did a lot of canvassing by phone, as it became increasingly difficult to get past all those remote-controlled gates in Houghton. If one did gain access, one was lucky not to be torn to pieces instantly by rottweilers. I was pretty confident that I could tell by the tone of voice when I phoned, whether I could mark the canvass card 'for' or 'against'. The 'fors' were always pleased I had taken the trouble to contact them. The 'againsts' said bleakly, 'We know what we doing.' So did I. No verb, no vote.

By 1966 I had acquired the seniority to occupy a front bench in Parliament. I approached Jack Higgerty, still Chief Whip of the United Party, to ask him to arrange this. Higgerty hemmed and hawed and puffed on his cigar and said he'd think it over. Fuming, I went to Cape Town station to collect my luggage which had arrived by train. There I ran into J. E. Potgieter, National Party Chief Whip. Before I could say anything he said, 'Hello Helen. You will be on the front bench this session.' I told him of my encounter with Higgerty and he laughed, 'Leave it to me.' I found my nameplate on an opposition front bench, next to Abe Bloomberg, a United Party representative of the Coloured people.

We in the Progressive Party would refer to Abe, a shrewd lawyer and leading light in Cape horse-racing circles, as 'Honest Abe, the people's choice'. My private name for him was 'Mr Fixit', based on my bemused observation of his ability to do this. He had three United Party colleagues in Parliament: the other White representatives of the Coloured voters. One of them, Bill Holland, was a notorious alcoholic. One day, shortly after the session began, an agitated Mr Barnett, one of the three, rushed in and said, 'Where is Abe? I must find him or Bill will be found guilty for the third time of driving under the influence.' That would have meant six months' imprisonment without the option of a fine. Bill would then have automatically been disqualified as an MP, a prospect that rather pleased me, as I knew the Progressive Party had a good chance of winning the ensuing by-election. Alas, it was not to be. Apparently Mr Fixit fixed it and Bill's case did not come to court.

After the 1966 election, the Nats held two-thirds of the seats in Parliament. They occupied the entire government side of the House of Assembly, more than two rows of benches on the opposition side and all the cross-benches. This meant that I was not only faced with Nats and flanked by Nats, but had them behind me as well. I found it distinctly unnerving to turn around and find several sets of beady eyes fixed on me with unremitting hostility, not to mention all the uncomplimentary interjections when I was making a speech.

In 1970 after the same sad story of a solitary Houghton victory had repeated itself, I said bitterly, 'Five more years alone with that bloody mob!' My remark was overheard by a journalist and appeared in *Life* magazine. On arrival in Cape Town for the session I was sent for urgently by the Speaker, Mr Klopper. A copy of the article was on his desk and he said a complaint had been lodged by a Nationalist MP and that I must apologise in the House. I resisted this instruction for almost the entire session. The Speaker then sent for me again and said he was under pressure from the National Party caucus to insist on my apology. Knowing how much I relied on his co-operation in allowing me to participate in debates, I reluctantly stood up in the House and said that the remark had not been intended for publication, but since some members had found it offensive, I apologised.

5

Confronting Verwoerd, Vorster and Botha

During the years that I was the lone Prog MP, two Prime Ministers held office: Dr Hendrik Verwoerd, who was Minister of Native Affairs and then Prime Minister from 1958 to 1966; and Balthazar John Vorster, Minister of Justice and then Prime Minister from 1966 to 1978. I also had the dubious honour of coping with P. W. Botha, Minister of Coloured Affairs and of Defence before he became Prime Minister from 1978 to 1983 and State President from 1983 until 1989.

Verwoerd, Vorster and Botha were as nasty a trio as you could encounter in your worst nightmares. They were ably assisted by a posse of equally unpleasant Ministers of Bantu Administration and of Police and Justice. Special mention in this regard must go to M. C. Botha and Jimmy Kruger.

Dr Verwoerd was an extraordinary man. He was not South African by birth, but came to the country with his Dutch parents when he was two years old, and lived his life as a devoted Afrikaner. He harboured a deep conviction that he had a divine mission to maintain White civilisation on the southern tip of the Black continent of Africa.

I have to admit Verwoerd was the only man who has ever scared me stiff, and I suspect he had much the same effect on his own caucus and on the United Party, then the official opposition. Here was a man who could stand up in Parliament and talk for more than two hours without a note, building up an argument so convincingly that one sat there nodding one's head like a zombie, until one realised that his entire argument was built on a false premise, for example, that there were no urbanised Blacks, that they all belonged in their ethnic areas and that was where they must exercise their political rights. In practice, the policy aimed at 'freezing' the number of Blacks living in the urban areas, restricting further migration from the rural areas and utilising only migrant Black labour in the urban areas. To this was added Verwoerd's ruthless implementation of forced removals – one of the most appalling aspects of apartheid. It involved the forcible uprooting and 'resettlement' of Black communities into the Native Reserves or Bantustans. The policy aimed *inter alia* at eliminating the so-called 'Black spots'. These were usually rural lands which had been acquired by Black tribes through purchases from White farmers before the Land Act of 1913 (extended in 1936), which severely restricted the right of Blacks to acquire land.

In some cases 'Black spots' consisted of land granted by the government of the day in recognition of services rendered, such as that given by the colonial government of Queen Victoria to the Mfengu people of Tsitsikama in the eastern Cape, for their support of the White settlers during the Sixth Border War (1834) against other Black inhabitants. This gesture of gratitude did not prevent the removal at gunpoint of the Mfengu people some 143 years later, from their fertile lands to an area more than 250 miles away – land which could not provide for them even at subsistence level. (Their own land was sold to White farmers for an average of R229 per hectare. Today the land is valued at R5000 per hectare and the Mfengu are engaged in a determined fight to regain their ancestral home through appeals to the government and by court action. They may well succeed in the 'New South Africa'.)

Verwoerd's Grand Apartheid scheme included the relocation of urban Black townships into other urban areas already so designated such as the removal of the Sophiatown community to Meadow-lands in Soweto. The endorsement out, or expulsion of 'illegal' Black town-dwellers, was yet another part of this heinous scheme.

The Native Reserves into which removals took place were already heavily overpopulated and overstocked with cattle and other livestock. There was scant preparation for the reception of people 'resettled' in those distant areas: often only the erection of row upon row of tin latrines on small demarcated plots. Their former homes, schools and churches were demolished and live-stock disposed of with minimal compensation. Entire communities, together with their meagre possessions, were loaded on to trucks under the supervision of armed police and transported many miles into the Reserves.

From the middle of the seventies Dr Verwoerd's Grand Apartheid scheme had been partially accomplished, as four of the ten Bantustans became 'independent': Transkei, Bophuthatswana, Venda and Ciskei (known as the TBVC states). Of course they were independent in name only. They relied on the Republic of South Africa for the major part of their revenue, so-called 'foreign aid', and they were dependent on the earnings of migrant workers in the Republic. Moreover they were recognised as independent states only by each other and by South Africa. Six Bantustans remained as self-governing areas.

I had a number of sharp exchanges with Verwoerd when he was Minister of Native Affairs as well as when he became Prime Minister in September 1958. That year he made his famous prediction about the future of Blacks in so-called White South Africa, saying that from 1978 Black migration to the cities would be reversed and Blacks would be returning to the by then prosperous homelands: 'The rising graph [of migration into the cities] will continue to rise until the year 1978 and then it will fall.'[1] Five years later I challenged Verwoerd with a more realistic assessment of the consequences of his predictions, asking

If thousands of Blacks went streaming back to the Bantustans, leaving White farmers deprived of their labour force with fields and livestock untended, and mine owners with their empty compounds and stationary shaft wheels; and factory owners with their silent, motion-less, machinery, whether all the guns of the Defence Force would not be used to stop these people, and to turn them back into the White Republic of South Africa so that they once again could dig our gold, plough our fields and man our factories, as they have always done, and as they always will do.[2]

To which Cas Greyling (National Party MP for Ventersdorp) replied: 'That is her death knell that has tolled. The speech of the Honourable Member for Houghton is a picture that could only be conjured up by a lunatic.'[3]

Verwoerd also informed Parliament that the Afrikaner would rather be poor and White than rich and mixed. I was sorry he was not alive to witness how wrong he was when the boycotts by Black customers in Boksburg and Carletonville took place in 1980 after the far-right Conservative Party tried to put the clock back and reintroduce apartheid in those small mining towns. Threatened with bankruptcy, the White shopkeepers soon accepted the repeal of the Separate Amenities Act, Verwoerd's assessment notwithstanding.

When, in 1966, Verwoerd spoke sympathetically about Ian Smith's Unilateral Declaration of Independence in Rhodesia (to which he never gave *de jure* recognition), I said that the less we in South Africa had to do with those rebels, the better. Verwoerd then told me he had written me off. I retorted, 'And the whole world has written *you* off.'

In 1960 there was an attempted assassination of Verwoerd at the Witwatersrand Agricultural Show at Milner Park in Johannesburg. An English-speaking South African named David Pratt shot Verwoerd at point-blank range as he stood on the podium after making a speech. Pratt sent a .22 bullet through Verwoerd's face, but did not succeed in killing him. Verwoerd's burly bodyguard fainted. (Pratt, who was charged with attempted murder, but never stood trial, was sent to a mental institution. The following year he committed suicide.)

Verwoerd was taken to hospital and returned to Parliament less than two months later, when he proceeded to give one of his customary lengthy speeches, minus notes. A friend who was sitting in the Visitors' Gallery during this *tour de force* said to me afterwards, 'Good God – didn't that bullet do anything to Verwoerd?' 'Sure,' I replied. 'It cleared his sinuses.'

Verwoerd made one of his first public appearances after the attempted assassination at the fiftieth anniversary celebrations of Union on 31 May 1960 in Bloemfontein. He was obviously more convinced than ever that divine guidance was with him, a sentiment not shared by the dove which he tossed into the air crying, 'There goes the symbol of South Africa's peace and prosperity.'

The astute bird dropped like a stone.

★

On 6 September 1966, the House assembled to discuss the Prime Minister's portfolio.[4] We were anticipating a long and busy afternoon as Verwoerd always talked at length on such occasions. In the event, the afternoon session ended abruptly.

The bells were ringing, as they do at a quarter past two every working day in the South African Parliament (except on Fridays when they ring at ten a.m.), when we all trooped in to take our seats. I sat down on my front bench, and a messenger handed me a letter, which I began to read. The Prime Minister came in and took his seat. Suddenly I heard a strangled cry and looked across the aisle of the House, only a few yards from my seat, where a small group had crowded around the Prime Minister's desk.

'Good Lord, what's happened?' I asked my neighbour on the next bench, a member of the National Party, who replied excitedly, 'Didn't you see that man attack the Prime Minister?'

I wondered for a moment whether one of the members of the United Party had gone crazy, leaped across the floor and punched Verwoerd on the nose. I then heard another strangled cry, and as the group opened out I saw somebody being dragged along the aisle of the House by a few Members. It was the man who had attacked the Prime Minister, not an MP but a parliamentary messenger. Before my astonished eyes he was dumped opposite my desk, while members pulled at his clothes and pummelled him. After another scuffle, he was dragged out and presumably handed over to the police in the Lobby of Parliament.

While I was watching all this with utter amazement, down the aisle of the House from the direction of the Prime Minister's desk dashed the Minister of Defence, P. W. Botha, arms flailing and eyes bulging. He stopped opposite me, shook his finger at me and yelled in Afrikaans, 'It's you who did this. It's all you liberals. You incite people. Now we will get you. We will get the lot of you.' And he blundered out of the House. I was astounded at this attack and said to the Members on either side of me, 'Good God, did you hear that?' Those on the right of me, who were United Party members said, 'Yes, what a thing to say.'

One of the MPs went to the Speaker's dais (the Speaker came in only after the Members were seated and the bells had stopped ringing) and announced, 'The Prime Minister has been seriously injured. Will you all kindly vacate the Chamber?' Soon afterwards the Prime Minister was rushed to hospital by ambulance.

When I went out into the Lobby with everybody else, I was beside myself with rage at Botha's accusation and the threat implicit in what he had said. I decided I could not let it go unchallenged. I went to see R. J. McFarlane, the Secretary of Parliament, who was a sympathetic official, always helpful and responsive. I told him of Botha's attack on me. He took a strong view of the matter and said, 'Well, my goodness me, one can't threaten a Member of Parliament the way he threatened you.' We agreed that he would report it to the Speaker.

By then we knew that Verwoerd was dead. Parliament was adjourned for the day. The following morning, I received a message to go at once to see the Speaker. On my arrival in Speaker Klopper's chambers, I found Botha there as well.

The Speaker turned to Botha, and said very sternly, 'Well, Mr Botha?'

Botha glared at me and growled, 'In terms of the rules of the House, I apologise.'

I lost my temper on hearing what I regarded as the most ungracious apology imaginable. I turned to the Speaker and asked, 'Do you expect me to accept an apology like that?'

The Speaker was distressed and said, 'Oh, please, calm down. We're all in such a nervous state. I do ask you to accept this apology. It would be very bad if we had any more scenes in Parliament.'

I turned to Botha, 'How dare you talk to me the way you did?'

'What did you expect?' he replied. 'There was my leader dying at my feet.'

'I'll tell you what I expect,' I said. 'I expect you to control yourself. You're the man behind the guns in South Africa. You're the Minister of Defence. It would be a sad day for all of us if you can't control yourself.'

He got up in a rage and said to the Speaker, 'Well, I've apologised and she can take it or leave it.' He flounced out of the room.

I turned to the Speaker again, 'Now, do you really expect me to accept that apology?'

'Well,' he said, 'I know he did the wrong thing. And he didn't apologise properly. But I do ask you to accept it in view of the circumstances and particularly as I myself want you to do so.'

Had I taken the matter further, in terms of the rules of the House, I would have had to use the first opportunity to move that a parliamentary select committee be set up to enquire into Botha's accusation and threats. That opportunity would have been immediately after the expressions of condolence by members of the different political parties.

The Speaker had always been more than fair to me, and I therefore felt I had a certain obligation not to put him through this ordeal. I promised to let him know and left his office.

I then consulted my two advisers in Cape Town: Colin Eglin (who had taken over the leadership of the party) and Harry Lawrence. Both advised strongly that I accept Botha's apology, however unsatisfactory. I sent a note to the Speaker: 'In deference to your wishes, and because of the unfortunate circumstances surrounding this whole incident, I have decided to accept Mr Botha's very unsatisfactory apology.' Within about ten minutes, the Chief Whip of the National Party, J. E. Potgieter, appeared in my office and said, 'I want to tell you we are very sorry about Mr Botha's outburst and we wish to thank you for not taking the matter any further.'

Although I felt better after Potgieter's visit, I vowed never again to speak to Botha on any personal basis; only on official business would I have anything to do with him. And from that day I never greeted him, though I had much to say to him across the floor in Parliament, especially after he became Prime Minister in 1978.

Verwoerd's assassin was a swarthy illegal immigrant named Demetrio Tsafendas, half-Greek and half-Portuguese. He was a temporary employee taken on by the Chief Messenger, and had obviously not been properly cleared by security. Indeed, the whole security situation was very lax until then. Every day, I would slip into the garden adjoining Parliament, through an unlocked gate (no policeman in attendance), walk through the garden to an unlocked side door in the office block of the House (no policeman in attendance), past the Prime Minister's office (no policeman in attendance), and take the lift to our offices on the second floor, and was never challenged by anyone to produce identification.

Tsafendas was charged in court, found to be insane, and was detained for life at the State President's pleasure. Those who are declared insane – be they murderers or other persons found guilty of a capital offence – are not executed in South Africa. South Africa executes only sane people, or did so until the moratorium on the death sentence in 1990. Since there are no institutions for mentally unsound murderers, Tsafendas is still in a maximum security prison in Pretoria twenty-five years on, reportedly in death row, and will probably spend the rest of his life there.

The most extraordinary thing about the removal of Verwoerd from the political scene was the eerie absence of almost any reference to him in Parliament in the years immediately after his assassination. It seemed as if there was a conscious effort to forget him, to exorcise his memory. That is, until the Herstigte Nasionale Party (HNP) under Albert Herzog, broke away from the National Party in 1969 after a Maori was permitted to come to South Africa with the All Blacks rugby team. Albert and his three MPs (I called them 'the quaint quartet') voiced many recriminations about the undermining of Verwoerd's concept of apartheid. All the HNP candidates lost their seats in the 1970 general election and the ghost of Verwoerd vanished again until the formation of the far-right Conservative Party under Dr Andries Treurnicht in 1982, after Prime Minister P. W. Botha had declared in favour of 'healthy power sharing'. (Evidently the Progressives' policy constituted 'unhealthy power sharing'.) From then on, a great deal more was heard about the betrayal of Verwoerd's sacred ideals.

Balthazar John Vorster succeeded Verwoerd in 1966. He was a different cup of tea altogether – pragmatic, down to earth and with no pretensions to divine missions.

Although Vorster's objective, like Verwoerd's, was the maintenance of White domination, he was more at home with the concept of baasskap [domination] than with Bantustans, and displayed a tough attitude to any opposition. He knew full well that the security of the state depended on maintaining a strong army and a strong police force in a country where unpopular laws pressed hard on the majority of the people, who were denied the right to voice their objections and were not consulted about the laws that governed their lives. I was convinced that there would not be many changes in basic government policy under the new Prime Minister, though there might be changes in emphasis.

Significantly, Vorster retained the Police portfolio. Make no mistake, though not the philosopher Verwoerd was, Vorster knew what apartheid was all about. In a significant speech on 24 March 1961 when he was Deputy Minister of Education, Arts and Science, he had told us what his version was. Speaking on the occasion of South Africa's leaving the Commonwealth, he said:

> I do not know what awaits South Africa. I do not know whether we shall continue to exist as a nation. I believe we shall do so, because we were placed here in South Africa for that purpose. But if it should happen that this nation must go under, let us then go under because it is our fate and not because it is our fault.[5]

I had much to do with Vorster before he became Prime Minister, when he was Minister of Justice and Police, responsible for piloting through Parliament in the 1960s the first Bills giving powers of detention without trial. I paid many a visit to the Union Buildings in Pretoria to see him on behalf of detainees. Security was lax there too in those days; one simply walked past an old fellow (probably a Boer War veteran) dozing in the entrance, ascended a flight of stairs and entered the Minister's anteroom. No identification was demanded and there was no search for weapons. Vorster gave me a courteous if chilly reception on those visits and always offered me coffee. I would reel off all the complaints I had received from the relatives of detainees: no visits allowed, rumours that detainees were kept in solitary confinement, locked up for twenty-three hours out of twenty-four with nothing to read but the Bible.

Vorster once paid me the 'compliment' of saying I was worth ten United Party MPs; I thought this was an understatement. He also told me that I allowed myself 'to be used too much', implying that I was one of Lenin's 'useful idiots'. And he had a point. I was used by people who had political views and aims very different from my own, ranging from those who supported the banned Communist Party to extreme Black nationalists. But, as I told him, as long as he locked people up without trial, I had no option.

I had many sharp exchanges in Parliament over his interpretation of the General Laws Amendment Bill, ubiquitously known as the Ninety-day Detention Law, which gave the Minister and senior police officials power to imprison any person incommunicado without trial for ninety days, and the manner in which it was implemented. During the no confidence debate at the beginning of the 1964 session I attacked Vorster for the lack of supervision of conditions in which the detainees were held, in prisons and police cells scattered throughout the length and breadth of the country. Despite a general instruction that they be held under the Awaiting Trial Prisoner Regulations, it was absolute nonsense to equate the conditions of awaiting-trial prisoners and those of detainees:

> Awaiting-trial prisoners are not kept in solitary confinement; they are not locked in single cells for twenty-three out of twenty-four hours of the day; they are allowed access to their lawyers and they are entitled to reading material as a right; they are entitled to visitors and to various other concessions. I want to make the categorical statement that as far as I can see, the conditions under which the ninety-day detainees are being held throughout the country in prisons and in police cells are worse than the conditions under which detainees were held under the declared state of emergency in 1960.
>
> . . . [Furthermore] the Minister refuses to disclose the instructions he has given to the people whose duty it is to administer this arbitrary law that he has passed.

I went on to talk about the abuses that took place under the Ninety-day Law:

> As if detention, being locked up without recourse to the courts of law or to legal advice is not bad enough, this system involves the refined torture of solitary confinement. I believe this is a disgrace to any so-called civilised country . . .
>
> . . . There is another form of torture, the use of which is denied, and that is physical torture, unlike mental torture, about which many allegations have been made. I have dozens of statements made by non-White detainees. They all allege different forms of physical torture. Throughout the length and breadth of the country, prisoners kept in solitary confinement with no connection with each other have made statements that they have been tortured. There are allegations about being hit with sticks, with bare fists, with hosepipes, of people being punched and kicked, of people being beaten with straps and batons. There are many allegations about electric shocks being given in order to induce people to make statements. The Honourable Minister wanted

the names of the people so he could have the cases investigated, but the Minister would not give any indemnification that these people, if they make statements and have been discharged, will not be re-arrested. I read some appalling allegations that had been made in the case of a man called Looksmart Ngudle, who was a detainee under Ninety-days. Looksmart Ngudle died in detention. It is no good the Minister simply coming to the House and denying these things. It is no good his Commissioner of Police and his Commissioner of Prisons simply saying it is a lot of nonsense. This whole thing lends itself to abuse.

There can be no detailed supervision of a law like this, and therefore it is quite likely that the Minister doesn't know, the Commissioner of Police doesn't know and the Commissioner of Prisons doesn't know. Apart from the torture, almost without exception non-Whites complain about the rotten food they are receiving in these jails . . . of filthy cells, of no toilet facilities, no toilet paper, no utensils for eating, not enough blankets and worst of all, about the constant intimidation and threats by the warders.

Now let me come to the magistrates, these famous magistrates, who are supposed to be visiting these people weekly. Many of their statements mention quite specifically that complaints were made to the magistrate about filthy cells, no change of clothing, beating, assaults and so on. The complaints simply say 'I complained about the food and was told that this was not an hotel.' 'The magistrate sat in the car and the interpreter said that the magistrate was not interested in such things as electric shocks.' Others reported assaults to the Chief Warders. What was the result? They were beaten up again, not by the Chief Warder but by the very men who had assaulted them at first.

Vorster interjected: 'I asked you specifically to give me the names and so far you have not done so.'

I thought the Honourable Minister follows court proceedings and statements in the newspapers about his department religiously. They have all been reported in the press. But I will give them to him. Then there are people who go from police station to police station. They are moved and their relatives are not told where they are. Should people have to go from one police station to the other to find out where their relatives are being held?

I also said that there were cases of persons serving not one lot of ninety days, but two. There were even cases of people serving their third term of ninety-days' imprisonment, and there were at least three women who had served more than one ninety-day stretch. The Minister had said that such people only had to talk and they would go free. I asked:

At which stage does the Minister decide or the officers in charge of these
people decide that they do not in fact have the information which he
required? How, anyway, does he ever decide that the information
given under those conditions can ever be reliable evidence? The
Minister is not trying to extract confessions from these people; what he
seeks is information about other people's alleged misdemeanours.[6]

There were many cases where the statutory time limit of ninety
days was ignored. One example was the case of Albie Sachs, who
was detained for 168 days. The story is told in his book *The Prison
Diary of Albie Sachs.* (Albie has returned from exile and is now a
member of the Constitutional Committee of the ANC.) Another
was Ruth First, who was held for 117 days. Ruth, a dedicated
communist, was the wife of Joe Slovo (later to become chairman of
the South African Communist Party after it was unbanned in
1990). She was detained in 1963, released after ninety days and
taken to a public phone booth supposedly to call her relatives to tell
them to come and collect her. Before she could do so, she was re-
arrested, and once again put into detention. She then apparently
suffered a nervous breakdown and, as it appeared from the book
she wrote later, and also from the film *A World Apart*, scripted by
her daughter, she attempted suicide while in Pretoria Prison.

I was telephoned one evening by a well-known woman communist, who said to me, 'I am asking you as one woman to another
to intervene in Ruth First's case. We hear that she is in a very bad
way mentally. Won't you ask Mr Vorster to release her and let her
leave South Africa on an exit permit?' Exit permits in those days
were given to people on the strict condition that they were not
allowed to return to South Africa. They also had first to obtain
acceptance from the country where they intended to live.

I replied that I had an appointment the following week to see
Vorster to discuss other issues, and I would certainly raise the case
of Ruth First and would request an exit permit for her.

Shortly afterwards, however, the phone rang again and this time
it was Ruth First's mother, who said angrily, 'I hear, Mrs Suzman,
that you wish to interfere in my daughter's case. Kindly do nothing
of the kind. The Blacks must know that Whites are prepared to
suffer just as they are suffering.'

I replied, 'Mrs First, you have been misinformed. I have no

desire to intervene in your daughter's case. I was phoned by one of your friends and at her request I agreed to speak to Mr Vorster about Ruth when I see him next week. But of course if you don't want me to do so, I will drop it immediately. I have more than enough work on my hands,' and I put down the phone.

Half an hour later the phone rang again. This time it was Bram Fischer, the leader of the Communist Party in South Africa before it was banned in 1950.

He said smoothly, 'Is that my favourite MP?' And I said, 'Come off it, Bram, you have very little choice.' Then he said, 'I know you have just been spoken to by Mrs First. Please ignore what she said and meet us tomorrow morning.' I agreed somewhat reluctantly and met Bram and Mrs First as arranged.

Mrs First said abruptly, 'Well, it seems that Ruth really is in a bad way, so kindly raise her case when you see Mr Vorster.' I agreed to do so, without much enthusiasm.

When I met Vorster, I told him I had been informed that Ruth First was in a serious state of depression and added, 'I am sure you don't want a suicide in prison.' That was a shot in the dark, for at the time I had no idea Ruth had attempted suicide. In retrospect, I felt sure Vorster did know, for he agreed quite readily to my suggestion that he should grant her an exit permit.

Soon afterwards Ruth was released and left South Africa for England. She later went to Maputo in Mozambique and taught at the Eduardo Mondlane University. She was murdered there in 1982, blown up by a letter-bomb sent by unknown agents, about whom many had dark suspicions, much fortified by evidence which later emerged about South African security police death squads.

During the first session in 1967 under John Vorster as Prime Minister, I noted with interest that he had made an effort to transform his image from that of a tough policeman wielding a truncheon and wearing a helmet (as he was often portrayed by Dave Marais, the *Cape Times* cartoonist), into a benign-looking sportsman with a putter, wearing a golfer's cap. He talked about an outward policy towards the Black states and actually hosted a lunch for some Black Malawi delegates. He was prepared to allow one or two persons of colour to be members of visiting sports teams, such as the Maori in the New Zealand rugby team.

I was glad to have the opportunity to tell Vorster face to face during the 1969 session that I had seen the survey in the *Sunday Times* which said that over 70 per cent of the White population thought he was doing a good job, and only 0.3 per cent thought he was no good. I said I wanted to stand up and be counted among the 0.3 per cent.

Indeed in some ways he was even less sensitive to the oppressive nature of apartheid than his predecessor. During the no confidence debate in 1971 I quoted his comment to the London *Daily Telegraph* correspondent that 'he was not aware that there were any annoying elements in apartheid'.[7] I suggested several examples of 'annoying elements' he might experience were he not a White South African: having his wife endorsed out of the urban area if he were a Black man, or suffering arrest under the Pass Laws; or being Group Areaed out of his home or business if he were a Coloured or Indian; not to mention the impossibility of finding a golf course where he would be allowed to play his favourite game. I told him that his second comment to the same journalist – that it must be 'just as annoying for a White man when he could not go into a Black or Coloured restaurant as it is for a Black or Coloured person not to be allowed into a restaurant serving Whites'[8] – was one of the silliest remarks I had ever heard him make. I suggested that he should go into the townships heavily disguised as a human being to experience at first hand what it was like to be a Black South African.

Vorster was impervious to the hardships endured by the thousands of Black, Coloured and Indian people subjected to forced removals or threatened with them. I first witnessed the iniquities of resettlement during Vorster's regime in 1969, when Father Cosmas Desmond, a Catholic priest (on whose book *The Discarded People* the moving TV documentary *Last Grave at Dimbaza* was based), took me to visit some dismal areas in Natal – Limehill, Vergelegen and Uitval – where thousands of Black people had been dumped. At Limehill, more than 700 miserable victims were living in tents or shacks with hardly any facilities. There was no piped water, there were no clinics, no shops, no schools and, above all, no jobs within reach. Within a period of five months after being 'resettled', seventy-three people, mostly children, had died.

Later that year in Parliament, I raised the plight of the people removed to Limehill and elsewhere into the rural homelands, quoting from a departmental circular issued from the Secretary of Bantu Administration in 1967:

> 'It must be stressed here that no stone is to be left unturned to achieve the resettlement in the homelands of non-productive Bantu who are presently residing in the European areas. The Minister has given instructions that the resettlement in the homelands of thousands of superfluous Bantu families at present residing in the European areas of the Republic must enjoy the highest priority.'[9]

The removals policy shoved people back into the Bantustans without any proper planning or care for their survival. I asked:

> Who are the non-productive, so-called superfluous Bantu? They are the aged, the unfit, the widows, the women with dependent children. These are the words used in the departmental circular. I want to ask the Minister . . . are these not the most vulnerable, the most defenceless people in the population? 'The human factor,' added the circular 'must never be lost sight of in the problem of resettlement.'

I said that the human factor had never been considered at all, let alone lost sight of, and all these people shared one common factor – they had been ruthlessly uprooted. As a result, they all lived in extreme poverty, most lacked employment opportunities or income unless they were the lucky individuals who would get the few perks going, such as trading store or petrol station licences, or possibly liquor store licences.

> People have been put on the veld, some of them in mid-winter, and given tents which they probably did not even know how to erect; they were left there with no proper medical attention, no proper facilities for schooling and no proper shop facilities for obtaining necessities.

I stressed too the gross hypocrisy of the government's claim about the preservation of Bantu culture while at the same time effectively causing the breakup of the extended family system:

> People were linked by a system of reciprocities in the old Bantu culture. There were no abandoned orphans, deserted wives and no widows with dependent children. They were all absorbed in the huge extended

family unit. There was lifelong security and everybody shared the
common fate. Be it famine or be it feasting, everybody shared the
common fate. This is not so now. We are breaking down Bantu culture
and we are putting nothing in its place. We are not allowing these
people to absorb the benefits of Western culture. What sort of
conditions are these likely to lead to? . . . Do Honourable Ministers for
one moment stop and think of what situations they are creating in the
urban areas with this broken family life? The whole emphasis of the
future labour pattern is being put on migratory labour . . . A vast
problem of crime and delinquency is going to have to be solved by our
children, because the conditions which are being set in the urban areas
of South Africa, for the African people . . . are going to lead to the
most terrible conditions of crime and delinquency.[10]

A Nationalist MP dismissed my speech as containing 'more hatred
and malice' than he had ever heard before.

No attempt was made by Prime Minister Vorster to alleviate
these conditions, nor did he react when I visited the aptly named
Stinkwater resettlement in the Transvaal and reported that I had
been to see the Minister of Bantu Administration, M. C. Botha,
about this pathetic place. With characteristic callousness Botha had
said that all the people moved there had been illegally in the urban
area anyway. And when I asked him if he didn't think it a good idea
to ensure that there was adequate water and other essentials of life
before moving people, his reply was: 'There is a hand pump – you
are spoiled, you should have grown up on a farm like me. I had to
use a hand pump too.'

In 1974 Vorster made a speech in which he asked the world to 'give
us six months', implying that change was in the offing. I told him
he had aroused great expectations in the United States, which I had
been visiting at the time, and I advised him as one golfer to another
that having made his backswing he had better follow through.

That year, however, the case of the Mayen people in the
northern Cape, who were threatened with a third removal, evoked
no sympathy from Vorster. I read out a letter written to me on
behalf of their chief Jeffrey Mosike:

'There is a very strong rumour that the State President would order that
we be cleared with short notice out of Mayen before long. I and my
subjects feel that this would be the worst crime that this government of
ours will have perpetrated.'

The letter claimed that the title deed to Mayen had disappeared in the Deeds Office in Pretoria, but that it had definitely existed 'and now was being treated merely as a scrap of paper as Hitler called the non-aggression pact he had signed'. Addressed as 'Most respectful Mother Suzman', I was asked to make representations to the State President on behalf of the Mayen people.[11] I did so, without success; the Mayen were removed into Bophuthatswana. (Now, encouraged by the recent repeal of the Land Act and of the Black Administration Act of 1927,[12] they are fighting through court action to return, and to declare invalid the premature sale of their land to White farmers, a sale totally at odds with undertakings given in Parliament concerning the redistribution of land.)

Yet another type of forced removal received little sympathy from Vorster or from his Minister of Community Development, Blaar Coetzee. This was the forced removal of Indian and Coloured people in both the rural and urban areas under the Group Areas Act. Under this Act, in almost every city and town throughout South Africa since shortly after the Second World War, Indians had been slowly but surely dispossessed of their homes and their businesses. If they were not moved some twenty miles out of town, as was the case in Johannesburg (where the Indians were moved from Fordsburg, near the city centre, to Lenasia, seventeen miles away), then in the little country towns throughout South Africa they were moved two or three miles, across the railway tracks or near the cemetery, away from the national road and from the centre of town, where they had their shops and earned their livelihoods. And though they had been forced to move, they received not one penny of goodwill for their businesses. They were forced to sell their properties at valuations far below their real market value. When Indians stayed on uneasily under permits in their existing businesses, they could not improve or expand those businesses, which often slowly deteriorated and closed down. At every opportunity I raised the iniquities that took place under forced removals and Group Area proclamations.

When the original Group Areas Act was introduced in 1950, and gave powers to a board to determine the right of ownership and occupation of land and property on racial lines, the Minister of Interior solemnly informed Parliament that its objective was to ensure racial peace and to eliminate friction, and that it would not be discriminatory. He said that all the racial groups in South Africa would be affected by the effort to sort out the complicated pattern of South African urban settlement. This turned out to be blatant sophistry.

My questions to successive Ministers over the years revealed that, overall, half a million Coloured and Indian families had been removed since the Act was first implemented in the 1950s, compared to very few White families. Compensation paid to those people removed from the suburbs of Cape Town, Durban and Johannesburg was minimal, nothing like the prices later gleaned by White purchasers, who simply tarted up those little houses with coloured awnings and paint and resold them at enormous profit. The Coloured and Indian people were moved out of the suburbs and resettled elsewhere.

Towards the end of his regime, Vorster had had a bellyful of me. He turned nasty and sarcastic, and the many unpleasant exchanges between us in Parliament led even Louis Louw, parliamentary correspondent of *Die Burger*, the most influential Nationalist newspaper in the Cape, to write an article entitled 'Why so hard on Mrs Suzman?'

A story going the rounds told of a photographer pleading with the grim-faced Vorster: 'Won't you please smile, Mr Prime Minister?' And Vorster, his mouth turned firmly down, replied, 'I *am* smiling.' I would relate this anecdote, suitably demonstrated, as apocryphal, until one day I received a call: 'Mrs Suzman, that story is not apocryphal – I was the photographer.'

Vorster's smile was not in evidence on the afternoon I came out of Parliament to find a long line of grim-looking Ratels (armoured cars) in the road, as if the total onslaught of which he had so often warned us had commenced. 'What's going on?' I asked Tim Patten, the *Star* correspondent who was observing the scene. 'Oh,' said Tim, 'it's a public relations exercise. There are Cabinet Ministers in the Ratels and they are about to go down Adderley Street to the Castle [down Cape Town's main street to the battlement built by the Dutch East India Company in the days of Jan van Riebeeck in 1652]. Go and look in the slat in the front

Ratel,' said Tim. I did so and recoiled in horror – there, unmistakably, was the ferocious eye of John Vorster glaring at me.

Vorster was succeeded as Prime Minister in 1978 by P. W. Botha – my *bête noire*. A three-headed *bête noire*, he was first Minister of Coloured Affairs, then Minister of Defence, and then Prime Minister. I had a singularly hostile relationship with him in all three roles, stretching over many years.

My first brush with him was as Minister of Coloured Affairs, when the government was trying to abolish the separate representation of Coloureds in Parliament. The Progs had won the two provincial seats in the Cape in March 1965, with our candidates Dr Oscar Wollheim and Ogies van Heerden. It was therefore probable that in the pending elections we would win the four parliamentary seats, which covered the same area.

One Prog in Parliament was regarded as a pain, four more would be unendurable. A Prog victory would also be seen as a clear refutation of the government's claim that the Coloured people were beginning to accept apartheid. As a result one heard much intimidating talk in Parliament, not only from P. W. but from the White representatives of the Coloured people, and in particular from my benchmate, Abe Bloomberg. Their seats were in danger. The Progressive Party was accused of exploiting the Coloured vote, and of 'buying' Coloured votes with bottles of brandy.

I made many angry denials and interjections when accusations of buying votes were made against the Progressive Party. Botha's response was, 'The Honourable Member for Houghton must stop chattering. She is in the habit of chattering continually. If my wife chattered like that Honourable Member, I would know what to do with her. There is nothing that works on my nerves more than a woman who continually interrupts me. She is like water dripping on a tin roof.'[13]

It was the election of the two Progs to the Cape Provincial Council in 1965 that started the whole sorry onslaught on Coloured representation in Parliament. Despite all the dark insinuations about irregular practices, not a single charge was substantiated in evidence before the Commission appointed to enquire into 'improper interference with voters'. All these sinister 'irregularities' boiled down to 129 registration forms not having been properly witnessed by Commissioners of Oaths out of the 20,000 additional registrations effected by the Progressive Party. This so-called offence was trifling compared with the irregularities that took place at White elections: dead voters rising from their graves to mark their ballots, long-sought missing persons appearing at the polls, absentee ballots disappearing in transit. And yet no one ever suggested disenfranchising White voters as a result. I had a go at both the government and the official opposition and was amused to watch the grins on the United Party faces fade as I swung round on them, while the Nat faces became wreathed in smiles.

Three Bills emerged as a result of the Improper Interference Commission Report. (The word improper was removed by ministerial amendment and the title became the Prohibition of Political Interference Bill, which was just as well, because the original version, as some wag said, was suggestive of rape.) The first shameful piece of legislation represented a further intrusion into the right of free speech and freedom of association across the colour line. It prohibited multiracial political parties, and thus killed the small Liberal Party and deprived the Progressive Party of its non-White members, who were suspended at their request. They asked us to continue to play our part in Parliament and so exercise whatever influence we could muster.

The second Bill extended the life of the sitting Coloured Representatives to 1971, thus giving them a remarkably lengthy parliamentary life of nine years. Thereafter the Coloured representation in Parliament was to disappear altogether. The third Bill, also passed in 1968, made provision for a Coloured Persons Representative Council to be elected by the Coloured people on a universal adult franchise throughout the country. Despite the shortcomings of the system of separate representation (and these were legion), it had at least provided four voices in the Parliament which made all the laws that affected the lives of the Coloured people. This was patently far more valuable than a Coloured Council which could not pass a single law without the approval of the Minister, or any law which affected existing laws.

To Botha's fury, I reminded him on several occasions that it was he who had master-minded the destruction of District Six in Cape Town in 1966 when it was declared a White group area. District Six was an area close to the city centre, long inhabited by Coloured people, 30,000 of whom were ruthlessly uprooted and dumped under the Group Areas Act on the Cape Flats, fifteen miles out of town, on windswept, sandy dunes with no vegetation except wattles. The removal took place before the rail link to the city centre had been completed, thus involving the people in heavy additional transport costs. The community was particularly bitter because District Six was situated at the base of Table Mountain, close to their places of work in the nearby industrial areas, and steeped in its own long-standing traditions. It was a slum, there is no denying that; but it had a vibrant communal life and many advantages other than proximity to the city. There were several mosques and schools and it was a tightly knit community which guarded its interests fiercely. Like Sophiatown, it could have been upgraded *in situ*.

Today District Six is a barren hillside, with only a couple of mosques and churches remaining, which the government, with typical hypocrisy, did not destroy, presumably because the powers above would note their actions. A technical college has been erected there and is multiracial. Few Whites, interestingly enough, have taken advantage of the fact that they could have bought property or land in District Six and used it for residential purposes; a pall of guilt hangs over the area. With the repeal of the Group Areas Act in June 1981, District Six is now open to all races. Just what advantage will be taken of this by the Coloured community, which was expelled twenty-five years ago, remains to be seen.

Anything to do with the military aroused much emotion in P. W. Botha. I especially infuriated him when I recounted his activities as a Nationalist Party organiser during the Second World War, when he encouraged National Party supporters to break up United Party meetings and to harass men in uniform.

In 1972, when he was Minister of Defence, I raised the issue of the treatment of Jehovah's Witnesses refusing military service. I was amazed at his furious outburst. I held no brief for Jehovah's Witnesses, as indeed I held no brief for a lot of the people on whose behalf I interceded. I did not necessarily agree with their policies or views; the cause was simple justice.

Under South Africa's conscription law, White men were called up at eighteen years of age to serve one year as recruits in the army (later extended to two years and reduced again to one year in 1990); thereafter they were liable for two weeks' military service every year until they were fifty-five years old. Jehovah's Witnesses, because of their religious convictions, refused the call-up and were charged. The usual sentence was two years in detention barracks at Voortrekkerhoogte army base near Pretoria. On their arrival (according to parents who came to see me in great distress), the boys were ordered by the officer in charge to put on uniforms. They said, 'We cannot. Our religion does not allow us to wear a uniform,' at which stage the captain in charge of the detention barracks would say, 'You are refusing to obey a lawful order: six months' solitary confinement.'

One mother told me that her son had served four consecutive periods of six months' solitary confinement: 'Mrs Suzman, when I went to see my boy he had forgotten how to talk because there was no one for him to talk to.'

When I raised the matter in Parliament during the Defence Vote, J. N. Rall, a Nat MP, commented, 'Wherever the enemies of the state crop up, there one finds the Honourable Member for Houghton.'[14]

Botha went further:

> I place her, together with her party, in the position of champions of all those people who contravene laws and who want to create chaos in South Africa, of all those who want to commit crimes against the state . . . She represents all those people who break laws and want to banish order.[15]

I did not take kindly to that remark and immediately rose on a point of order. I tried to get him ordered to withdraw it. But the Chairman of Committees was very weak, unlike Speaker Klopper, who would have done so without hesitation. I reported it all to the Speaker afterwards who said, 'I wasn't there when it happened. I would have made him withdraw. But you know perfectly well that Mr Botha is a very difficult man.' I said, 'That is precisely why he should be disciplined.'

Botha had mellowed somewhat about the Jehovah's Witnesses the following month when a Defence Amendment Bill was introduced, largely, I conjecture, because of the intervention of the newly appointed head of the South African Defence Force, Commandant General Admiral Biermann, who no doubt was in the Officials' Bay during the original debate. Thereafter, after serving a sentence of not less than twelve months' detention for refusing to don a uniform, conscientious objectors could not be charged again with such contravention. Botha could not, however, resist saying that Jehovah's Witnesses were 'a positive danger to any decent civilised society and should know that they must expect no sympathy from this Parliament'.[16] Nor could he resist a swipe at me, saying, 'The two of us are poles apart – the less we say to each other the better.' I replied, 'I agree with that.'

Behind Botha's outburst was an obvious personal dislike for me, which was mutual. I remember one occasion in later years when we were having an all-night debate. Having made my speech, I was half asleep in my seat at about three o'clock in the morning, when Botha got up, and I heard my name being mentioned. That woke me up. He had said, 'The Honourable Member for Houghton, it is well known, does not like me.' I sat up and interjected, 'Like you? I cannot stand you.'[17] On that same occasion he said, 'The Honourable Member is going to America tomorrow to receive an award from people who are South Africa's enemies.' I replied, 'You leave us with no friends so I have to accept awards from our enemies.'

I was, in fact, going to New York to accept a Human Rights Award from the United Nations on the occasion of the thirtieth anniversary of the signing of the Universal Declaration of Human Rights.

6

The Years Alone: 1961–74

I. Fighting for the Rule of Law

During my first few years as the lone Progressive Party Member, I was confronted by a series of vicious laws designed to undermine civil rights and to intensify discrimination against Blacks.

In pursuit of Dr Verwoerd's mad dream of Grand Apartheid, the government introduced one law after the other, extending discriminatory practices and subjecting South African Blacks to more and more restrictions on their mobility and on their right to seek a livelihood in the urban areas, and depriving them of a normal family life by making it very difficult for wives and children to join the male migrants legally. Had the government deliberately tried to create an unstable society, it could not have done better. I described one example of this crazy policy in a letter to my daughter Francie in December 1961:

> Have had a bloody week trying to get to the bottom of the Alexandra Township removal scheme. The official explanation was that it was a slum clearance scheme and there would be fine new houses at Diepkloof where the former residents would go and a lovely new spacious suburb for the remaining citizens at Alex. Well, I had a phone call at 6 a. m. from an African asking me to do something about Alex. There are police raids night after night, hundreds of women are being arrested as illegal residents, fined R10 or two weeks and told to clear out, where to no one knows or cares. I got hold of young Pogrund, *Rand Daily Mail* African Affairs reporter, and together we've been visiting the township and sitting in at the courts. A sickening sight. One wretched African after the other, an average of one case per thirty

seconds. If anyone pleads not guilty, the case is immediately postponed so back to gaol goes the poor devil anyway. We will expose the whole damn business. He in the press, me when I go back to Parliament.

The normal process of the law maintains law and order only when the majority of the people to whom the laws apply accept and approve of them. However, as the late Professor Julius Lewin of Witwatersrand University once said, 'The theory of human equality which inspires the Rule of Law and the theory of racial separation which inspires the South African government have come into collision over and over again. A government determined at all costs to enforce apartheid in the teeth of all legal and practical difficulties, will abandon the Rule of Law.' That is precisely what happened in South Africa. Powers which circumvented the courts, due process and *habeas corpus* followed in quick succession.

The first of these was the far-reaching Sabotage Act, which defined sabotage and gave arbitrary powers to the government to place people under house arrest. It was introduced in Parliament in 1962, during my first session alone. It is significant that for over a week after the Bill was published no one knew if the official opposition (the United Party) would fight it. Only after the English-language press, including the United Party's strong supporters, the *Cape Argus* and the *Sunday Times*, had shown their hand, and when protest meetings and marches organised by the Progs in places like Johannesburg, Durban and Cape Town had demonstrated public reaction against the Bill, did the United Party finally decide to oppose it. Max Borkum, my campaign manager, was now the chairman of the Progressive Party on the Witwatersrand, and he organised a huge protest march through central Johannesburg. We also held a public meeting at the Johannesburg City Hall which was very well attended. In particular, we protested against the house arrest of the first victim of that law, Helen Joseph, who had done sterling work among the unfortunate people banished to distant places under the Native Administration Act of 1927. I said at the meeting that during the debate on the Sabotage Act I had sat on my green bench in Parliament, watching a shiver run through the ranks of the United Party, looking for a spine to run up.

Perhaps the best way to convey some of the strains of that session is to quote from a letter to Francie in June 1962:

Have had a perfectly fiendish week in Parliament – what with the committee stage of Vorster's Sabotage Bill and me with seventeen amendments to move and call divisions on. The United Party was furious at having let me take the lead and call the tune, but I got in first so they had to lump it. I thought I'd pass out at the end of the second day, as I couldn't leave the House for one second and we were sitting mornings too. My old bladder must have suffered irreparable damage. A Nat gent said to me in the lobby, 'God Helen, we can think of ten Progs we would rather have here instead of you – why did they pick on you?' To which I replied: 'For that very reason'.

Looking back over the past five months I really don't know how I have kept up this cracking pace. I've spoken on every major issue and have invented a few too from my side. The United Party are furious at all the publicity I've had, so are now going around saying that all my speeches have been ghost-written for me, that I have a huge team working in the background and so on. If only it were true! . . .

My anonymous admirer, 'Yok',[1] is apparently also incensed and literally bombards me with his charming postcards addressed to 'Der Yiddishe Know-All from Houghton'. They arrive like homing pigeons and advise me to go stick my long Jewish nose into the Knesset and leave nice Christian Parliaments to nice Christian gentlemen. Ah well, as long as it stays at postcards, I don't mind. What I do mind is the rebirth of fascist armies under Robey Leibbrandt[2] with the connivance of the Minister of Justice, according to an answer he gave me in Parliament. These are the bicycle-chain swinging types that go round breaking up meetings and can become a real menace at any liberal gathering.

The 1963 session was even more stressful. My opening gambit that year was to use the No Confidence debate to quote the closing speech in his defence made by Nelson Mandela at his trial for treason and sabotage, just before he was sentenced to life imprisonment. I thought Members of the House should know what was being said by Black leaders in South Africa.

'Always we have been conscious of our obligation as citizens to avoid breaches of the law, where such breaches can be avoided; to prevent a clash between the authorities and our people, where such a clash can be prevented; but nevertheless we have been driven to speak up for what we believe is right, and work for it and try to bring about changes which will satisfy our human conscience. Government violence can only do one thing, and that is to breed counter-violence. We have warned repeatedly that the government, by resorting continually to violence, will breed in this country counter-violence among the people, until ultimately if there is no dawning of sanity on the part of the government, ultimately the dispute between the government and my people will finish up by being settled in violence and by force. Already there are indications in the country that people, my people, Africans, are turning to deliberate acts of violence and of force against the government in order to persuade the government in the only language which this government shows by its own behaviour, that it understands.'[3]

The Nationalist Member who spoke after me, Dr L. I. Coertze, said, 'I want to congratulate the Honourable Member for Houghton, Mrs Suzman, on her new leader, Mandela.'[4]

The 'dawn of sanity' was, alas, suppressed for many years. Instead, on 24 April 1963 the Ninety-day Detention Law (the General Laws Amendment Bill, to give it its official title) was introduced. As I have said, this was the first Law that allowed detention without trial, without a state of emergency having been declared. The official opposition supported it, and I was the sole voice of opposition. One Nationalist newspaper summed up the situation: 'The United Party lay down like curs.' In fact the United Party had panicked, lest it be accused of hindering the Government in dealing with Poqo, the militant underground movement of the Pan-Africanist Congress, which had been responsible for the murder of four Whites at Bashee Bridge in the Ciskei.

I had expected the United Party to oppose this Bill, because it had voted against the Sabotage Act the previous year. I thought that nobody in their right minds on the opposition side could give the government these powers, especially as the Bill also contained a second fundamental breach of the Rule of Law, the notorious 'Sobukwe Clause' (Section 4), aimed solely at Robert Sobukwe, the leader of the banned PAC. Thereby he could be held in prison by the Minister indefinitely, by annual extension, after he had served the three-year sentence imposed on him by the courts for organising defiance of the Pass Laws at the time of the Sharpeville massacre in 1960. De Villiers Graaff, the United Party leader, made a speech criticising the two major clauses in the Bill: Section 4 and Section 17 (the ninety-day detention without trial clause). But then inexplicably he announced that the United Party would vote for the Bill at second reading. I was utterly appalled that the official opposition intended to support the Bill in principle.

Graaff sat down after his announcement and the Speaker said, 'I put the question' – which was his way of calling for the next MP to stand up. I looked around the House and nobody stood up. I expected a member on the government side to stand up; nobody did. I looked at the United Party. Nobody stood up. The Speaker repeated, 'I put the question', and I realised that if I did not immediately stand up to speak, the Bill would be passed without a single opposing voice in Parliament.

I made what was virtually an extempore speech in which I told the opposition what I thought of its craven attitude. I warned the government that 'long before the final chapter of the struggle that is going on in this country is written, a great number of people, who were formerly peace-loving, will be driven to desperate acts of recklessness.'[5] A Member interjected, 'Go to Ghana and enjoy freedom there.'[6] I suggested that government members who believed that Blacks had no genuine grievances 'should imagine themselves in a Black skin for one day of their lives and let them see whether it was easy to get a job, to move freely around the country of their birth, to live where they wished to live and to have their family live with them.' I added 'it was the very failure of moderate African leaders to achieve any improvement in the everyday life of the Africans that had led to the rise of extremist leaders in South Africa.'[7]

The Minister in reply thanked the official opposition for its support, implied that I was in the communist camp, and sat down.

The Speaker said, 'I put the question? Any objection?'

My lone voice was heard saying 'Yes.'

Then he said, 'Will those in favour say "Aye".' Nat and United Party Members shouted 'Aye'. 'Will those against say "No".' My lone 'No' was heard. 'I think the "Ayes" have it,' said the Speaker. And I stood up and said, 'Divide', thus forcing a physical division.

As procedure laid down, the bells of Parliament rang for three minutes, Members streamed in and took their seats. The doors were locked. The Speaker stood up and said, 'The question before the House is . . .' and he put the question, and ordered those in favour to take their seats on his right; those against, on his left. I sat alone in a sea of empty green benches, while the whole of the official opposition crossed the floor and packed themselves in among the Nationalist MPs. It was a dramatic sight.

The United Party voted against the two offensive clauses (4 and 17) at the next stage of the debate, the committee stage, but at the third reading, the final stage, again supported the Bill. I commented that one felt giddy observing their gyrations. The Minister again thanked the United Party for its support and said that, as usual, mine was the one discordant voice. The United Party was so fed up with the humiliation of crossing the floor – reported with gusto by the English-language press – that it negotiated with the government Whips for a new voting procedure. Four members had to support a call for a division before Members would have to cross the floor physically, otherwise the names of the minority would simply be recorded. As I was the lone Prog, and would remain so until 1974, my name was often recorded as the sole objector to government measures, without opposition members having to cross the floor when they supported the government.

After the debate on the Ninety-day Bill, I had mail from all over the country, and from the US, Australia and the UK, including a letter from the women Fellows of Girton, Cambridge. Albert Lutuli wrote:

> I take this opportunity to express my deep appreciation and admiration for your heroic and lone stand against a most reactionary Parliament . . . I most heartily congratulate you for your untiring efforts in a situation that would frustrate and benumb many . . .
>
> For ever remember, you are a bright Star in dark Chamber, where lights of liberty of what is left, are going out one by one.
>
> This appreciation covers your contribution since you entered Parliament as member of the Progressive Party. This meritorious record has been climaxed by your fittingly uncompromising stand in the rape of democracy by Parliament in the debate that made law, which was one of the most diabolic bills ever to come before Parliament.
>
> Not only ourselves – your contemporaries, but also posterity, will hold you in high esteem.

I had surprisingly few abusive letters, but a telegram from Robey Leibbrandt read, 'Hope your attitude on Minister Vorster's anti-communist bill is warning to all *goyim*.'[8] To this I did not reply.

However, after the twenty-ninth of April 1963, when the Ninety-day Bill was passed, the attacks on me in Parliament intensified to such an extent that several newspapers commented on it. On 30 May the *Natal Witness* carried a headline, 'Break Suzman Campaign May Have Been Planned'; their parliamentary correspondent wrote:

> New threats were made, more damning than those made yesterday when Mrs Suzman was accused of moving heaven and earth to stir up racial friction. I understand that the present outburst is not merely political banter, but a caucus-organised plan to break the spirit of Mrs Suzman. The apparent reason for this is that the Nats are desperately anxious to present to the outside world a picture of all Whites being behind the government. Mrs Suzman is a thorn in their side and because of the wide press following for her, they are anxious to silence the lone opposition voice. A Nationalist Member . . . said, 'The time has come for us to take action. She has the press on her side and the press is playing her off against the United Party. She is a danger to us in the House.' Loud 'hoor-hoors' [hear-hears] greeted this remark . . . He added, 'She is sweeping up racial hatred in this country, she pleads for the non- Whites just when it suits her.' Other interjections were hurled across the floor at Mrs Suzman, who sat unflinching, were 'You are a political pest,' from Mr Cas Greyling, 'You are the biggest political enemy of this country,' Mr G. P. van den Burg. And Mr J. F. Schoombee shouted something about Mrs Suzman's 'pestilential politics'.

The correspondent reported that 'Mrs Suzman appeared to thrive on these remarks and came back time and time again with her attacks on Bantu policy. She certainly appeared in no way to be losing her spirit.'

Other newspapers also sprang to my defence. The *Rand Daily Mail* had a leading article the following day, in which it criticised the bitter attacks on me from the government benches. It was a particularly unpleasant time for me and I was grateful to a United Party Whip, Gray Hughes, for coming to my defence by protesting against the implicit threats in the Nationalist attacks on me that session.

A couple of weeks later, on 18 June, the Minister of Justice, Vorster, unleashed a broadside at me, implying that he would be committing a breach of security in giving confidential information to me. He accused me of associating with people in whom he had no confidence. 'I will think twice before I give her confidential security information,'[9] Vorster declared. 'Mrs Suzman hit back hard at the Minister,' reported the *Rand Daily Mail* on 19 June:

'There is nothing treacherous or illegal or anything other than democratic in assisting people to provide legal defence in our courts of law,' she said. Mr Vorster said that Mrs Suzman moved in certain circles of which he was not too sure, like the Defence and Aid Fund. He accused Mrs Suzman of acting as a front for them and giving them information. Mrs Suzman asked, 'Are you accusing me of treason?' Mr Vorster said, no, but he was afraid she might at some time or another slip up and give these people information they should not have. Mrs Suzman said she took strong exception to Mr Vorster's remark. 'I shall continue to do my duty. I believe there are things that need airing in South Africa.'

During the 1964 session, I moved a Private Member's Motion under the parliamentary rule which allowed a Member to debate a special subject. My Motion asked for the repeal of all enactments allowing detention without trial. In introducing it, I said:

Vast powers outside the law that have been taken by successive Ministers are used in ever widening circles, very often against people who were never the intended victims when the law was first made, very often for reasons which were never advanced in the first instance by Ministers introducing the law, and in a manner not even contemplated or actually allowed in the Statute. Arbitrary powers which are not subject to public scrutiny in the courts of law have an ugly habit of getting out of hand, of being used more and more recklessly to control any opponents of the ruling power.[10]

I commented that perhaps the saddest part of this whole sad story was that thousands upon thousands of White South Africans had become conditioned to all sorts of inroads on basic freedoms, and concluded my speech by saying that 'The time has come for us to take stock, to put a halt to the tragic decline in civil liberties in our country, because I believe that if the present trend is allowed to continue, South Africa will not only have lost civil liberty, she will have lost her soul.'[11]

I obtained no support for my Motion. Not a single MP from the United Party even spoke on it, let alone voted for it.

In March 1964, Dawie, the parliamentary correspondent of *Die Burger*, the National Party organ in the Cape, praised my performance in Parliament:

She is busy building up a reputation as a parliamentarian that has even aroused the admiration of her enemies. She has had something to say on every important point that arises in the House, and even if she has a team of helpers outside Parliament, she is the one who has to carry the message into the House. And she is doing this well. Not that it will help the Progressives much, for the fact remains that if there was an election tomorrow, she would not have a hope of retaining Houghton.

However, as I've already said, I held my seat in the general election of 1966. My victory was welcomed by the Black newspaper, *The World*, on 31 March 1966 with the headline, 'Mrs Suzman is our hero, say Reef Africans':

Africans today hail the victory of Mrs Helen Suzman in the Houghton Constituency during the General Election yesterday. Some leaders described it as the news of the year for Africans. Many township people sat next to their radios last night waiting for the results. Radio Bantu today did not make any mention of Mrs Suzman's victory, but other services of Radio South Africa gave the news in their early morning bulletin. There was widespread jubilation in buses and trains from Soweto and other townships today as news flashed that Mrs Suzman had retained her Houghton seat. Mrs Hilda Mashinini, a well-known Orlando resident, said that her victory was a tangible demonstration that there were Whites willing to live normally and decently in accordance with known standards of civilisation and Christianity.

Another Black township paper, *Post*, commented on 3 April:

The all-White election had gone according to the *Post* forecast – a huge swing to the right. The Nationalists are back in power as our rulers with the biggest majority ever. The only exception – a glorious exception –was in Houghton, where Helen Suzman increased her majority from 564 in 1961 to 711. It was a magnificent performance against heavy odds. How that woman worked! Her machine was streamlined – beautiful, relentless.

The *New York Times* commented on 1 April 1966:

The voice of conscience of Mrs Suzman will be heard with gratitude far beyond South Africa's borders by free men and those struggling to be free. There is basis for believing that as the sole voice of the voteless, she actually represents more South Africans than all the other Members of Parliament combined.

Back in Parliament for the short session following the election, I wrote home (15 October 1966):

I had a hellish week in Parliament having had to make speeches on five different subjects on four successive days. Committee of supply is always murder for me, because one vote follows the other in swift succession, and I had to prepare speeches for example, on Coloured Affairs, Bantu Education, Bantu Administration, Labour and Justice, practically at one and the same time, since we were sitting morning, afternoon and night at that time. If I wanted to get into any of these Committee stage debates, I had to be in my seat all the time, since it was a matter of popping up and down in the hope of catching the chairman's eye for a ten-minute go. Very exhausting, but I suppose it had its uses.

Hard on its heels came the next session early in 1967, when the government introduced the third and harshest of all the measures undermining the Rule of Law: the notorious Terrorism Act. Once again I cast my solitary vote against a major piece of legislation that subverted due process. The United Party, to its everlasting shame, voted for this Act with its far-reaching Section 6, which gave powers to the Minister to impose indefinite detention on any person and to hold him or her in solitary confinement for purposes of interrogation, for which they were heartily thanked by the Minister of Justice, Mr Piet Pelser. He added:

> As far as the Honourable Member for Houghton is concerned, it is a question of east is east and west is west and ne'er the twain shall meet. We simply do not see matters in the same light. She has always interceded for elements that seek to bring about the downfall of the White man in this country. I did not think she would go so far as to intercede even for terrorists. Even with dealing with terrorists, I cannot get the support of the Honourable Member for Houghton.[12]

A. N. Steyn, Nat MP for Graaff Reinet added his complaint: 'One is getting sick and tired of this constant nagging of the Honourable Member for Houghton about the rule of law. As soon as the Government takes drastic action to combat an evil which is threatening the safety of the state, the clarion call of the rule of law echoes from the Honourable Member.'[13]

And another Nat MP, A. L. Schlebusch, delivered the coup de grâce: 'To the Honourable Member for Houghton and those of her mind I want to say that a liberty which has been built up over more than 300 years with the blood and the tears of the Whites, will not be jeopardised simply because we have to respond to the ridiculous criticism levelled by her and her henchmen.'[14]

The vote was put, and as fewer than four Members supported

the demand for a division, my name was simply recorded in the minority, and there was no physical division.

The Terrorism Act was described by *Beeld*, one of the major newspapers supporting the National Party, as 'giving the police a free hand to act without legal restraint'. As a senior police officer observed jubilantly when the Act was passed, 'This is a mighty weapon in the hands of the police.' And so it proved to be. More than seventy people died while being detained without trial under the Ninety-day Law and under Section 6 of the Terrorism Act (later Section 29 of the Internal Security Act of 1982).

I said, in moving my amendment that the Bill be read 'this day six months' (the most extreme form of parliamentary opposition), that in this Bill the government was giving unprecedented powers to the Minister and to the police to use emergency measures without having to declare a state of emergency. It completely excluded the jurisdiction of the court. The government as usual pleaded 'necessity' to justify itself. I was reminded of the dictum of William Pitt: 'necessity is the plea for every infringement of human freedom. It is ever the excuse of tyrants, it is the creed of slaves.' I pointed out that this particular Bill was not going to be the last of its kind, because nothing was ever done to counter the causes of disorder. Instead the screws were tightened as apartheid was relentlessly implemented. The government's method of dealing with the escalation of Black resistance over the years, as the disastrous effects of apartheid legislation were felt, was to use the big stick, to curtail protest and civil rights more and more.

With these three Acts – the Sabotage Act, the Ninety-day Detention Law and the Terrorism Act – 'due process' and the Rule of Law were utterly destroyed in South Africa. The government had empowered itself to crush all resistance to its relentless extension and implementation of apartheid.

The thin red line that separated lawful dissent and subversion became ever fainter.

II. *Fighting the Apartheid Laws*

In 1962 a Bill to amend the 1950 Population Registration Act was introduced by the then Minister of Interior, J. de Klerk, father of today's State President, F. W. de Klerk. The 1950 Act (commonly known as the Race Classification Act) was the foundation stone of apartheid. Every South African citizen was racially classified at birth, or retrospectively, as White, Coloured or Black. The Coloured classification embraced seven sub-groups: Cape Coloured, Griqua, Malay, Indian, Chinese, Other Asiatic and Other Coloured. It was possible for the same person to be classified 'White' under the definitions clause of one Act (such as the Group Areas Act) and 'Coloured or Black' under the definitions clause of another Act – what I described as the chameleon-like character of South Africans. With even more drastic consequences, members of the same family could be classified differently, for example one Coloured and one White.

Perhaps the best indication of the crazy nature of the law came from the definitions clause of the Act itself:

A White person means a person, who

- (a) in appearance obviously is a White person and who is not generally accepted as a Coloured person, or
- (b) is generally accepted as a White person and is not in appearance obviously not a White person.

In deciding this thorny question the Act laid down

- (a) that the person's habits, education and speech and deportment and demeanour in general shall be taken into account.
- (b) in the absence of proof that any person who was not a Black, was generally accepted as a White person, it shall be assumed that he was generally accepted as a Coloured person.

The Act went further (lest any person slip across the colour line). Sub-section (c) stated that

- a person shall be deemed not to be generally accepted as a White person unless he is so accepted in the area in which or at any place where he is ordinarily resident, is employed or carries on business, mixes socially or takes part in other activities with other members

of the public, and in his association with the members of his family
and any other persons with whom he lives.

Racial classification was the make or break factor in South African
life; it determined whether one would enjoy first-class, second-
class or third-class citizenship. Every year hundreds of people
changed their racial classification. For example, a question I put in
Parliament in 1962: 'How many Coloured persons had applied to
be reclassified as White?' elicited the answer '700', and of those 529
had succeeded in their applications, four had failed and 167 were
still awaiting a decision.[1]

Twenty years later a similar question elicited the information
that 794 persons had been reclassified in a bewildering range of
transformations including Chinese, Indian, Malay, Coloured,
Black and White.[2] In 1989 just two years before the Race
Classification Act (Population Registration Act) was repealed,
1142 persons applied to be reclassified and 275 were unsuccessful.[3]

There were several loopholes in the Act whereby the courts had
over the years given a number of decisions against the Race
Classifications Board and in favour of persons objecting to their
classification, and the 1962 amending Bill attempted to close those
loopholes. It arose out of two notorious cases which had made the
headlines: the Singh/Song cases.

The Singh case involved an Indian man and a White woman,
who left South Africa because of the Prohibition of Mixed
Marriages Act, married in Rhodesia and returned to live in
Durban. They were arrested and charged under the Immorality
Act, since South African law did not recognise the validity of their
marriage. They were acquitted on a technicality, as the state could
not prove domicile. Mrs Singh tried to get herself reclassified as
Coloured under the existing Act, which defined White by relying
on 'acceptance and appearance', with more emphasis on acceptance, and there was a possibility that she would succeed because she
had been accepted by her Indian in-laws.

Mr Song was a Chinese man from Durban who managed to get
himself reclassified from Coloured to White on the grounds that he
was generally accepted as White. As I said in the debate, to
accomplish this feat, Mr Song produced a petition signed by 350

White people, and testimonials from the YMCA and from White schools attended by his daughters. Unfortunately, his attorney did not apply to have Mr Song's family reclassified at the same time. By the time anybody thought of this, the Act had been amended, giving more emphasis to appearance. Furthermore, the amending Bill introduced the criterion of descent: that is, if a person admitted he was of Coloured or of Black descent he could not be classified as White and vice versa.

This put paid to both Mrs Singh and Mr Song. Mrs Singh had no hope of succeeding in her application to be reclassified as Coloured, and unable to live with his Coloured family in a White group area, Mr Song had himself reclassified back again from White to Coloured.

Further amendments to the Population Registration Act in 1967 heralded yet another attempt to define the indefinable and provided a further example of the government's obsession with race and colour. As I told the House, the basic reason for the introduction of the amending Bill was the exasperation of the then Minister of Interior, P. M. K. le Roux, at the numerous successful appeals against current classifications. Furthermore, even under the existing restrictive definitions, there were several court decisions which upheld appeals by aggrieved persons. That slack was now taken up and it would henceforth be very difficult indeed for persons wishing to 'go up' a notch in South Africa's colour-conscious society. Descent was now the over-riding yardstick, for all whose parents were already classified. They represented the vast majority of citizens, since most people had by then been issued with identity documents specifying their racial group.

Many little equations applied to this Bill. If the parents were classified White, then the children were White. If the parents were both classified Coloured, the children were Coloured; and if the parents were both classified Black, the children were Black. But White plus Coloured equalled Coloured. The other sub-groups – Malay, Indian and Chinese – were not equated. Then, too, there were illegitimate children with one parent unknown, and those people not yet issued with identity documents. They were 'sorted out' by the Board, which used all kinds of criteria – such as inserting a pencil into the hair on the head of the would-be 'changeling' to see if it would remain there or not – criteria which, I said, would make South Africa the laughing stock of the world.

As already stressed, among the worst of the apartheid laws were the infamous Pass Laws which dehumanised Blacks into units of labour. Unless they fell into certain categories laid down by law, they spent their entire lives as migrant workers, seeing their families in the rural areas for one month each year.

I hated the sight of police vans driving around the streets of Johannesburg, picking up Blacks whose documents were not in order. Black fingers could be seen sticking through the mesh wire in the vans and one knew that the vast majority of the captives inside were not thieves or muggers, but Black South Africans who had committed the 'sin' of looking for work in the urban areas without the required permit.

In 1964 a particularly vicious Bantu Laws Amendment Bill was introduced. This diminished the much valued privilege of 'Section 10(1)(a) Blacks' – a category defined in the Bantu Urban Areas Act as those who were either born in the urban areas or who had been resident there for fifteen years, or who had worked for one employer for ten years – who could remain unimpeded in the urban areas, and allowed their wives and children (unmarried daughters, and sons under the age of fifteen) to live with them. I opposed the Bill vigorously:

> One can only say that in the last analysis, because these laws apply only to Black men – laws which nobody would dare to impose on White men in this country – the only conclusion one can reach is that the government does not consider the Black man as a human being. It does not regard him as a person with the normal aspirations of a human being and the normal aspirations to have a secure family life. This Bill is the very essence of *baasskap* [domination]. It ignores all the fundamental concepts of human dignity. It strips the African of every basic pretension that he has to being a human being, to being a free human being in the country of his birth, and it reduces him to the level of a chattel, to the level of a servant. Already by existing legislation, laws which have been put on the Statute Book with monotonous regularity as far back as 1923, and which practice has been continued by successive governments and accentuated over the last fifteen years, the African is harassed almost beyond endurance – by Pass Laws, by Influx Control, by labour regulations, by restrictions on mobility, by restrictions on employment: all designed to maintain a cheap supply of labour.[4]

L. J. C. Bootha, the National Party Member for Rustenburg, replied,

> When the Honourable Member gets up in this House, she reminds me of a cricket in a tree when it is very dry in the bushvelt. His chirping makes you deaf but the tune remains the same, year in and year out. I should like to give the Honourable Member for Houghton a little advice. Look, if South Africa is so bad that she really cannot live here together with us on this side, English-speaking and Afrikaans-speaking (unfortunately just for luck we have no Jews on this side) there are other countries and places that will heartily welcome her.[5]

To which another Honourable Member on that side contributed 'Ghana'.

Until 1964 owners of places of public entertainment in South Africa could permit multiracial attendances. However, at Verwoerd's insistence, the government now began to enforce a proclamation originally passed in 1957 (Proclamation R.26), and transferred the decision to government officials: permits were now required for even casual attendance of 'disqualified persons' at places of entertainment such as theatres, concert halls, sports stadiums, race courses and so on.

I raised this bureaucratic absurdity in Parliament during the 1965 session describing Proclamation R.26 as 'a sort of Nationalist variety of the Mad Hatter's tea party'. There were six different criteria and no one knew which took precedence over the others or whether it was a combination of factors. Apart from six criteria, to add to the confusion there were four separate ministers to deal with. And of course these different ministers made different decisions, based on different criteria in applying Proclamation R.26. Thus all the decisions were ad hoc, by grace and favour of permits granted by ministers who did not have to give any reasons whatever for granting or refusing a permit. (Originally Proclamation R.26 applied also to attendance at church, but this was modified after widespread protest from the Anglican Church which threatened to defy the law, while the Dutch Reformed Church expressed reservations about this attempt to interfere with its right to make its own decisions.)

Cultural and social events were in a turmoil. The most

disgraceful incident of all was the refusal to grant permission to St Dunstan's organisation to hold a mixed banquet for ex-servicemen who had been blinded in the service of their country. I commented in Parliament:

> When those Coloured servicemen were given facilities for a separate banquet, the chairman was not allowed to attend, because he was a White man, and we had the shaming incident of one of the ambassadors having to stand outside the doorway to read a message to the ex-servicemen who were Coloured. If ever there was a case of confusion worse confounded, it was this unbelievable muddle over Proclamation R.26.[6]

Blaar Coetzee, MP for Vereeniging (later Deputy Minister for Community Development and Bantu Education), rose to say: 'If they want to mix in politics, they have only themselves to blame.'

Another incident I cited involved a Red Cross parade of forty schools, from which children from Coloured schools were banned. I ended up by saying that the government were deliberately piling insult upon insult, and further restricting the leisure pursuits of thousands upon thousands of South Africans classified as non-Whites. There seemed no end to the abysmal selfishness of White South Africa.

G. de K. Maree (MP for Namaqualand), who spoke after me, said: 'I want to tell the Honourable Member for Houghton that if she accepted the accepted policy of South Africa, she would have no difficulty in understanding the rules in connection with admittance to places of entertainment.'[7]

After Vorster became Prime Minister in 1966, Deputy Minister Blaar Coetzee became my favourite target. He made a highly satisfactory substitute. He was a large, tough man very much in evidence in the House, and he sat right opposite me.

In 1969, while he was Deputy Minister of Community Development, I visited the Indian community at Rustenburg, north of Pretoria, at their request. They told me that their properties had been acquired by the Group Areas Board for R73,000, and resold less than two years later for nearly five times as much. I thought this was an absolute disgrace, and said I hoped the government would see its way clear to grant the Rustenburg Indians the small corner of the town which they had requested. They had been there since the days of Paul Kruger, President of the Transvaal Republic, who had granted them freehold rights at the turn of the century in recognition of their assistance to local Afrikaner farmers in tiding them over financially during the 1896 rinderpest scourge, which had ravaged their cattle. But Paul Kruger's successors were little moved by old-time obligations. On the contrary, their utter hostility to Indian traders was typified by a comment by Coetzee, at a place called Warmbaths in the Transvaal (an apt name, because that little statement got him into plenty of hot water): 'I am sick and tired of seeing young Indians sitting on shop counters as if there were no other occupations open to them.'

Coetzee threatened to force Indians into other occupations if they didn't heed his advice. In fact only about 23 per cent of Indians were employed in commerce, and I asked him what other avenues of employment were open to them, what with the acute lack of training facilities, job reservation and inter-provincial immobility, not to mention the crippling effects of Group Areas proclamations. The Minister said the advice he had given to Indians was similar to the advice given to Afrikaners in the thirties: to diversify their occupations, to branch out into other occupations and become clerks, roadworkers, fitters and turners. Needless to say, he made no mention of the efforts by the state to help Afrikaners in those days through free and compulsory education, vocational training, and the so-called 'civilised labour policy', which meant jobs created by the state for unskilled Whites, as well as the reservation of all skilled work on the mines for Whites.

Blaar Coetzee eventually controlled two important portfolios – urban Blacks and Bantu (Black) education. I castigated him for his mean action in closing the Black night schools in Johannesburg and Cape Town, and criticised the policy of locating Black high schools in rural areas only. I deplored the desperate shortage of teachers, and the unfairness of expecting the poorest section of the population to finance most of their children's education and of refusing to provide free text books, while White children received free schooling and free books.

At the end of the 1970 session, before the general election due that year, Blaar (who was always making wild prognostications)

came across to my bench and said, 'Well Helen, I am sorry I won't
see you here next session.' 'Oh really,' I replied, 'are you not going
to stand for re-election?'

During the following session, however, we were constantly
engaged in brisk acrimonious exchanges. He had staked his
political career on accomplishing Verwoerd's aim: to reverse the
flow of Black labour away from the 'White' towns and back to the
Bantustans by 1978. His theme song was, 'I shall stop, reduce and
reverse the flow of Blacks.' Addressing the Federated Chamber of
Industries, Coetzee used a dramatic phrase: 'It is tantamount to
suicide for Whites to allow the flow of Blacks to the
Witwatersrand, to increase or to continue.' Some of the steps he
had already taken to ensure that no additional Black could be
employed unless registered by August 1966, actually had no
statutory authority. When I challenged him and accused him of
using departmental directives instead of laws to enforce policy, his
reply was characteristic: 'So sue me.'

Coetzee would sometimes accost me in the Lobby after one of
our rows: 'That was a good one, hey Helen? I always enjoy a good
fight with you.' It might have been amusing if one did not know
the enormous power he wielded. Several years later I objected to
his appointment as South African ambassador to Italy; a more
unlikely diplomat it would be hard to imagine.

The measure which created most interest in 1967 was the Planning
Bill, introduced by the new Minister, Dr Carel de Wet, fresh from
his ambassadorial post in London and suave of manner. I found
him very different from the tempestuous man from Vanderbijl-
park who had entered Parliament when I did in 1953. (Many
members of the class of '53 were occupying Cabinet benches by
then, including Vorster, M. C. Botha, Carel de Wet and Coetzee.)
When Verwoerd reported to Parliament in March 1960 on the
unrest in Sharpeville, it was de Wet who made the incredible
remark that he was 'concerned that when there are riots, whether
on the part of Whites or on the part of Blacks, if it is necessary to
shoot, only one person is shot dead'.[8] Verwoerd attempted a
mollifying explanation, but the damage was done.

It was also de Wet who stopped me in the Lobby after I had made one of my usual speeches advocating rights for Black people, and said, 'You must be mad, Helen. If we do what you suggest, what do you think will happen to your children?'

'Carel, if you don't give other people rights, you won't have children to enjoy the rights you have. They will not be alive.'

'Nonsense, we can hold the situation for my generation and for my children's generation, and after that, who cares?'

The Planning Bill was based entirely on apartheid ideology, namely the government's determination to reduce the number of Blacks in 'White' metropolitan areas such as the Witwatersrand, Cape Town and Durban. De Wet believed that urbanisation was closely connected to political demands, and seemed to think that Blacks out of sight had ceased to exist.

After one interview with the business community, de Wet informed the House there was no point in further consultation, since he now knew that commerce and industry were against the principle of the Bill. I could not think of any democratic country in the world where the government would pay so little attention to the very people whose enterprise, initiative and risk-taking had been responsible for phenomenal growth in the country, and whose taxes were to a very large measure the source the government relied on to pay for the services it provided. Conversely, people who supplied the brains of commerce and industry and mining had largely abdicated their political responsibility by leaving the vast business of running government to those who were hopelessly ill-equipped to do so.

Until now, economics had been stronger than politics in South Africa. I was not at all sure that this would be so in the future, because tough and dedicated young men in Vorster's Cabinet were determined to carry out the government's policy. Instead of Verwoerd's equation of poor and White versus rich and mixed, South Africa could easily end up poor and mixed.

It was ridiculous to expect that the impoverished, overstocked, overpopulated Native Reserves, Bantustans or homelands (or whatever picturesque name one gave them), could ever provide sustenance for their existing populations, let alone for all those singing hordes that by 1978 were meant to be marching back there from the White areas. This was especially so because, as I have said,

White capital and enterprise were not permitted to invest in the
Native Reserves, despite that recommendation in the Tomlinson
Commission Report which Verwoerd had rejected. But even with
White capital and enterprise, it was all a pretty hopeless proposi-
tion. So now expectations were directed to the border industry
plan. Industries were to be sited on the borders of the Reserves, and
the African labour they used would troop across the borders in the
mornings and go home to sleep at night in the Reserves; they could
also use dormitory labour, which went home at weekends. So
ideally two birds would be killed with one stone – ownership of
industry would remain on the White side of the border and labour
would be resident on the Black side.

In 1970 M. C. Botha, Minister of Bantu Administration,
proudly announced that the implementation of the Physical
Planning Act had prevented something like 260,000 additional
Blacks from coming into White areas. 'If you take a conservative
estimate and multiply it by five for dependants,' he said, 'more
than one and a quarter million Blacks have been prevented from
increasing the number of Blacks in the urban areas.'

I asked:

> What has happened to those people? Where are they? That is what I
> should like to know; where are these would-be work seekers, who
> would have been employed by the extension of industry in the existing
> industrial areas, had the Honourable Minister not prevented them from
> coming in? He does not tell us that he has condemned them to a life of
> poverty and idleness in the Reserves. He cannot tell me that all those
> people are employed in border industries. He knows perfectly well that
> the number of jobs created by border industries is a drop in the ocean
> compared to the number of jobs that existing industries in the White
> industrial areas are offering to non-White workers and particularly to
> Blacks.[9]

In 1969, the abolition of the death penalty was the subject of my
Private Member's Motion. I made it quite clear that although I was
in favour of abolition, all I asked was that the House appoint a
commission of enquiry into the subject. Interestingly enough, the
South African Parliament had never before debated the death
penalty, although this issue had been the cause of much con-
troversy in parliaments all over the world. Yet this was one

country, I felt, where it should be debated, because unlike other countries we had added to the list of capital offences over the years. Furthermore, reprieves in South Africa had dropped and we were responsible for 47 per cent of all civil death sentences in the free world, according to a United Nations report. The previous year, 1968, we had executed 119 people. Murder accounted for 90 per cent of the death sentences imposed. In Europe, only Spain, France, Ireland, Turkey and Greece retained the death penalty for murder. Many states in the US had abolished it; and indeed in the past two years no one had been sent to the electric chair, although over 400 men and women were on death row. South Africa remained rooted in her adherence to the death penalty.

Not a single MP supported my plea, not even for an enquiry; this, despite the fact that the United Party spokesman for Justice had made it known privately that his party would allow a free vote in the debate. The United Party moved an amendment favouring the retention of the death penalty, but asking for an automatic right of appeal. All the Nat members were eagerly in favour of retention; they seemed to assume that there were thousands of would-be murderers, straining at the leash, ready to do people in if the death penalty were abolished. That there were alternative methods of punishment, such as life imprisonment, seemed not to occur to them or to the United Party. That the violence and crime in our society required not only punishment but the closest investigation to determine causes of crime also escaped them.[10] (So South Africa was to continue hanging an inordinate number of people until 1990, when a moratorium on the death penalty was introduced.)

As I wrote to the family:

By the time the United Party and Nationalists had finished with me you'd have thought I was in favour of murder, rape, treason, sabotage, terrorism, child stealing, kidnapping, armed robbery and housebreaking with aggravating circumstances.

Identifying me with the promotion of violence was a favourite tactic of my opponents throughout my political career: 'She is against the death penalty – she is in favour of murder.' Because I opposed all measures allowing detention without trial, the counter-propaganda extended to depicting me and the Progressive Party as 'soft on communism, soft on security'.

Moreover, both the government and the United Party devoted a good deal of propaganda to creating the impression that I was in favour of a permissive society. Thus my solitary vote against the Drugs Abuse Act of 1971 meant I had to be in favour of drug-taking. I had indeed opposed this measure, which the Minister of Welfare boasted was the harshest, the most drastic anti-drugs law in the world. The Bill drew no distinction between hard-line drugs and marijuana, the personal use of which carried a mandatory minimum prison sentence of two years. If a person was in possession of 115 grams or more of marijuana, he or she was deemed to be a peddler and the minimum sentence was five years' imprisonment. The court had no discretionary powers except to give suspended sentences.

I was well aware of the widespread use of marijuana (or *dagga* as it is called in South Africa), among the Black population. I roundly condemned the Act, saying it would inevitably lead to the jailing of thousands of Black people for what was a cultural habit. I had discussed my proposed stand against the Bill with the leader of the party, Colin Eglin, knowing that drug abuse was a political hot potato. To his credit, although the next election was never that far away, Colin said I should do what I thought was right. I have no doubt that as a result of my opposition to the Drugs Act, the Progressive Party lost votes in the 1974 general election.

During the five years following the implementation of the 1971 Drugs Act, there were over 80,000 convictions for the use or possession of *dagga*; the vast majority were Blacks. After 1973, when the right of the courts to give suspended sentences was removed by an amending Act, thousands went to jail. Neither the prison officials nor the judges could cope with the drastic effects of the law, and in 1978 it was amended. Complete discretion was restored to the courts. One of my most vehement critics in 1971, Alf Widman – then a United Party city councillor – had accused me of 'trying to lead the youth of South Africa astray'. By 1978 he took a different line: 'This is a feather in the cap of the Member for Houghton. If I may say so on her behalf, she can say, "I told you so." ' He had by then become a Progressive Federal Party MP.[11]

I used Parliament to raise many other contentious issues: I pleaded for clemency for Bram Fischer, the communist leader serving life imprisonment, and for other political prisoners. I took up the cudgels for the playwright Athol Fugard who had been denied a passport for several years. I raised the absurdity of the censorship regulations which classified Africans with children of other races under the age of twelve. As I told the Minister of Interior:

> There is a long list of films which African adults are forbidden to see, like children under the age of twelve of other racial groups. Adult whites, Coloureds and Indians are allowed to see these films. But adult Africans are prohibited . . . I think this is a gratuitous insult to the African people and what is more, they think so too.

A Nat MP interrupted: 'You mean the Bantu peoples?'

> No, I do not. I mean the African people . . . I am not interested in changing definitions like the honourable member for Waterkloof. He thinks when he changes a definition, he solves the problem. He does not. There are still thirteen million Black people, African people to deal with in this country.[12]

I raised the astonishing case in which two men, one White and one Black, were sentenced to death for murder – the White man was reprieved, the Black man was hanged. I mentioned the extremely high daily average prison population; I criticised the trigger-happy police who shot people who were attempting to avoid arrest; I complained that far too little was spent on social welfare and too much on defence. I raised the appalling shortage of housing in the urban areas and the special disabilities of African women, and asked the Minister not to build any more Orwellian, single-sex hostels at Alexandra Township on the outskirts of Johannesburg. Here I actually had support from the Deputy Minister of Bantu Administration and Development, Punt Janson, who said he was not happy with the hostels at Alexandra and did not regard Blacks in urban areas as 'temporary sojourners', or as being 'only casually here', expressions used frequently by his Nat colleagues. He said that Blacks would be in the White urban areas for many years and it was necessary to make them as happy as possible. He got enthusiastic headlines and cheers from the opposition benches.

It was quite extraordinary to note how punch-drunk we had all become, because what the Deputy Minister had said was completely self-evident. Everybody knew perfectly well that Blacks were in the urban areas to stay. We already had third generation Blacks born in the urban areas, so why all the excitement? It was because we had all been so long excluded from power that we leapt at every crumb of comfort offered to us, and it was a sad reflection on our state of mind. Verwoerd knew his customers when he wrote his doctoral thesis many years before. Its title was 'The Blunting of the Emotions'.

However, this euphoria was dissipated the following day by M. C. Botha, Minister of Bantu Administration, who came into the debate with all guns blazing, giving everybody merry hell, especially the Progressive Party for daring to have talked to Black leaders in the homelands. These activities, he alleged, amounted to political terrorism, bordering on the treasonable.

7

In and Out of the House: 1961–74

Those turbulent years were very lonely. I did not once have a meal in the Members' private dining room. Meals there tended to become informal caucus meetings as, by custom, Members sat at tables with their party colleagues. Unless I was entertaining guests in the public dining room, I had a sandwich in my office. I especially missed the camaraderie of drinking with my chums in the Members' pub after the House adjourned, and all those lively postmortems on the day's events.

'The solo years'[1] also entailed a great deal of very hard and sustained effort – the conscientious ethic fostered by Sister Columba and the stamina inherited from Sam Gavronsky stood me in good stead. I did not have a team of researchers and speech writers, as many people imagined. South Africans MPs do not receive the generous allowances paid to US congressmen to employ as staff bright young political animals lured to Washington from Ivy League universities.

South African MPs rely almost entirely on party secondments. I had a secretary and a researcher but no speech writer. Not surprisingly, the defeated Prog candidates went back to their former occupations and were busy trying to make a living. I consulted those who lived in Cape Town, among them Colin Eglin, Harry Lawrence and Clive van Ryneveld. I would send Bills flying around the country to experts whom I knew shared my political views, asking for advice and points I could use in debates. Sometimes their replies came back in time; sometimes they came back after the Bills had already been passed by Parliament. Sometimes they didn't come back at all.

Barbara Mouat, my secretary, was calm and efficient and looked
after me like a mother hen. Jacqueline Beck, my researcher, was
indispensable. She had a law degree, was bilingual in English and
Afrikaans and was a great help in analysing proposed legislation.
She was also skilled at extracting relevant material from newspapers which I could use for speeches and questions. I was a keen
participant in the committee stage of Bills and in the Votes of
various Ministers, where Members were entitled to deliver ten-
minute speeches. Those short speeches often took a long time to
prepare as one had to condense a lot of material. On average I
tackled about fifteen different Ministers each session – as a random
examination of Hansard indexes reveals. With Jackie's help, I put
hundreds of questions during those years: an average of more than
200 a year, most concerning treatment of Black, Coloured and
Indian people – on housing, education, forced removals, Pass Law
offences and other matters. I also asked many questions relating to
civil rights and the Rule of Law – detentions, bannings, whippings,
police brutality and executions. So infuriated was one Cabinet
Minister that he shouted in Parliament, 'You put these questions
just to embarrass South Africa overseas.' I replied, 'It is not my
questions that embarrass South Africa – it is your answers.'

My questions, and the answers to them, elicited a great deal of
useful information. They provided facts and figures which were
used by researchers (and also, no doubt, by anti-apartheid
organisations) worldwide. The South African Institute of Race
Relations, in their valuable annual surveys, featured many of my
questions and the Ministers' answers. I often smiled when I
recollected the foolish advice given to me by a Natal Whip of the
UP when I was a new backbencher: 'Avoid putting questions –
they are just a cheap way of getting publicity.'

I had the heavy responsibility of representing not only the voters
of my own constituency but the thousands of Progressive Party
supporters throughout South Africa. I had to put our party's view
on every important bill that came before Parliament and on all the
abrogations of the Rule of Law. I could seldom leave the debating
chamber as I had no Whip to inform me when a measure on the
day's agenda would be debated, or indeed if the agenda would be
altered, or to take points of order on my behalf when unparlia-

mentary remarks or interjections were hurled at me – some anti-semitic, some sexist, others just plain hostile. I especially missed Harry Lawrence at those times. He would have helped me cope, for example, with one Nat MP who sat close by, hissing 'neo-communist, sickly humanist' every time I spoke in the House.

However, not all my colleagues on the government benches were hostile. A number seemed to regard me with amazed fascination. Most of them had large, docile wives brought up in Calvinist fashion to be respectful to their parents and to their husbands. Here was this small, cheeky female with a sharp tongue which she used without regard to rank or gender. Some were shocked, but a few were amused and one or two actually liked me.

Fanie Labuschagne, a National Party member for a rural seat, was very friendly. He would often send me a chocolate across the floor of the House, having popped it into an envelope, after I had made a speech, with a little note saying 'I don't agree with a word you say but . . .' On one of my frequent visits to Washington DC, I ran into Fanie who was there on behalf of the Maize Board, or some such non-governmental organisation. He invited me to have a drink and after we had imbibed a couple, Fanie leaned forward and asked confidentially, 'What are you going to tell the chaps here about us, Helen?' 'The truth Fanie,' I replied, 'only the truth.' Fanie groaned loudly, put his head in his hands and said, 'Oh God!'

My popularity with National Party MPs increased enormously in the period following Israel's spectacular victory over the Arabs in the Six-Day War in 1967. Nats who used to pass me by in the Lobby with eyes averted, stopped me, shook my hand and congratulated me, saying 'Mooi skoot, Helen' [good shot], as if I had been personally responsible for Israel's military feat. They presumably identified with Israel because it was a small be-leaguered nation surrounded by dark-skinned enemies. Being Jewish, I became an instant surrogate Israel. Of course, the flip side was that when Israel did not vote against anti-South African resolutions at the United Nations, I came in for a goodly dose of abuse, all of it anti-semitic.

Apart from the demands of Parliament itself, I received an astonishing amount of mail containing innumerable appeals from

people wanting assistance, hardly any of whom were my constituents, and most of whom did not have a vote. The volume of
letters that poured through my mailboxes in Cape Town and in
Johannesburg was immense. They came from home and abroad,
from the rich and the famous, the poor and unknown and the
merely curious. Most of all, though, they came from ordinary
people – people who believed that I could solve anything, that my
position made it possible for me to work miracles. As I reported to
my constitutents in 1970:

> I . . . do very little for you as individual constituents – instead, I seem to
> have become the honorary ombudsman for all those people who have
> no vote and no MP – they write to me in their hundreds, asking for help
> over pass problems, housing problems, jobs, bursaries, trading
> licences. I get requests for everything from a set of golf clubs to a bus. I
> get pleas for help from Indians over group areas removals, from
> coloured people over accommodation and race classification problems
> (I've even had three white men wanting to be reclassified as Malays or
> 'other coloured' as our quaint definition calls them – and actually
> succeeded in one case after the gentleman swore he was the illegitimate
> son of an Egyptian.)
>   I get dozens of pathetic letters that are smuggled out of gaol, and
> many appeals for help from banned people. Sometimes I manage to get
> conditions alleviated – often not. But my desk here and in Cape Town
> is a sad harvest of the seeds of apartheid.[2]

Reference books (pass books) that were invalid, confiscated
passports, imprisoned relatives, exiled friends, housing problems,
financial problems, personal problems, employment problems,
legal disputes – there was nothing South Africans (and sometimes
non-South Africans from neighbouring countries), Black and
White, seemed to believe that the Member for Houghton could not
put right. Sometimes I could. Often I couldn't. But no letter went
unanswered. So conditioned was I that on occasions I found myself
answering anonymous letters.

I had an interesting exchange of correspondence with Mrs Marie
van Zyl, who was the president of the Kappie Kommando, a
women's organisation so named because its members wore clothes
of a style used in the days of the Great Trek of 1836, including a
deep rimmed bonnet [kappie] to shade the intrepid pioneer ladies
from the African sun when they trekked in the ox-wagons across
the veld.

I had given an interview to a Sunday newspaper in which I was asked my opinion of the ladies of the Kappie Kommando, who were very right-wing and reactionary. I simply said, as a throw-away line, 'Oh well, they really belong to the days of witch burning.' I received a letter from Mrs van Zyl.' She was clearly very angry, but she wrote in polite terms. She addressed me as 'Geagte Mevrou Suzman' [Dear Mrs Suzman] and went on in Afrikaans to say that the Kappie Kommando women were proud of their old-fashioned ideas and she would like to remind me that her ancestors had taken the Bible across the mountains to the savages on the other side. 'And what', she asked as an anti-semitic sideswipe, 'were your ancestors doing at that time, Mrs Suzman? Die uwe [yours faithfully] Marie van Zyl.' And she drew a little sketch in profile of the kappie worn by the ladies, really rather cute. So I wrote back, also in polite Afrikaans, 'Geagte Mevrou van Zyl, My voorgangers was besig om die Bybel to skryf. Die uwe, Helen Suzman. [Dear Mrs van Zyl, My ancestors were busy writing the Bible. Yours faithfully, Helen Suzman.]' That was the end of that correspondence, but some months later I received a threatening letter from Mrs van Zyl, and this time I took it more seriously. I wrote to her sternly and said that it was an offence to threaten a Member of Parliament and that if she continued in this vein, I would hand her letter to Mr Speaker and ask him to take the appropriate steps. I never heard from her again.

I received a good deal of anonymous hate-mail throughout my years in Parliament – some of it just abusive, some of it threatening and most of it anti-semitic. I dubbed that lot my 'fan mail', and usually it went straight into the waste-paper basket. However I kept a few samples – full of old world charm!

I also received many phone calls of the same kind, usually in the dark watches of the night. My method of dealing with these late-night callers was simple: I blew a loud blast down the phone with the shrill whistle I kept handy. I recommend this method to victims of heavy breathers. One seldom hears the same voice again.

I arrived home one weekend to find Mosie with a large envelope in his hand. He said, 'I don't want you to open this letter. It looks very suspicious to me. I think it may contain a letter bomb.' I ridiculed the idea but then looked more closely at the envelope addressed 'To Helen Suzman, Friend of the Blacks in South Africa'. It was stuck down with a piece of string and sealing wax and on the back it had 'From Friends in Amsterdam'. I said to Mosie, 'Well what shall I do with it?' He replied, 'I think you should ask Arthur [his lawyer brother]. He knows everything.' So I phoned Arthur, who said, 'Mmm, sounds very suspicious. You should ask the Jewish Board of Deputies. They know everything.' So I phoned the Secretary of the Jewish Board of Deputies. 'Oh' said he, 'it sounds very suspicious and we did actually have a letter bomb only a couple of weeks ago from Amsterdam. I suggest you get in touch with John Vorster Square, [Police Headquarters]. They know everything.'

So I phoned the commanding officer at John Vorster Square: 'Colonel, I feel a bit silly about this, but there appears to be a possibility that a large envelope I have received contains a letter bomb. What shall I do with it?' 'Oh, mevrou [madam],' he said, 'take it seriously. We have had a number of letter bombs recently and we have special means of detecting them. Stay where you are, don't open the letter and I will send somebody immediately to collect it.' About half an hour later the doorbell rang and there stood an enormous policeman with a shoe box in his hand. He asked (in Afrikaans) for the letter. I took it out of the drawer in the entrance hall. 'O, wees 'n bietjie versigtig, mevrou [be a little careful],' he said nervously and opened the shoe box. I put the letter in and he clapped the lid shut as if he had caught a mouse. Off he went.

I heard nothing from John Vorster Square for the next three days. Then, overcome by curiosity, I phoned the commanding officer again and asked, 'Oh Colonel, what about that letter I sent you?'

'Ja, it looked very suspicious, Mrs Suzman,' he said, 'we sent it to the CSIR [Council for Scientific and Industrial Research] in Pretoria; they have a special detecting device. It was not a letter bomb.'

'Then what was in it, Colonel?'

'Pornographic literature,' he said.

'Oh well, send it back.'

'Not for the eyes of a lady,' he replied disapprovingly.

1a My father and mother, Frieda and Samuel Gavronsky, photographed together, about 1915. My mother died when I was born, and I first saw a photograph of her – this one – when I was fifty-five years old.

1b Auntie Hansa. We lived with her until my father remarried.

1c Myself, my father, my sister Gertrude.

1d My father with Debbie, my stepmother, photographed in 1952.

2a With my daughters, Patricia and Frances, photographed in 1953 when I first went into Parliament.

2b and **c** The 1961 election: *right* my campaign photograph and *below* victory smiles — Patty, my husband Mosie, myself, Francie.

SURVIVING THE STORM

3 The Solo Years: *top* cartoon depicting my lone survival; *middle* a chat with Speaker Klopper in the House of Assembly; *bottom* cartoon captioned 'Mrs Suzman's Stilettos', a reference to my opposition to the 90-day detention law.

4 1962:
top left speaking against the Sabotage Act at the mass protest meeting at City Hall, Johannesburg. *Top right* the march of 13,000 people organized by Max Borkum in support of the protest. Shortly after this picture was taken, they were attacked by hooligans.

In Zambia with Kenneth Kaunda in 1970 and (*bottom*) in Dakar in 1971 with Gary Ralfe, Colin Eglin and Bava Diouf. My visits to African countries were much criticised by the South African government.

5 Campaigning:
above with Irene Menell in 1981,
photographed for elections for
Parliament and the Provincial
Council; *below* with Selma Browde
(Provincial Council Candidate) and
our campaign manager, Max
Borkum, outside the polling booth
in my constituency of Houghton
(1974).

Above success in
1974 – celebrating
with René de
Villiers;
below with Jannie
Steytler and Harry
Oppenheimer at the
Progressive Party's
National Congress
(1974).

6a With my colleagues outside Parliament: the 'sextuplets', the six successful Prog. candidates, photographed in 1974, (from left to right: René de Villiers, Colin Eglin, Gordon Waddell, Alex Boraine, Rupert Lorimer and Frederik van Zyl Slabbert).

6b With my family at 'Blue Haze' in 1974: Mosie, myself, my grandson Danny, Francie, my granddaughter Josie, my son-in-law Jeffrey Jowell, Patty.

7a Seeing for my-self: in the Black township of Klip-town, near Johannesburg, 1973.

7b Outside the Houses of Parliament observing the police dispersing marchers protesting against the removal of squatters on the Cape Flats in 1981.

7c With Ken Andrew at a squatter camp outside Cape Town in the winter of 1981 after shelters had been demolished by officials.

8a John ('I *am* smiling') Vorster, in an armoured car, glimpsed in Cape Town, 1978.

8b With the parents of Dr Neil Aggett, the trade union leader who died while in detention in 1982. This photograph was taken at the inquest. *Right* same-size reproduction of a letter about Neil Aggett smuggled out of prison. I still have the original.

The following week exactly the same sort of envelope arrived and I wondered whether the first might have been a decoy duck. Should I go through the whole ridiculous procedure again? Or should I just take a chance? I took a chance. I ripped it open and there indeed was more pornographic literature, quite interesting stuff and very unusual. The pages had been cut from glossy magazines in Holland and the photographs depicted lurid scenes of Black men and White women having sex. And across the top was written, 'This is what you want for South Africa, you bitch.'

Throughout those years alone I was constantly badgering civil servants for permits, passports, paroles, and was also taking action on what were normal, everyday responsibilities of parliamentarians in democratic countries, but which in South Africa always seemed to require the stamp of ubiquitous officials – to such an absurd degree that I remarked bitterly in Parliament that it seemed one half of the population of South Africa was occupied with granting permits to the other half.

Then, too, there were all those curious aspects of life in South Africa which I felt I had to observe firsthand if I was to speak with authority on them in Parliament. Forced removals, actions of the police at protest meetings or at funerals, the treatment of prisoners, procedures in Pass Law courts, all required my personal attention.

I spent hours dictating speeches to Barbara, not only for the debating chamber but for the scores of meetings I addressed outside Parliament: protest meetings, university meetings, party public meetings. During election years all these demands intensified to a horrific degree. Looking back, I marvel that I survived. 'It's because you really are a Basuto pony, Ma,' said one of my daughters. 'You've got stamina.'

I was also on the itinerary of every visiting journalist or overseas politician. Although at times I felt like a surrogate Kruger Game Park, the stream of visitors included several whose presence in South Africa contributed to our struggle against the apartheid regime.

Robert and Ethel Kennedy visited South Africa in 1966. It was at the height of the confrontations between the students at the liberal

English-medium universities and the government. Student leaders had been banned and forced to live a twilight existence, forbidden to attend classes or participate in political activities or gatherings – the latter defined as consisting of more than two people. Some students were 'house-arrested' – confined to their homes from 6 p. m. to 6 a. m.

Robert Kennedy's visit and his passionate espousal of liberal values were immensely encouraging to those under siege. He boosted the morale of all of us under attack, and for once we felt that we were on the side of the angels. His stamina was remarkable. I accompanied him in Cape Town for one day. He started at dawn by visiting factories where he spoke to workers; he then held a mid-morning *kaffeeklatsch* with a group of women; gave a lunch-hour talk to businessmen; paid an afternoon visit to a Black township, where he spoke to many individuals; and ended his day at a mass meeting of students at the university. His address to the students closed with these inspiring words:

> Few will have the greatness to bend history itself, but each of us can work to change a small portion of events and in the total of all those acts will be written the history of this generation. It is from numberless, diverse acts of courage and belief that human history is shaped. Each time a man stands up for an ideal or acts to improve the lot of others, or strikes out against injustice, he sends forth a tiny ripple of hope, and crossing each other from a million different centres of energy and daring, those ripples build a current which can sweep down the mightiest walls of oppression.

On his return home, Bobby sent me a letter thanking me for the effort I had put into his trip to South Africa and he added: 'You are an inspiration to all of us. Those of us who live in a different atmosphere under different circumstances and yet are struggling with the same kinds of problems may become weary and discouraged at times. But we shall always find the stimulation to continue knowing that Helen Suzman never gave up.'

During the solo years I was fortunate indeed to have had H. J. Klopper as Speaker. He was a hardline Nationalist and the first chairman of the Broederbond in 1918. The Broederbond (literally Bond of Brothers), a secret organisation to which only male Protestant Afrikaners could belong, aimed at achieving exclusive political power for Afrikaners through a network of social, economic and cultural subsidiaries. Its success was evident: many Cabinet Ministers, top-ranking civil servants, prominent board members of major organisations, belonged to the Broederbond from the time the National Party took power in 1948. Many of those in command of Afrikaans newspapers and of state-controlled radio and television are Broeders. Afrikaner economic interests have been well served by the Broederbond, especially in the insurance, building society and banking sectors of the economy, and many Afrikaners have been given preferential treatment in obtaining important and lucrative government contracts.

Klopper later joined the far-right Conservative Party, after his retirement. So our political views were poles apart. Nevertheless, throughout those years that I was the lone Progressive in Parliament, Speaker Klopper would send for me at the beginning of every session and make a little speech: 'Well, I don't agree with a word you say, but it is my duty to see that minorities have their rights in this House. I am going to see that you get time to speak whenever you want to.' And he did. Without his help I couldn't have functioned. I would send him a note when a debate began, asking, 'Would you please put me on your list of speakers?' And the old man would look up and catch my eye, nod at me and smile. I had only to stand up thereafter and he would 'see' me. It was very important to be 'seen' when I wanted to be 'seen', and not at twenty minutes past ten in the evening, when those who were not asleep on their benches had gone home. During those years the Speaker probably allowed me, a minority of one, more speaking time than ten other MPs together.

I fell foul of Speaker Klopper only once. While I was out of the debating chamber during a particularly noisy after-dinner session, he announced that he would not permit any further interjections. I resumed my seat and, as was my wont, soon interjected. Blaar Coetzee demanded that I should be sent out of the House and the Speaker ordered me out. As I was on my way to the exit, M. C. Botha shouted 'Good riddance', on which the Speaker chucked him out too. Next day I informed the Speaker that I had not been present when he had issued his instruction, and apologised to him. Our friendly relations were resumed.

*

I was, moreover, to my surprise, allocated a Private Member's Day almost every year, which enabled me to highlight some of the worst aspects of life under the Nationalist regime. Looking back on my parliamentary career, I get a certain satisfaction from knowing that many of the Private Member's Motions I presented, although severely criticised at the time by both government and official opposition, were eventually reflected in official policy.

In 1962, for example, I introduced a Bill to repeal those sections of the Immorality Act which made sex across the colour line a punishable offence, and also to repeal the Prohibition of Mixed Marriages Act. The original Act of 1927 confined its prohibition to sex between Whites and Blacks ('Europeans and Natives' in the nomenclature of those days). In 1950 this was extended to include Whites, Coloureds, and Asians. I pointed out that this grim law had some shocking side-effects, such as suicide, murder and blackmail.

Between 1950 and 1960, 7000 people had been prosecuted and nearly 4000 convicted, under Section 16 of the Immorality Act, with all the accompanying glaring publicity. So indoctrinated were many South Africans about the 'disgrace' of miscegenation that, even if subsequently found not guilty by the courts, prosecution was enough to result in suicide. Vorster insisted that the existence of these laws was justified by the fact that so great a stigma attached to charges under the Immorality Act, and alleged that my liberal tendencies would naturally lead me to condone immoral relations across the colour line.

Despite Vorster's allegations I returned to the attack, and in 1971 introduced a Bill with the same objectives. There had recently been some ludicrous events in Excelsior, a small Free State dorp. A crop of Coloured babies appeared there, although there were no Coloured adults living in the little town. It was obvious that the babies were the product of miscegenation, and police investigations resulted in several charges being laid under Section 16. Excelsior was invaded by dozens of eager pressmen – South African and foreign – anticipating salacious stories and juicy headlines. The charges were eventually dropped, as it appeared that the Black women who were arrested had been beaten up during investigation and their evidence would not have been admissible in court. When at long last the offensive Section 16 of the Immorality Act was repealed in 1985, nearly 11,000 people had been convicted under that Section. Many more were charged and found not guilty, but their reputations were in tatters and their jobs lost. During the debate in 1985 when the Act was repealed, government members were astonished at the statistics I produced. Over twenty years earlier, in 1962, when I originally moved for the repeal of Section 16 of the Immorality Act and of the Mixed Marriages Act, I was accused by Jimmy Kruger (later Minister of Justice) of not understanding the mores of South Africa. Evidently by 1985, the mores of South Africa had changed.

These laws made South Africa ridiculous throughout the world. As I had predicted in my Private Member's Motions, their absence made little difference to the social fabric of South Africa. Citizens did not leap across the colour line in their thousands into one another's beds, either within or outside matrimonial bonds, after the repeal of these two grotesque examples of apartheid. It gave me much satisfaction, incidentally, to remind smug American audiences that, although there had been no prosecutions for many years, a law against mixed marriages existed in the state of Mississippi until 1988.

In 1963 my Private Member's Motion explored the need for minimum wages for Blacks, who were grossly exploited in many sectors of the economy. Surveys revealed starvation wages. Blacks had no bargaining power and were immobilised by the Pass Laws and the Masters and Servants Act, under which it was a criminal offence for a Black farm labourer to break his contract and leave his employer. Moreover, they were restricted to unskilled work by job reservation and by closed shop agreements. I also raised in Private Member's Motions the manpower shortage and the need to train and use our entire population; the advantages that would accrue from free and compulsory education for all South African children; the urgent necessity to overhaul the laws pertaining to Blacks in the urban areas; and the evils of the migratory labour system.

In the sixties I had much to say about the widespread and

indiscriminate use of the Suppression of Communism Act against opponents of the government. Dr Raymond (Bill) Hoffenberg, who had to leave South Africa on an exit permit, was one such example. His sin? He was chairman of the Defence and Aid Fund, which provided legal assistance to people accused of 'political crimes'. He was forbidden to teach students or to enter provincial hospitals. I thought how really crazy the government was to force a brilliant man like Bill to leave the country. He became Professor of Medicine at Birmingham University, president of the Royal Society of Physicians in England and was knighted. Today he is Master of Wolfson College, Oxford.

Ruth Hayman was another such case: she was a member of the Liberal Party, and a courageous lawyer who defended many people accused of crimes against the state. She was banned and placed under house arrest; she could no longer practise and eventually had no option but to leave the country, going to London in March 1967, where she occupied herself by teaching English to Asian immigrants.

Such travesties passed unnoticed, but what did cause a sensation was the second heart transplant performed in Cape Town in 1968. A Coloured heart went into a nice Jewish gentleman. It was ironical to read the mealy-mouthed and hypocritical comments by the Afrikaans press and by the Dutch Reformed Church dominees [clergymen]. They could hardly object to an event so favourable to South Africa's image, but if ever there was racial integration, this was it – rather more intimate than sitting beside a Coloured person on a park bench.

The following year a ludicrous incident put paid to South Africa's participation in international cricket for more than twenty-two years. When the MCC did not at first select Basil d'Oliviera, a Coloured man born in Cape Town but resident in Britain, to play in the English team against South Africa, Louwrens Muller, the Minister of Police, triumphantly announced this omission at a National Party meeting in Potchefstroom. The cheers of his audience resounded halfway round the world. Then, when the MCC eventually included d'Oliviera after one of its original selections dropped out, Prime Minister Vorster refused to allow the team to visit South Africa. This was the beginning of

Africa's continuing anguish about exclusion from international sport.

It was not only in the field of sport that Muller demonstrated his astounding insensitivity. There was a horrifying incident where a number of people had been arrested and then transported in a police van, in which there was no ventilation. It was a very hot day, and when the van finally arrived at its destination, several people inside were found to be dead. I asked Muller whether the government would consider making an *ex gratia* payment to the dependants of the victims. He replied: 'The South African police cannot adopt the attitude of Father Christmas.'[3]

During the parliamentary recesses, which usually lasted for six months, I travelled to foreign parts. England and the United States were frequent destinations: to visit my daughters, give lectures or receive honorary degrees. Over the years, Israel, Australia, Germany, Russia and China were also on my itinerary, but, as a politician living in an African country, I made it my business to see as much of that continent as possible. Thus I travelled widely in Africa, often infuriating the National Party press which commented bitterly that it was strange that I could get visas 'to visit Black African countries which denied flying-over rights to her own country' and which did not usually give access to those carrying South African passports.

In December 1970 I went to Zambia to visit President Kenneth Kaunda. The Whites I met there were understandably bothered about the economic reforms Kaunda had recently introduced, which were undisguised nationalisation with scant compensation. Many businesses were given a year to hand over. I was pretty sure what the repercussions would be on the economy. It was unlikely that any foreign capital would come into the country in the future. President Kaunda and I got on very well on a personal level. He was full of smiling charm, but shrewd and uncompromising about *die volk* [the Afrikaners] and their machinations in the Portuguese territories in Africa, and he made it clear that he loathed the Smith regime in Rhodesia. We had a two-hour luncheon, during the course of which a portable radio was brought in and we listened to the news, which was followed by a fierce attack on those African states engaged in dialogue with South Africa. Later, when we strolled past a table on which there stood a bowl with a single fish swimming around in it, I couldn't resist commenting, 'I see you have solitary confinement in Zambia, too, Mr President.' Kaunda was not amused.

The following year, I made a six-country trip through West Africa, East Africa and parts of southern Africa with Colin Eglin. The most vivid account of this comes from letters written to my family. From a letter dated 9 October 1971:

Which country shall we talk about – Senegal, The Gambia or Ghana? I can't offer you the Ivory Coast, alas, as President Houphouet-Boigny chickened out. He cancelled our appointment at the last minute, very probably because he was busy negotiating an official mission to South Africa and thought it might be jeopardised if he received John Vorster's opposition. Anyway we have chalked up two Presidents so far – Senghor of Senegal and Jawara of The Gambia, and one Prime Minister – Busia of Ghana.

The Senegalese came up trumps – lunch with Ministers, official cocktail party and a most satisfactory interview with President Leopold Senghor, who received us with much ceremony, including frock-coated attendants. He asked many questions about South Africa which largely centred on the issue which loomed large in Black Africa: dialogue or no dialogue with South Africa. We said 'yes', providing the dialogue was not confined to Nats, but included Africans and other non-White leaders in South Africa and people like ourselves who are strongly opposed to race discrimination. Senghor, who is a great Francophile and poet, presented each of us with a copy of his poems, warmly inscribed.

Bava Diouf, the editor of the main paper in Dakar, *Le Soleil*, interviewed us for nearly two hours, quite the most penetrating interview I have ever experienced in all my years in politics. Off the coast of Dakar is the little island of Goree, once notorious as the slave trade depot. We visited the old slave fort, the last outpost before the wretched captives were transported to the West Indies and America with a horrifying death toll en route. We were told a ghastly story in Dakar about the bishop who used to have his throne brought to the dockside so that he could baptise the poor wretches before they were thrown into the hold – saving their souls in advance.

With Abidjan out, we found ourselves with a day in hand, so we decided to dash over to The Gambia, where, with US ambassador Ed Clarke's help, we had fixed an appointment with the President, Dr Dauda Jawara, at a moment's notice. It was a mere 220 miles each way, including a half-hour trip by launch across the estuary of the Gambia River to get to the capital, Bathurst. The whole place is an historical anomaly, scrapped over by the British and French in the nineteenth century when they were busy carving up Africa. Its main source of revenue – smuggling. In the days of slavery, no doubt it was a big centre. We spent a couple of hours with the President. He is a vet., trained in Edinburgh – charming, knowledgeable and nobody's fool. More questions about dialogue.

Our next port of call was Ghana. We had been told we would be met by protocol people in Accra, but nobody appeared at the airport and we were kept hanging around for about an hour while a suspicious immigration officer phoned the Prime Minister's office to check our story – all this despite the fact that we had seven-day visas for Ghana. Anyway the guy finally pitched up and rescued us, and from then on it was roses, roses all the way – an official car, an escort, the lot. We had a meeting with the Deputy Minister of Foreign Affairs and his staff, and fielded many penetrating questions about South Africa. In the afternoon there was champagne with the Prime Minister, Dr Kofi Busia. He was, like the other heads of state, deeply interested in the mechanics of dialogue in such a way as not to appear to support the apartheid regime. The press kept us busy for three hours thereafter, some pretty hostile, others not.

Then off to a late supper in a little dive where our host ordered a great local delicacy – cane cutter – which turned out to be rat! . . . We are now winging our way east, the sun is just rising and we shall soon touch down at Addis on our way to Nairobi, which is our next port of call. Then Tanzania, maybe Malawi and home. I think we will have a much trickier time this side of Africa, because it has many South African exiles and freedom fighters, all bitterly opposed to any contact with White South Africans, including liberals. Hold thumbs for us.

Actually, East Africa proved as warm and as hospitable as the other side of the continent, with Nairobi especially open-hearted in its welcome.

We had an informal meeting with the Attorney-General, Mr Charles Njonjo, and a long talk with Vice President Daniel arap Moi. Colin and I were given a rousing cheer by the Kenyan MPs who banged on their desks when the Speaker, Mr Mati, announced that we were his guests in the House. Quite overcome, we were, rather different from my usual reception in Parliament! I really loved Nairobi, which is a lovely green, cool city. I can't say the same for Dar, which is hot and muggy, tatty and rather depressing. We had been warned that we would probably be met by pickets at the airport from the PAC and the ANC who have bases there. But in the event, nothing more than a statement in the local press greeted us, saying we were 'Trojan horses from

Pretoria', 'the grinning friends in the enemy camp', and the 'ambassadors of merchant democracy', whatever that might mean. I imagine that once President Julius Nyerere had agreed to meet us, none of these people would really dare to have a public demonstration against us.

Of all the African leaders we met, Julius Nyerere was undoubtedly the most impressive – friendly and extremely intelligent, though he made it absolutely clear that he was irrevocably against dialogue with South Africa under present circumstances, and fully committed to the freedom fighters. He had some amusing and ironical remarks to make about his so-called alignment with the Red Chinese.

'Funny,' said he, 'when I had Canadian officers training my army, nobody said I was aligned with the West. But now that I have seven Chinese training my troops, everybody says I am aligned with the communists.' I asked him why he needed 20,000 Chinese workers to build the Tanzam railway line – he replied '20,000 Chinese are teaching 100,000 Tanzanians *how* to work.' As we said goodbye to Nyerere, he held my hand and said, 'Mrs Suzman, when all this is over, the role that you played will be remembered.' I was very touched.

Our final stopover was in Malawi to see the President, Dr Kamuzu Hastings Banda. He's a rather tough, self-important, ebullient little fellow who made no bones about the fact that he was much more concerned with the economy of his country than demonstrating that he was totally anti-South African. He reckoned that Malawi was dependent on South Africa for jobs and he had to take note of that.

(Some years later, I reflected that he had done a remarkable job in looking after some three-quarters of a million refugees from Mozambique, even though the human rights record of his government with his own citizens was pretty dismal.)

After returning home at the end of October, I wrote again to my daughters:

I have been home for just over a week. . . . that the great African adventure . . . was an inspired idea is clear, for everyone I have met since my return, and I am not referring to the crowd of Progs who met us at Jan Smuts Airport with wild enthusiasm, but just the ordinary apolitical citizen, has been excited over the idea of White South Africans making contact with leaders in Black Africa. Of course the Nat press has been extremely nasty, firstly ridiculing the whole venture as 'a journey to nowhere by nobodies', with a cartoon depicting Colin as Tarzan and me as Jane, and then as the reports of our cordial reception from Dakar to Dar came streaming in, they ranted about our conniving with South Africa's enemies, consorting with murderers, beswaddering [slandering] our country and all the usual nonsense.

Our response, as reported by John Ryan of the *Rand Daily Mail*, was that if only the government would take its courage in both hands and show some evidence of real change in South African politics instead of relying on mere dialogue, the doors of Black Africa would be thrown wide open. It took another twenty years before the South African government was able to produce such evidence of change and enter those open doors.

John Worrall, the *Cape Times* correspondent who travelled with us throughout the tour, wrote: 'The Suzman–Eglin "Talking to Africa Mission" was a smash-hit success by any standards. Never before has such a tour been undertaken by South African political leaders. They have broken right through the apartheid wall, and the repercussions must be widespread and profound both in and outside the Republic. Never has South Africa had such roving ambassadors – charming, sincere, hard-working, patient – and the public relations impact is bound to be very considerable.'

In 1972 Colin Eglin, Ray Swart and I went to Venda, a Black homeland in the northern Transvaal which later became an independent Bantustan. We visited the President, Chief Mphephu, an insignificant, uneducated, unintelligent man. We flew in a small plane to Louis Trichardt where Mosie's driver, Wilson Rapunga, met us and drove us to Sibasa, the seat of government. When we got there I was astonished to see Wilson drop to his knees, crawl up to Mphephu's chair and make obeisance. When he came back to us I said, 'Good heavens, Wilson, did you vote for that awful man in the elections?' 'No,' he said, 'but it is our custom to kneel before the Chief.'

We stayed overnight with the Commissioner-General of Venda, Mr de Wet Nel (the former Minister of Bantu Administration) at his official residence. Dinner was served at about 6 p.m. and our hosts retired to bed immediately afterwards. Colin, Ray and I wandered around the house, looking for something to drink. We had been offered nothing on arrival and were dying for a Scotch and soda. Nothing was to be found. I learned afterwards that they were busy drying out old de Wet Nel. This was a lesson to me, I might add: never to travel without my quarter bottle of Scotch safely tucked away in my hand luggage.

De Wet Nel himself was a real character. He used to go into a paroxysm of rage at any mention of the Black Sash, whom he called 'Meddling old aunties who go around inciting Africans to break the pass laws'. When he was the Minister he had grimly warned Members of Parliament to be careful what they said in the House of Assembly, because only the other day, he told us, he had been motoring in the Transkei (another 'independent' Bantustan) and what did he see but a Bantu on a bicycle with a Hansard tucked under his arm! He received many gifts of karosses (animal skins) and other articles from the tribesmen among whom he lived and he had a great collection of artefacts. De Wet Nel was also much interested in Black folklore. He was a keen believer in the myth of the white crocodile which lived at the bottom of a lake and dragged maidens down to its lair.

On 1 May 1972 the Speaker allowed a special half-hour debate to enable the House to depart from its agenda to discuss the illustration in the newspaper *Wits Student*, published on 21 April 1972. The motion to adjourn to discuss 'this matter of urgent public importance', was brought by the Member for Carletonville, J. C. Greyling, one of my most persistent critics. He was horrified at this student publication.

On the front page was a picture of a student bending over a lavatory pan with the caption, 'Ah, the Prime Minister, I presume?' This led to fulminations of fury from the Member for Carletonville. He said the government had the key to open or close the doors of the university, and it would use that power if the universities could not enforce discipline. The council of the university and the Vice-Chancellor, Professor G. R. Bozzoli, had already apologised to the Prime Minister. This was apparently not enough for the Member for Carletonville, who suggested that the parliamentary subsidy to the university should be cut. I pointed out that it was not the National Party that subsidises universities, but the tax-payer, and added that there was going to be a howl of laughter throughout the civilised world at this latest example of South African idiocy. 'Indeed the world might well reach the conclusion that South Africans have gone round the bend.'[4] The Nationalists, I said, were 'flushed with their success' at a recent by-election in the Cape.

The Minister of National Education, Senator J. P. van der Spuy said: 'This matter does not concern a mean joke or a bit of filth involved in student fun; this matter concerns an attempt to act in a subversive way.'[5] I replied that the debate on the *Wits Student* was probably the silliest debate in all my years in Parliament.

Far more sinister for the universities, however, was their inclusion in an investigation instigated by the government in 1972. The Schlebusch Committee (later converted into a commission) was appointed explicitly to investigate the subversive activities of four organisations: the South African Institute of Race Relations, the University Christian Movement, the National Union of South African Students (NUSAS) and the Christian Institute. The South African Institute of Race Relations was exonerated. The University Christian Movement was in any case almost defunct. NUSAS was declared an 'affected organisation' and thus forbidden to receive money from abroad, and eight White students were banned. Later (no doubt to show it did not discriminate on the basis of colour) the government banned eight Black Students.

The Christian Institute was a church organisation founded by the courageous Dr Beyers Naude in 1963. He was a senior member of the Broederbond and the moderator of the Synod of the Dutch Reformed Church in the Transvaal. He resigned from the Broederbond when he became the Director of the Christian Institute and the Church promptly removed his status as a minister. In 1975 the last of the Schlebusch Commission reports appeared. It dealt with the Christian Institute and unanimously declared the Institute to be a danger to the state and recommended that statutory provisions be used against it. This gave the government the green light to declare the Christian Institute an 'affected organisation' thus denying it access to overseas funds, which effectively crippled it. Two years later, the government used the Suppression of Communism Act to ban Beyers Naude and the Christian Institute, together with seventeen other organisations. (In 1980 Dr Naude left the Dutch Reformed Church and became a member of the Black Dutch Reformed Church Africa (DRCA).)

When the Schlebusch Committee was first appointed, I warned the United Party in Parliament not to touch it with a bargepole, advising them to leave it to the Nats to sit on the committee, communing with themselves like yogis contemplating their navels. I said that in the unlikely event of my being asked to serve on it, I would certainly refuse. I warned that it was a McCarthy committee, a witch hunt, and would lead the United Party to disaster.

The United Party did serve on the Schlebusch Commission. It did lead them to disaster. This was the beginning of the final break-up of the party, whose four MPs on the Schlebusch Commission signed the reports containing its disgraceful recommendations. Graaff had said his men would serve as watchdogs. I could only comment that these watchdogs had no teeth – they did not even utter a warning growl when they signed the interim reports.

The pressures in Parliament continued unabated. I wrote to my daughters in September 1973:

> Labour, justice, prisons, police, economic affairs and foreign affairs votes are all coming up in quick succession and having to be spoken on. It's the hideous preparation for these short ten-minute speeches that takes so much time and then the sitting around for endless hours, hopping up and down like a jack-in-the-box trying to be seen by the chairman. I had a nasty brush with the nasty little deputy Minister of Police, one Jimmy Kruger, who was furious when I raised the issue of the police shooting persons attempting to escape from custody – ninety-two in the first two months of this year so far, including three teenagers who were pinching cars or committing other heinous crimes, which the police appear to treat as capital offences. Instead of expressing regret for all this, as one might have expected, he turned on me like a maddened snake, accused me of treachery and said I wanted the police to be killed in executing their duties. Did you ever!

The Community Development Vote of that year resulted in a curious little exchange between the Minister, A. H. du Plessis, and me about the Nico Malan Theatre in Cape Town and civic theatres elsewhere. I suggested that they be made 'international venues', like Jan Smuts Airport, so that people of all races could attend performances. The Minister replied, 'Whites have rights too.'[6] Now, who ever would have thought that in South Africa?

I also had to do battle with a horrible rackrenting landlord in Houghton. All the tenants of his flats were terrified of him. He resorted to a variety of dirty tricks: abusive phone calls, hoaxes of a sinister kind, denying the use of the lifts to delivery men, blocking parking spaces, locking all servants' rooms. I warned my daughter, Francie, that if I was found strangled in a ditch on Houghton golf course or buried in the sand in a bunker, to remember it was this mafia gent who dunnit.

Nineteen seventy-three marked twenty years of parliamentary service for me. On 14 June the Progressive Party organised a banquet in Cape Town to mark my twenty-first session in Parliament. It was attended by more than 500 people and the toast was proposed by the KwaZulu leader, Gatsha Buthelezi. He said I was 'the one flickering flame of liberty amidst the darkness that is such an enveloping feature of South African politics . . . the lone voice of millions of voiceless people'. He presented me with a Zulu carving depicting a Black woman holding Africa aloft. The inscription reads, 'To Helen Suzman MP from Gatsha Buthelezi and family and many voiceless people'. Colin Eglin presented me with a silver and onyx paperweight inscribed '1953–1973 – To Helen Suzman from the Progressives with love and admiration'.

In those days I had a very cordial relationship with Gatsha, and we exchanged friendly letters over many years. He now prefers to be called Dr Mangosuthu Buthelezi.

He was repeatedly labelled a puppet of Pretoria by the ANC-in-exile because he was the chief minister of a Bantustan. I thought this judgement unfair. Neither the ANC nor his Black detractors at home gave him credit for the fact that he had accepted this post after consultation with Chief Albert Lutuli and the ANC. Nor did they give him credit for his steadfast refusal to take independence for KwaZulu, thus frustrating the Grand Apartheid aim of Dr Verwoerd and preserving South African citizenship for six million Zulus. I knew too that the National Party government was hostile to Buthelezi. Many barbed remarks in Parliament implied that he was a pawn of the Progressive Party and that his speeches were written by me. He also had problems in obtaining a passport to travel abroad.

My relationship with Gatsha in the mid-seventies was such that I sent an urgent message to Ulundi, the capital of KwaZulu, asking him to fly to Johannesburg to intercede in an impending confrontation between Zulu migrants living in the Mzimhlope hostel and the local residents in Soweto. I had received frantic phone calls warning me that a bloodbath was imminent. Buthelezi came immediately and I am convinced that his intervention prevented a further catastrophe. I visited Ulundi two or three times at his invitation and was warmly received there and at Groutville where I attended the unveiling of Albert Lutuli's tombstone in July 1972, together with Ray Swart and Alan Paton.

Our friendly relationship suffered a setback, however, shortly before the 1974 election. We crossed swords over the so-called Mhlabatini Declaration of Faith, initiated by Harry Schwarz, then United Party leader in the Transvaal. Schwarz and Buthelezi signed the declaration, which in fact embodied Progressive Party principles rather than those of the United Party. I construed this as a ploy to win seats from the Progressive Party at the forthcoming general election and made a statement to the press in which I said, somewhat tactlessly, that Chief Buthelezi had 'unwittingly' lent himself to this strategy. Buthelezi resents criticism from any quarter and invariably responds at length both in the press and privately. There was an angry public rebuttal and a reproachful letter to me.

We eventually restored a cordial relationship, and I was gratified that in response to nagging from me he urged the government to amend the Natal Code under which Zulu females were perpetual minors in law.

In latter years my relationship with Buthelezi again deteriorated. He strongly resented my comments about the humiliating treatment meted out to him by the PAC at the funeral of Robert Sobukwe. Thereafter we saw little of each other. In the early eighties it seemed to me that he could have done more to try to halt the violence that erupted in Natal between his Inkatha Freedom Party and the allies of the exiled ANC. Still later, the revelation that the government had funded two Inkatha rallies in 1989 and was secretly giving financial support to UWUSA (United Workers' Union of South Africa), his trade union organisation, out of a government Defence Department slush fund further alienated me. Both Buthelezi and de Klerk claimed they were unaware of this funding. If true, it was not a good excuse, for they should have known. I criticised this action strongly in my presidential address to the South African Institution of Race Relations in 1991.

Despite the scandal of the slush fund affair and Buthelezi's later curious association with the right-wing Concerned South Africans Group (COSAG) he remains a key figure in negotiations for the new South Africa. He is, after all, the leader of the largest ethnic group in the country and is a skilful and experienced politician.

At my Report-Back meeting in 1973 I thanked my constituents for their forbearance in putting up for all that time with a representative who had paid little attention to normal constituency issues. The voters of Houghton apparently realised that they had served their interests well by maintaining a voice in Parliament to speak up for the disenfranchised millions, a representative who refused to compromise on individual liberty, civil rights and the Rule of Law.

I in turn was convinced that I represented a point of view which still existed in South Africa – despite intimidation, despite the bullying of the government and the toadying of the one-time anti-government forces – a point of view which needed to be stated unequivocally on a hundred and one issues. My job in Parliament was to be the disputing voice expressing that point of view. It was not to indulge a passion for opposing, as was often suggested by my detractors; it was to provide an outlet, a means of expression for all those who were not prepared to conform to the bizarre practices known as 'the South African way of life', as if this very phrase was a justification for the most shameless discrimination and the most inhuman policies.

The most helpful allies I had during all my years alone in Parliament were the political correspondents. I formed many lasting friendships with the men and women in the Press Gallery and with foreign correspondents from overseas papers whose support gave me great encouragement in my more despairing moments. In March 1966, shortly before the election, Joseph Lelyveld, then on his first stint as *New York Times* correspondent in southern Africa (later author of the Pulitzer Prize-winning book on South Africa, *Move Your Shadow*, 1985) published a lengthy article, 'Minority of One in South Africa's Parliament' in the *New York*

Times Magazine. At the end of it he asked whether there was any point in my going back to Parliament where 'she can only repeat herself and can't possibly make any headway'. He answered that the choice at present was not 'between revolution and moderation but between speech and silence'; if a tragedy was unfolding in South Africa, then while the community was moving inexorably to its doom, the task of speech and interpretation was left to individuals of strong character. He ended with my comment to him: 'Those who can talk must continue to talk.'

I also had support from many diplomats and visiting academics during those years, notably the British ambassador, Sir John Maud; the Canadian ambassador, Charles Woodsworth; the American ambassadors, Bill Edmondson and Bill Bowdler; and Robert Birley, a former headmaster of Eton who came to South Africa to teach in the Department of Education at Wits. They, and many others, were aware of the intricacies of South African politics and their encouragement was of enormous value.

The reason for the extensive coverage of my speeches, and for the support I was given from diplomatic quarters, was that I unequivocally opposed abrogations of human rights, exposed police brutality and the iniquities of forced removals, and asked awkward questions at every opportunity. This was all headline stuff and I certainly got headlines. When National Party and United Party MPs sourly accused me of seeking publicity, I had a simple reply: 'Say something worthwhile and you too will get headlines.'

This axiom, incidentally, was just as effective with the government-supporting Afrikaans press whose headlines were frequent, albeit hostile. Their cartoonists had a field day depicting me as a hideous hook-nosed prototype from *Der Stürmer*, with heavily bejewelled fingers, about to devour a Christian child for breakfast. One morning after a particularly repulsive cartoon of this genre had appeared in *Die Transvaler*, I happened to be visiting a prison. The warder's wife to whose care I was entrusted after the official inspection and before tea, looked at me intently in the ladies' room, and I could see clearly the balloon above her head with *Die Transvaler*'s cartoon in it. She blurted out 'Ag, Mrs Suzman – you not so bad!'

8

Prisons and Prisoners

Visiting prisons became an important part of my job as an MP, for I realised that prisoners are the most helpless of human beings. I often wondered why judges and magistrates who, unlike MPs, could visit prisons without first obtaining permission, did not make more use of this entitlement. I was convinced that it was of paramount importance to make the authorities aware that someone was keeping a watchful eye on the prisons, and for the prisoners to know that somebody from outside was interested in their welfare.

South Africa's prison population is large, averaging more than 100,000 each year, higher pro rata than that of the UK and the US. Ordinary criminal jails are grossly overcrowded. Among the worst sufferers are the awaiting-trial prisoners who spend many months locked up before their cases come to court. During that period they do not have recreational or study facilities. I had no doubt that the creation of statutory criminals through the Pass Laws was a major cause of the huge number who were locked up and my visits to the magistrates' courts where such cases were tried confirmed this assessment. I likened their procedures to sausage machines which churned out 'criminals' – one every two minutes – convicted of the 'crime' of looking for work without the required permit.

As I have related, my first experience of visiting a prison was in 1960, when I investigated the conditions of the detainees held during the state of emergency. My continuing interest was stimulated by a notorious case in 1965 in which the government prosecuted the *Rand Daily Mail* for publishing a series of articles about prison conditions. This allegedly violated Section 44(1)(f) of the Prisons Act, which made it an offence to publish anything about conditions in a prison without taking reasonable steps to verify with the prison authorities that the facts were correct. Obviously it was very difficult to verify facts detrimental to the prisons. Nevertheless, the *Rand Daily Mail* published a series of articles based on sworn affidavits given to them by warders and ex-prisoners. Harold Strachan, an art teacher in Durban who had served a sentence of three years in Pretoria Central jail for sabotage, was a main source of information.

The *Rand Daily Mail* and their publishers, South African Associated Newspapers, were promptly prosecuted, as were all the *Mail*'s informants, who one by one were found guilty under the Prisons Act. Thus began a sequence of cases which took nearly four years to come before the courts, cost the newspaper something like R300,000 and in effect lost the editor, Laurence Gandar, his job. Gandar, one of the finest editors ever to run a newspaper in South Africa, was a courageous opponent of the apartheid regime, as was his African Affairs reporter, Benjamin Pogrund, who had written the offending articles. Strachan was banned when the reports appeared, was charged and found guilty under the Prisons Act and sentenced to another eighteen months in jail.

As a close friend of Laurie Gandar and his wife Isobel, and of Benjy, I went to court whenever possible to attend the hearings. Gandar was utterly self-possessed and full of spirit facing the hectoring cross-examination of the prosecutor. I wondered if even the state didn't occasionally have a qualm, especially when people like Lord Devlin (a judge of appeal in the British House of Lords who had come to South Africa to observe the trial) and William Rees-Mogg, editor of the London *Times*, were present. Rees-Mogg gave valuable evidence for the defence. However, I had only to remind myself that this was a political case and I came back to earth. The state assembled an unbelievable bunch of liars. One old lag who appeared said that I had often given him tea and had tried to convert him to my 'leftist' way of thinking. Needless to say, I had never seen him before in my life. He also claimed that Gandar had offered him a job on the *Rand Daily Mail* and R1000 if he would besmirch the prison system.

Shortly after the case started, I asked the Minister of Justice for permission to go to Pretoria Central to see if the conditions had been accurately described by the *Rand Daily Mail*. At the prison, which I visited early in September 1965, it was clear that there had been an overnight transformation. Every prisoner was holding an eating bowl, glistening in the sun, whereas Strachan had alleged that their bowls were rusty. These were obviously brand-new. All the prisoners were wearing new jerseys and they told me that hot showers were now available. The taps in the ablution block had been repaired, so that they could clean their teeth over the washbasins and not over the lavatory bowls, as the *Rand Daily Mail* had reported. The whole prison had clearly been cleaned up for my visit.

I talked to various prisoners, and something very strange happened. I walked past a cell with the commanding officer of the prison, and there was a man cleaning the door. He stopped me and said: 'What are you going to do for me, Mrs Suzman?' I had never seen this man before, and I looked at him and said, 'Who are you and what do you want me to do for you? Do you need defence?' which was all I could think he could be wanting of me. 'Don't pretend you haven't seen me before,' he blurted out. 'Don't pretend you don't recognise me as the man who Gandar and that other man, Pogrund, brought to see you at your house in Houghton. Don't pretend you don't know me. You all offered me money if I would give evidence against the prison authorities.'

I turned to the commanding officer and said, 'This man is totally mad. I've never seen him before.' The man then put up his hand and said, 'Permission to make a statement, sir?' 'When you make your statement,' I said, 'remember my house is not in Houghton.'

I was told that his name was Paul Putter and I was pretty sure he had been put up to it as a trap, a feeling confirmed when he escaped some months later. He was recaptured and while waiting to be charged managed to send a message from the cells at the court to the *Rand Daily Mail* saying he wanted to make a statement. The *Rand Daily Mail* sent a lawyer and Putter made a statement alleging that the prison authorities had offered him remission of his sentence if he gave evidence against Gandar and Pogrund. He also said that he had been persuaded to sign a statement that Gandar had given him R30 to buy clothing, as a bribe to make accusations against the Department of Prisons.

Putter was re-sentenced. He then wrote me a letter from prison withdrawing the statement he had made when he was an escapee, and again accusing me of offering him a bribe, and threatening to expose me. 'I am going to get you, you dirty bitch!' he wrote. That letter was apparently smuggled out of jail in November 1966. I immediately sent a copy of it to the head of the Prisons Department demanding that steps be taken against this man who was making false accusations against me. I had no response, except for a formal acknowledgement of my letter.

A few months later, in February 1967, I was on the ferry going to Robben Island to visit prisoners – to be my first encounter with Nelson Mandela – and I was accompanied by the same official, General Steyn. I asked, 'By the way, General, why have you never followed up my letter about Putter?' 'Oh, Mrs Suzman,' he said, 'you know the man is just mad, we don't take any notice of anything he says or does.' But the following month the commissioner wrote to say that Putter had committed a breach of prison regulations by writing to me, and that for this offence he would be dealt with departmentally. As for the contents of the letter, the commissioner said I could take legal action against Putter, which I did not bother to do. I believe he subsequently died in prison.

Advocate Sydney Kentridge did an excellent job for the defence in the case against the *Rand Daily Mail* and in July 1969 the trial fizzled out like a damp squib. Gandar and Pogrund were found guilty on two counts: publishing false information about prisons, and not having taken due care to verify before publishing. The judge, in a six-hour judgement, added that he found them not guilty of knowingly publishing false information. He sentenced Gandar to R100 fine or three months in prison and Pogrund to three months' imprisonment suspended for three years.

It was a moral victory for the *Rand Daily Mail*, especially as on important allegations such as the use of electric shock on prisoners, the state was held not to have proved its denial. We drank champagne that night and a great weight was lifted from the defendants' shoulders. But imagine a case that dragged on for over three years, entailed seven months in court, cost the newspaper a huge sum of money, and ended with the kind of penalty imposed for negligent driving. It should never have come to court, and South Africa was given merry hell by all the important newspapers in Britain and the United States. But the state achieved its objective: for many years thereafter newspapers shied off reporting prison conditions.

I had an extraordinary experience with another prisoner, Andy S., who also had connections with the *Rand Daily Mail* case. He was the offspring of an Afrikaner mother and a Jewish father, and had evidently been in and out of trouble from his early years. My first contact with him was the receipt of a letter from Krugersdorp Hospital on the West Rand. He addressed me as 'Auntie Helen' and concluded by sending his love to 'Uncle Mosie'. This bogus nephew informed me that he had been transferred from Pretoria jail to the hospital because he had tuberculosis. He asked me to obtain parole for him on compassionate grounds. Intrigued by his *chutzpah*, I did so.

But parole did not last long and he was soon back in jail. Shortly afterwards, I was in court observing the *Rand Daily Mail* case and there was Andy in the capacity of state witness. I suspect he was offered remission to do this. While he was in the witness box, just before the lunch break, an affidavit was laid before him and he was asked whether he had made and signed the statement it contained. It was apparently a denial of the allegations Strachan had made and the *Rand Daily Mail* had published. He admitted the document had been signed by him. He then announced, 'None of this is true!' The prosecutor immediately asked that he be declared a hostile witness and the court adjourned for lunch. On resumption, the affidavit had disappeared – either down Andy's gullet or down the lavatory. No copy could be produced immediately and the case was postponed. I admired his courage, for he had laid himself open to a charge of perjury, and if indeed remission had been offered, the offer had flown out the window. He skipped the country next day and went to England with his English wife. The disappearance of this one state witness offset to a small degree all those defence witnesses who, having volunteered to give evidence on behalf of the *Rand Daily Mail*, had melted like the morning mist as the day for the trial approached.

A few months later I received a letter from a motor company in England informing me that they were contemplating prosecuting Andy for fraud. He had claimed to be my nephew and a political refugee. As their sympathies were on the liberal side, the letter went on, if his story was true they would not prosecute him. Could I verify it? I refuted the blood relationship, and concerning the political refugee claim I sent a number of cuttings from the local press on the 'hostile witness' incident. Whether this sufficed to rescue him I do not know, but a few years later I received a letter from the gentleman himself from Wormwood Scrubs, where he was a guest of Her Majesty. He asked me to let him know what the period of prescription was for perjury in South Africa, as he was due to be released shortly and had been told that he would be deported. Would I intervene with the Home Office? I followed much the same procedure I employed with the car company. It seemed to work. But not too long afterwards, he was back in jail. I doubt whether the Home Office was so magnanimous the second time round, but since Andy hasn't pitched up on my doorstep, I can't be sure.

From the mid-sixties on, I made a point of obtaining permission to visit the White political prisoners in Pretoria Central once a year. My original contact was with Bram Fischer, QC, the son of a former Judge President of the Orange Free State and a grandson of its former Prime Minister. He was a Rhodes scholar, a leading member of the Communist Party, and a brilliant advocate. Ironically enough, he was often retained as legal adviser by the Chamber of Mines, that pillar of the capitalist establishment in South Africa. He was the leader of the defence team at the 1964 Rivonia trial in which Nelson Mandela and seven others were charged with treason and attempting to overthrow the state by sabotage. After a trial lasting seven months, one accused was discharged and the rest were sentenced to life imprisonment including the one White accused, Denis Goldberg.

The following year Bram himself was charged with the same offences and was granted bail. He went to England to plead a case before the Privy Council there, and on his return to South Africa he jumped bail and disappeared. Heavily disguised, he evaded the police for several months, but was eventually arrested, charged and found guilty. He was sentenced to life imprisonment.

I visited Bram regularly. It was hard to reconcile this small mild man with anything violent or with his fervent belief in communism. He always assembled a concise list of grievances to hand to me. I remember being very touched when I arrived one day and he presented me with a bunch of flowers he had grown in the prison yard, where the authorities allowed him to use a small area for gardening. I learned of a spiteful little incident which arose because the prisoners had planted a fig tree in the yard. When the fig tree produced its first crop, the prisoners bottled the figs and put them in their fridge. The warder in charge of this group of prisoners was a highly excitable man. He discovered the bottle of figs, and became so incensed that the prisoners had done this without asking his permission that he had the fig tree chopped down.

This warder always cried on my shoulder when I emerged after seeing Bram, because Bram was quite unconcerned who was present when he reeled off the prisoners' grievances. The warder once said to me: 'They never tell you, do they, that I always allow them extra time when their visitors come? They don't tell you that I don't object if their letters are more than five hundred words, which is what they're supposed to be? All they do is complain, complain, complain.' I said, 'Calm yourself, captain, calm yourself. You must realise that a prisoner takes advantage of the fact that a Member of Parliament has come to see him, and therefore he wants to get as much advantage out of that visit as possible. He's not going to sit there extolling your virtues. What he's going to do is give me their complaints, so they can be attended to. You mustn't take it personally. There is nothing personal.'

Eventually, this man retired, or was transferred, and other warders were put in charge of the politicals in Pretoria prison. I was allowed to have a piped music system installed for the prisoners, and we built up quite a library of classical records, which I delivered to them each Christmas.

Right to the very end Bram was a convinced communist; nothing diverted him from that philosophy, not even what happened in Czechoslovakia or Hungary – nothing at all. My last visit was when he was dying of cancer, in a state hospital in Pretoria, under guard. When I walked into the ward where he was kept, I didn't recognise him; he had shrunk to a tiny mummy. He was fast asleep when I walked in and I said to the official, 'I hesitate to wake him up.' The official responded, 'Oh, Mrs Suzman, he sleeps most of the time, he's under drugs, so wake him up. He'll want to see you.'

I did wake him up, and he looked at me and said, 'Who is it?'

'Bram, it's Helen Suzman,' I said.

'Oh, well if you've come here to persuade me to change my mind and say that I will do anything to get out of here, I can just tell you . . .'

'Bram, calm down. I wouldn't dream of asking you to do anything or to give any undertakings. I know your views. I've just come to see you. How are you?'

He calmed down and said, 'Oh well, that's different.' He said to the warder, 'Fetch me my notebook,' which was on another table, and this chap jumped to it and gave him his notebook. 'These are the things that I want done,' said Bram, then he rattled off a series of requests, mostly on behalf of his fellow prisoners.

When I returned to Cape Town I went to see Jimmy Kruger, the Minister of Justice, about Bram. As usual he shouted at me the minute I walked into his office: 'Oh you and your communist friends.'

'Now look,' I said, 'let's not go through all that nonsense again. Bram is a friend of mine. That has nothing to do with his communism. I've known him for years. The man is dying, and it would be a very fine gesture of compassion if you would let him die at home and not in hospital or in prison.'

'Oh,' said Kruger, 'I can't do that.'

'Yes, you can. You phone his doctor and you'll learn that he only has a couple of months to live.' Kruger did phone, and Bram was flown in a military plane to Bloemfontein to stay with his brother, a doctor.

One day soon afterwards Kruger came up to me in the Lobby of Parliament. 'Yes, you and your communist friend,' he said. 'I hear Fischer is up having breakfast every morning. I'm going to send him back to prison.'

'You'll do nothing of the kind,' I said. 'You just leave him where he is. People who are suffering from terminal cancer often have periods of remission. Leave him.' And he did. Bram died a couple of months later, a tragic end to the tragic life of an exceptional man. I find it ironic that his name is seldom mentioned by any of the present-day activists who belong to the South African Communist Party. His tremendous sacrifice 'for the cause' is ignored, and few tributes are paid to his memory. His wife Molly, also a confirmed communist, died in a macabre car accident before he went to prison. They were motoring to Cape Town to celebrate the twenty-first birthday of their elder daughter, Ilse, who was a student at the University of Cape Town. En route they crossed a bridge spanning a dry river bed. Bram swerved to avoid an animal, the car left the bridge and fell into the only pool of water underneath the bridge. Molly was trapped in the car and drowned. Their only son Paul died in 1971 aged twenty-three. Bram was not permitted to attend the funeral.

After Bram died, I continued to visit the Pretoria jail with its White political prisoners annually. I was allowed to select one prisoner to represent them all and I chose Hugh Lewin, a young man sentenced to seven years for sabotage, whose parents were dead and whose wife had divorced him before he went to prison. Hugh was a member of the African Resistance Movement, which consisted mainly of misguided young members of the Liberal Party. He had been implicated in sabotage by another member who 'sang' under interrogation. When I first saw Hugh he had served only two and a half years of the seven, and it sickened me to think of this young life being wasted. I eventually managed to get permission for him to take an honours degree with the University of South Africa, the excellent extramural university which saved the sanity of many of the political prisoners. But he still had to spend endless hours sewing mailbags.

On one occasion I arranged for our group of seven Progressive Federal Party MPs to visit a local prison in Cape Town. We went in a small bus in the early morning of a cold rainy day in winter. I was dropped off at the women's section of the Roeland Street jail (now closed) and the others drove on to the men's section. I was greeted by a smartly uniformed young woman captain wearing a hat and carrying a baton. She led me to an open section of the prison and there, huddled under the roof of the verandah, was a sorry little group of white women prisoners.

'Môre, blankes' [Morning, Whites] barked the captain, 'Môre mevrou' came back the quavering reply. 'Het julle gebid?' [Have you prayed?] 'Nee mevrou' [No madam]. 'Nou ja – bid' [Well then, pray] and a few gabbled words of prayer ensued. 'Enige klagtes?' [Any complaints?] asked the captain with considerable menace in her voice. 'Nee mevrou' was the whispered reply. It would have been a brave prisoner indeed who complained in those circumstances.

The captain and I then crossed to the Black section of the jail. This time the prisoners were addressed by her as 'Môre, swartes' [Morning, Blacks]. For the rest the procedure was the same – no discrimination at Roeland Street! When the other Progs joined me, I related the story. For weeks afterwards, when a decision was taken in our caucus, someone would look around the table and ask menacingly, 'Enige klagtes?'

During the eighties a more humanitarian approach to prisoners was adopted by the authorities. I paid a visit to the new maximum security prison for politicals in Pretoria in November 1986 and saw all eight White prisoners together in a room. The new prison was really quite something – hot and cold running water in each cell, flush lavatories, beds, a mess room, a fine sunny exercise yard and, best of all, a carpentry shop, so that they no longer had to sew mailbags. Physical conditions were much better, but some regulations remained very strict: no newspapers, limited visits and no remission of sentence. I was allowed to visit them as a group year after year. After his release, one prisoner delivered a dozen bottles of Chateauneuf-du-Pape to me with a note of thanks from the group for my efforts on their behalf. Both the gift and the thought were much appreciated.

I also visited the White women prisoners at Pretoria jail fairly regularly. Their physical conditions were satisfactory. Two women, Barbara Hogan and Ruth Gerhardt, were of particular interest to me, Barbara because she displayed great spirit and Ruth – a Swiss citizen – because of the Swiss government's astonishing treatment of her. Barbara had received a savage sentence of ten years for advancing the aims of a banned organisation, the ANC, to which she belonged. Her 'crime' was giving the ANC information about Black trade union activities; she had not been involved in any violent act. The same judge who sentenced her gave a sentence of two years' suspended to members of the far-right Afrikaner Weerstandsbeweging (AWB) or Resistance Movement for illegal possession of arms. The judge referred to these thugs as 'decent and respectable people'. They possessed a veritable arsenal of arms, including AK47s and over 4000 rounds of ammunition. One of these 'decent people' was rushing around the countryside giving the Hitler salute. Barbara served seven and a half years of her sentence. I made several attempts to persuade the Minister of Justice to give her remission earlier, but she was released only in 1990 under F. W. de Klerk's amnesty. She is now employed as a senior staff member by the ANC in Johannesburg.

Ruth had been sentenced to ten years' imprisonment for acting as courier for her husband, Dieter Gerhardt. He was given a life sentence in 1983 for treason as a Soviet spy. He was a former commodore in the South African navy, stationed at Simonstown, the naval base from which for over fourteen years he was the eyes and ears of the USSR in the South Atlantic. He was released on 27 August 1992 after serving nine years in Pretoria Central Prison. I saw him on several occasions when I visited the political prisoners there, from whom he was physically separated. His release followed representations by Russian President Boris Yeltsin when he met State President de Klerk on his visit to Moscow in June 1992.

Ruth Gerhardt told me on one of my visits that the Swiss embassy in Pretoria sent a member of their staff to visit her regularly, but, she said, the Swiss government charged her a fee for each visit and unfroze her funds in Berne for that purpose. I was utterly astonished to hear this and tackled the Swiss ambassador in Cape Town. 'Yes,' he said, 'we are a small embassy. It is difficult to spare anyone for this task. It is government policy to charge for this service.' I obtained the name and address of the relevant Minister in Berne and wrote to him. He thanked me for my interest in Ruth's case and confirmed the policy of charging for the visits, declining to change it. Ruth and her husband are now together with their young son in Basle.

★

During the 1980s I paid several visits to prisons where detainees were held during the repeated states of emergency, mainly to make sure that they were not being subjected to the same brutal treatment meted out at St Albans Prison and other prisons in Port Elizabeth, as had been revealed by Dr Wendy Orr, a courageous young district surgeon.

So in October 1985 I went to the Johannesburg prison, dubbed 'Sun City' by Blacks. The jail, at Diepkloof just outside Soweto, is an enormous place, accommodating about 8000 prisoners. I went with my parliamentary colleague, Peter Soal, on a very hot morning, and the heat coming off that enormous concrete structure, which radiates out in wings to segregate the different categories, sexes and races of prisoners, was awesome. We were received courteously by the commandant and there was a senior member of the Prisons Department present as well. We were given access to all the detainees and spoke to them out of the officers' hearing. Not one complained of being roughly handled during interrogation. It seemed that the prison authorities at Diepkloof were careful to have detainees medically examined before and after interrogation if they were taken away by the security police, and to be present at interrogations if they took place at the prison. So we were satisfied on that score.

Of course, being locked up without trial was the major complaint, and some of the Black female detainees, mostly schoolgirls, were subjected to additional punishment by being put in cells which they complained had no ventilation at night. On inspection it certainly appeared that this was so, because the louvre windows were fixed so that they could not be opened, and solid iron doors were closed at night over the open bars of the cell. I made a big fuss and the officials promised that these detainees would be moved to other quarters the next day. Apparently the girls were very defiant and created a lot of noise and trouble, but that was no excuse for keeping them in conditions under which I, for one, would die of claustrophobia.

Thereafter I was kept busy sending reports to the Ministers of Prisons and Justice and of Law and Order, and giving interviews to the press. I was incensed at the reaction of the Detainee Parents' Support Committee, which made a statement to the press implying that my report about conditions at Diepkloof was naive and had undermined their efforts on behalf of detainees. I responded that I had had many more years of experience at such work than they for, as their name implied, they had only recently become active, only after their own children had been detained.

Over the years I received hundreds of letters smuggled out of jail by prisoners, asking me to obtain parole or remission or complaining about ill-treatment by warders, bad and inadequate food, and poor facilities for recreation. It was difficult to ensure in-depth investigation into these cases as letter smuggling is a punishable offence and I could not be certain there would not be repercussions from the prison authorities. My usual method was to use the name of a relative – the mother or wife of the prisoner – when reporting such cases; often, it actually was a relative who complained or asked for parole, remission or transfer on behalf of a prisoner. I was sometimes successful in these cases and also in those which the Black Sash referred to me. I cross-indexed complaints, naming the jails and identifying specific accusations of abuses in each one, and sent them to the Commissioner of Prisons. More often than not, he wrote to say the complaints had been investigated and were found to have no foundation. But I have no doubt that the fact that a beady eye was upon them had a salutary effect on warders' behaviour towards the prisoners.

This impression has been borne out by the comments of Breyten Breytenbach, one of South Africa's foremost writers and poets, in his book *The True Confessions of an Albino Terrorist*.

He wonders whether my 'regrettable failure' to meet him when I visited Pollsmoor Prison during his stay there was because I had been refused permission to see him or didn't know that he was there or didn't consider it of any importance. None of these reasons was correct. I did not ask to see him because I thought a visit from me might deprive him of a visit from his parents or his friends such as Van Zyl Slabbert. I was intrigued to read what Breytenbach wrote about my prison visits:

> I don't think it will be excessive to say that the prisoners, both political and common law, consider her as Our Lady of the Prisoners. She is

indeed a living myth among the people inhabiting the world of shadows. The quality of the food suddenly improves? Out of the blue a movie is shown on a Saturday afternoon? People have been sleeping for years on mats on the floor – 'sleeping camel' as we said, because the skin of the hips eventually becomes calloused – and now beds are made available? Prisoners would look at one another and nod their heads wisely and say: 'You see, Aunty Helen did it after all.'

At the same time she was, or is, considered as the final recourse for any prisoner, the ultimate threat of retribution or redress one would brandish when trying to get something done. I once heard old Johnny Blik in an exercise yard in Cape Town shout, beside himself with fury, at one of the warders: that he was not going to take things like this any longer, he was finished with this eating-shit business, he was going to go to the Head of the Prison and if that didn't work to the brigadier ('I'm not afraid of anybody!') and beyond that he would insist on seeing the commissioner himself, just let him come down here. And if he didn't get satisfaction by Jesus he was going to write directly to Helen Suzman. The remarkable thing is that it had the desired effect on the warder. It happened many a time that an old lag would sidle up to me to ask, out of the side of the mouth, if I had Helen's address please.

During my spell in Cape Town one prisoner actually slashed his wrists while in the court-cell below the courtroom one day, in an effort to force the authorities to allow him to see Helen Suzman. He was guilty of rape but he expected her to work a miracle and change his guilt into innocence. If I remember right she did see him and advised him to accept his fate.

They, the boere, to put it mildly, didn't like her overmuch. They detested her sharp eye and her sharp tongue and her fearless criticism of whatever wrong she saw. It was recounted to me by a fellow-inmate who had spent time in Kroonstad Prison (or Crown Town as we knew it) of how Helen Suzman came through there once. Since, however, the institution was at that time somewhat over-populated – not an uncommon occurrence – a good quarter of the prisoners, among whom he found himself squeezed, were actually hidden away, so that she would not notice the lack of living space.[1]

Perhaps it was an acquaintance of one of the old lags mentioned by Breytenbach who pitched up on my doorstep late one night, when I had flown from Cape Town for the weekend. He told me he had just been released from prison and had walked the six miles from the railway station in Johannesburg to my house to get help, as he had been told I was sympathetic to prisoners. I said rather irritably that I couldn't do anything for him at 11.30 p. m. and he should go back to town, spend the night at the YMCA and phone me in the morning. I gave him a R10 note which, in old lag fashion, he instantly reduced to the size of a postage stamp. I drove him to the nearest bus stop where of course there wasn't a bus in sight, so off we set for the YMCA. En route I asked him his name, what he'd been sentenced for, and how long he'd been in jail. Anderson, armed robbery, fifteen years. I wasted no time getting him to the YMCA, which to my great relief was open. I checked with Pretoria the next day, and they had a record of Anderson and of his release. I never heard from him again, but shortly after the Anderson incident, another ex-con arrived at my home. He kept me for an hour while he gave me (you will excuse it) a ball-by-ball description of the operation performed on him while he was in jail.

The attitude of many of the senior prison officials improved considerably over time, and the philosophy of rehabilitation replaced that of punitive retribution. Today the Department of Prisons has been renamed the Department of Correctional Services.

I believe that my visits over the years were partly responsible for some of the improvements in the system, though I certainly cannot claim all the credit. I was gratified that despite all those years of criticism in Parliament and nagging of successive ministers, I retired with considerable goodwill on the part of the Prisons Department. On my last visit to Pollsmoor in Cape Town, with a small group of PFP Members of Parliament, the public relations officer of the Department made a gracious speech commending me for my interest in prisons and my activities on behalf of prisoners.

This attitude was a far cry from the days when the prison authorities were prepared to use the wretched Putter to incriminate me.

9

Robben Island
– University for Leaders

Robben Island is set in Table Bay, about five and a half miles from the mainland at Cape Town, in a freezing sea with strong currents and prowling sharks. All the supplies, including water, have to be brought from the mainland.

To most South Africans, the island has a sinister connotation, rather like Alcatraz to Americans. It was a maximum security prison to which Black, Coloured and Indian prisoners were sent – about half of them political prisoners and the rest ordinary criminals. Escape was well-nigh impossible.

It was here that Nelson Mandela and his fellow Rivonia trialists were sent to serve their sentences of life imprisonment. There were many rumours about the harsh treatment they were receiving, and I therefore asked for permission to visit them. That was at the beginning of 1967.

I was appalled at the conditions I found there. When I arrived, I was taken to what was known as the single-cell section, which housed about thirty men, most of them serving long-term sentences for crimes against the state, such as sabotage and treason. Among them were the 'lifers', including Nelson Mandela, Govan Mbeki and Walter Sisulu of the Rivonia group.

I stopped at the first cell and said, 'Good morning, I'm Helen Suzman.' The prisoner, a Coloured man named Eddie Daniels, said, 'Yes, we know who you are. Don't waste time talking to us. Go and talk to Mandela at the end of the row. He's our leader.' I followed his suggestion and went straight on to Mandela. He was in one of the single cells: there were bars on the door through which one could look into the cell. Mandela is very tall, has very good posture and speaks excellent English. He also has an unmistakable air of authority. He stuck his hand through the bars and said, 'How do you do, Mrs Suzman, I'm very pleased to meet you.'

'How do you do, Mr Mandela,' I said. 'How are you and how are things here?'

'They are very bad indeed, I'm very glad you have come to see us.'

Although the commanding officer of the prison was standing right next to me, Mandela spoke quite frankly. He made no bones about his complaints.

He told me that there was a warden in charge of them who had a swastika tattooed on the back of his hand and that this warder had said to them, pointing to the swastika, 'Those are my political views and you will suffer for them, you communists.' 'We have a bad time, Mrs Suzman; that warder is a very tough man indeed,' said Mandela. At that stage they were doing hard labour, breaking stones in a quarry and collecting seaweed – including even older prisoners like Govan Mbeki.

'I'll certainly take this up with the Minister of Justice when I get back to the mainland,' I said. 'And what about everything else?'

He complained that the prisoners did not have enough visits, that they were sleeping on bed-rolls on the floor, and that the food was bad. Also, they were refused newspapers. The hard labour was very hard, and the warders were very strict.

When I got back to the mainland, I wrote a formal letter to Piet Pelser, the Minister of Justice, (Vorster was now Prime Minister) thanking him for allowing me to visit the island. I then went to see him. 'I've had a very interesting visit to Robben Island, and I've learned about a lot of shocking things.'

'What do you mean?' he asked.

'There is a man in charge of those prisoners who shouldn't be a prison warder at all, but in no circumstances should he be in charge of those political prisoners on the island. This man professes to be a Nazi, has a swastika tattooed on the back of his hand, and is giving them a very hard time indeed. What's more, I'm going to raise this in Parliament under your Vote. And that comes up in about two weeks' time, if I'm not much mistaken.'

'That's dynamite, Helen. You mustn't do that.'

'I know it's dynamite. It will be headline news all over the world. You had better do something about that warder.'

'Look,' said Pelser, 'I can't just dismiss him tomorrow because of what you say. That's very bad for discipline. But I promise you this. He will be gone before two weeks have passed.'

'Well, you'd better be sure of that, because I will know whether it has happened or not.' I was not sure just how I would know, but I thought the prisoners would get a message to me somehow. And indeed, that was exactly what happened. Mandela, who was charged with a breach of prison regulations, had his lawyer come to visit him on Robben Island. Prisoners were constantly at war with the authorities during those years because they were being treated so badly. The lawyer phoned me and said, 'Nelson Mandela has asked me to phone you to say thank you. The man has gone.'

From then on, I regularly applied for visits to political prisoners. As I have said, I was permitted visits on an annual basis to the White political prisoners in Pretoria jail, but permission to visit Robben Island, Pollsmoor Prison and elsewhere where Black, Coloured or Indian political prisoners were held, was given less frequently. Although I put in a request every year, seven years were to pass between my first visit in 1967 and the next time I was allowed back to Robben Island, due to the intransigence of the then Minister of Justice and Prisons, Jimmy Kruger. When I did eventually return, Mandela asked why I had not been to see him for such a long time. I replied that I had tried every year but was refused permission. I found that conditions had materially improved in the interim.

In May 1980, the new Minister of Police and Prisons, Louis le Grange, announced that he would reinstate undergraduate studies for the political prisoners, which to my dismay had been stopped by Kruger two years before. He also announced that he would permit newspapers for the prisoners, thus ending my long campaign for this concession. The day after this announcement, the Minister phoned me to say that one of the senior prison officials was going to Robben Island the following afternoon, and I could go with him if I liked. I leapt at the chance. At 2 p. m., duly insulated with anti-nausea tablets, accompanied by the senior prisons official, I set off across the choppy sea in the ferry boat. It took about an hour to reach the island. I spent over three hours there, saw every section of the prison, met the Rivonia group in the exercise yard and was able to chat with all of them. I spent half an hour talking to Mandela, whose spirit was unbroken though he had by then been in jail for sixteen years.

Almost two years later I returned to Robben Island on a formal visit organised by the Prisons Department for members from all three parties in Parliament. Mandela and four other prisoners had by then been moved from Robben Island to Pollsmoor, a maximum security jail on the mainland. We wandered around speaking to the prisoners. We went into the kitchen where a number of prisoners were peeling great mounds of pumpkin and carrots. One prisoner flourished a large knife on being introduced to me and said, 'Very pleased indeed to meet you, Mrs Suzman. I must tell you we were very surprised this morning when several sacks of green beans arrived. I knew something was going to happen, because we hadn't seen green beans for months and months.' The commanding officer, who had just given us a recital about the varied diet the prisons received, with about eighteen different types of vegetables, was not pleased with this man, and I wondered what would happen to him after we left the island. I also pondered the fate of the small Coloured prisoner who ran up to me and said, 'They very hard on us – they swear us and hit us.' A warder nearby who overheard the complaint, said, 'Ag, Mrs Suzman, it was just a kick up the arse.'

On one of my visits to Robben Island I inspected the library and found it had a good selection of books, ordered from the Cape Provincial Library. The librarian was one of the prisoners. I noticed, on the wall, a poster which had the faces of four South African authors on it: Alan Paton, Athol Fugard, André Brink and Nadine Gordimer (later Nobel Laureate). I asked the librarian if those were the prisoners' favourite authors. 'Yes,' he said. When I asked who was the most favourite, he said, 'Nadine Gordimer. We liked *Burger's Daughter* best of all,' which intrigued me because to some extent the story was based on Bram Fischer. I was amazed that Nadine's book, which had originally been banned in South

Africa and then later unbanned, was allowed to be read by the political prisoners on Robben Island. When I returned to the mainland, I phoned Nadine, who is a friend of mine, and said, 'Well, you will be interested to hear that you are the pin-up girl on Robben Island.' She was delighted.

In July 1983 I stayed in Cape Town for an extra day after the session ended in order to visit Nelson Mandela. I had repeatedly asked for this visit and had been fobbed off by Kobie Coetsee, then Minister of Justice and Prisons. I finally got permission, after articles had appeared in the UK press averring that the Pollsmoor authorities were treating him badly and were trying to break his spirit. I had received a letter from Winnie Mandela about this, so I put pressure on the Minister, who denied the allegations. I told him no one would believe his denials, but if I had a visit and found the allegations to be untrue and said so, I would be believed. However, if I found them to be true, I would also say so. The visit was arranged.

I had a long contact visit (unimpeded by bars or glass) with Nelson lasting over an hour, and also with Walter Sisulu, Ahmed Kathrada and three other long-term political prisoners. I saw their living quarters and their exercise yard, and was told that they had access to a small library. Because their section of Pollsmoor was a closed, maximum security jail, the prisoners were unhappy that all they saw were high walls and the sky. At least on Robben Island they could see grass and bush and the sea. But the rest – the food, medical attention, study facilities, access to newspapers – all were OK. As for Nelson's spirit being broken, that was absolute nonsense. We talked freely and he told me he was in good shape. I wrote to David Astor, editor of the *Observer*, describing what I had actually seen, and to British MPs David Steel and Denis Healey, who had written to the *Observer* on the strength of a rather exaggerated letter from Winnie, who must have visited Nelson on a day when he was feeling depressed. I knew my refutation of Winnie's claims would earn me the acute displeasure of the anti-apartheid movement, but I believed that the over-riding objective was to obtain the prisoners' release. Nelson and his fellow prisoners had been in jail for nearly twenty years. I was convinced that the case for their release was weakened by exaggeration.

One of Winnie's allegations was that Nelson had been forced to wear shoes that were too small for him, and as a result had to have a toe removed. When I asked Nelson how his foot was after the operation, he looked at me blankly, then said, 'Oh, you mean the toenail that was removed. That's fine. It was my fault really, as I ordered the wrong size shoe.' Winnie had obviously misunderstood the situation.

I went to see the Commissioner of Prisons in Pretoria and said that a complaint had been made to me by Mandela and the other prisoners that they saw only prison walls and the sky. I asked the Commissioner if he couldn't put troughs of earth in the exercise yard where the prisoners could grow either vegetables or flowers. That was done; another little improvement had been effected. For a prisoner, it is the small things that make a difference, because the big things in life – liberty and the right to lead an ordinary life – have been taken away.

My most in-depth discussion with Mandela took place in May 1986 at Pollsmoor Prison, after I received the permission I had sought for the previous two and a half years to revisit him. With Mandela's agreement, I took my colleague Tian van der Merwe with me. We first talked about personal matters and about his family, and reminisced about my previous visits – he reminded me that I had first met him on Robben Island in 1967, and I remarked that prison conditions had much improved since those days. We talked about Pollsmoor, and apart from delays in receiving letters he had no complaints. I asked about his health and remarked that he was thinner than when I had last seen him. He said he was well and had lost weight intentionally. He also said that at his own request he was no longer with the other five political prisoners. He wanted his privacy. We then discussed politics, on which he was very well informed, as he read all the local newspapers. He stood by what he had told an English visitor the previous year: that he was ready to help negotiate with the government and that he wanted 'to normalise conditions' in South Africa. He said that Chief Minister Buthelezi of KwaZulu, leader of the Inkatha Freedom Party, should be part of the negotiations; that he, Nelson, remained what he had always been – an African nationalist dedicated to the Freedom Charter, which set out the aims and principles of the ANC and had been adopted at a vast multiracial gathering in 1955. He said he was not prepared to split the ANC because some of its members were communists, though he was not a communist. He maintained he would take his freedom only unconditionally, and if fellow prisoners were also released. He was scornful of State President P. W. Botha's idea that he would be released on condition that Soviet dissidents Natan Scharansky and Andrei Sakharov were also released, together with Wynand du Toit (a South African prisoner of war, captured in Angola). Mandela commented favourably on the PFP's performance in Parliament and said he hoped we would remain there.

I emerged, as always, much impressed by Mandela's dignity and reasonable attitude. Despite all those years in prison, he retained a sense of humour, was not at all bitter, and obviously had outstanding qualities of leadership. There was nothing deferential in his relationship with the prison authorities. I had noticed this remarkable self-assurance at our first meeting in 1967, and my original impression was unchanged. One might have expected the long, dreary years of incarceration to have worn down his spirit. Not so; and I was convinced that this was the one man who would have the will and the authority to persuade the ANC and the government to suspend violence, and who could create the climate for negotiation.

I reported my conversation with Mandela to the press, and said I was convinced that his presence at the negotiating table was essential for a peaceful future, indeed that he was probably our last hope. I recommended that Prime Minister Botha should meet him. This must have infuriated the easily infuriated Botha, because I was refused permission to see Mandela for a couple of years thereafter.

All in all, I saw Mandela several times on Robben Island; twice when he was moved to Pollsmoor Prison; once in a luxury clinic in Cape Town, when he was recovering from surgery; twice at Victor Verster Prison, where he lived in a warder's cottage, attended by a White warder prior to his release (I lunched with him there on one occasion, and the warder cooked and served the meal).

In addition, I saw him whenever MPs from different parties, in the so-called prisons groups, paid official visits to the prisons. I have to say that I found my individual visits more useful.

On three occasions when I visited Robben Island, I saw Toivo Ja Toivo, the leader of the Namibian group, who had been jailed under the Terrorism Act of 1967. Indeed one section of that Act was passed specifically to enable the authorities to detain Toivo until they were ready to bring him to trial. He was the father of the South West African Peoples' Organisation (SWAPO), which waged war against the South African forces for the independence of South West Africa and its conversion into Namibia. In 1967 Toivo had been sentenced to twenty years' imprisonment, but the government released him in 1984, before his sentence expired.

The first time I met him was in 1975, and I found him a very formidable person. He was in the same section as the Mandela group, and was playing tennis in the recreation yard when I walked in. He was not wearing a shirt, but the minute he saw me, he stopped playing, walked across to the pole where his shirt was hanging, put it on and walked away. I said, 'I'd like to speak to Mr Toivo.' One of the officials said, 'Well, there he is. Go and try.' I went across but he was not at all friendly. I put my hand out and said, 'Mr Toivo, we don't know each other. I'm Helen Suzman.' He stared at my hand for a good five seconds before he shook it. And then he said, 'I will not speak to you in front of these people. I do not accept the jurisdiction of this prison or of this government over me and my people.' 'Mr Toivo,' I replied, 'I won't be allowed to speak to you alone, but I assure you we can speak freely. I'm going off to see other prisoners now, including Mr Mandela. Perhaps when I come back you will have made up your mind whether to speak to me or not.'

When I returned, Toivo had decided to speak to me, and for half an hour we sat in a little room, together with a prison official. Toivo and I talked generalities. I asked how he was, and whether he was well treated, and if there was anybody among his relatives I could arrange for him to see. Then I stood up, and this time he put his hand out. I shook it immediately and said how pleased I'd been to meet him. The official put his hand out, and Toivo gave it a disdainful look and walked right past him. 'Well, there you are,' the official said to me afterwards, 'you see the attitude. As a matter of fact, you're the only White person whose hand I've ever seen Toivo shake.'

The second time I saw him, he had grown a large bushy beard. He glared at me for a moment or two, then recognised me and stuck out his hand and shook hands firmly with me. I had only a few moments' conversation with him, as he was not prepared to talk in front of prison authorities. I simply asked him whether he was all right and he said 'yes', and whether there was anything I could do for him and he said, 'No thank you'.

When I saw him a third time, in 1984, there was no question whether he would talk to me or not; he talked immediately. This was three days before he was released. Neither he nor I knew that the government was about to send him back home and release him there. He gave me the name and address of his niece whom he said he would like to visit him, because his mother was too old to make the journey from Windhoek in South West Africa to Cape Town and then across on the ferry to Robben Island. I gather Toivo had to be pushed out of the jail at Windhoek, or wherever they took him in South West Africa, because he said he didn't want to be released unless all his SWAPO colleagues in jail were released as well. I thought he was a man of great strength, with an indomitable spirit. I wondered what his attitude to me, a White South African, would be should we meet in the future.

I found out later that year in New York at a lunch at the United Nations in honour of Bishop Desmond Tutu, who had just been awarded the Nobel Peace Prize. I saw this very large, very black, bearded man standing in a corner of the room and I thought, 'Good Lord, that's Toivo.' I went across to him and said, 'Remember me?' He looked at me and said, 'It's Helen Suzman,' and clasped me in a bear-hug – an emotional moment for us both. I asked him what he was doing in New York and he told me he was trying to expedite Namibia's independence. And when next I saw him it was at the independence celebrations in Windhoek in 1990 at the banquet I was invited to by the President-elect, Sam Nujoma. Toivo was now Minister of Mines, and he laughed when I said, 'Don't nationalise the mines – let *them* run them and you take a good chunk of the profits!' So far, the uranium and diamond mines of Namibia have not been nationalised.

Whenever I complained to officials or to successive Ministers of Prisons about conditions being grossly harsh or inadequate, changes took place, but I got stuck for a long time on two improvements I thought very important. One was the right of prisoners to have newspapers; the other was more lenient study privileges. The authorities often withdrew study privileges for very minor breaches of discipline. That meant a great deal to men who had been sentenced to life imprisonment, which in South Africa in those days generally meant just that; remission of sentence was rarely given to political prisoners. Eventually, after years and years of nagging, both changes were introduced. (I learned much later that the newspapers were at first mutilated by the prison censors, though I had been assured that there was no censorship.) Contact visits with relatives were also permitted from the 1980s. Remission of sentence, for which I pleaded year after year, took much longer to achieve.

All in all, conditions on Robben Island improved quite considerably over the years. The political prisoners, who have all since been released, were segregated from the ordinary convicts who did most of the maintenance work on the island or worked in the workshops. There had also been a separate section for the young convicts who were imprisoned after the Soweto riots of 1976, for crimes such as arson, sabotage or public violence. All of them are long off the island, because most received sentences of about five years. By the end of 1992 some 700 ordinary criminals were the only prisoners on Robben Island – now destined to become a tourist attraction.

Many people expressed shock when they learned that there were children under the age of eighteen on Robben Island, which had acquired a bad reputation. But it became a well-run jail, albeit strictly administered. The young prisoners were safer there than in any of the ordinary criminal jails. There are not enough places of reform or detention for children under the age of eighteen in South Africa, and they are often sent to the ordinary jails. But those on Robben Island were looked after by the political prisoners there, and were encouraged to study. They were protected from the sodomy and assault to which they could have been subjected in an ordinary jail on the mainland; they were not exposed to the violence endured by prisoners in other jails as a result of the shadowy sub-culture of the vicious gangs of hardened criminals incarcerated there.

Eventually the main issue for political prisoners became the question of remission, which for many years was implacably refused to this category of prisoner. In 1985 P. W. Botha announced in Parliament that remission would be considered if the prisoner renounced violence. He was referring specifically to Mandela, but when I asked if this would apply to other political prisoners, he said it would. (One Rivonia trialist, Denis Goldberg, was subsequently released for doing so, apparently after requesting and obtaining Mandela's consent. Renfrew Christie, another White political prisoner, also accepted Botha's offer. Mandela and the rest refused.)

Mandela issued a lengthy statement which his daughter, Zinzi, read at a United Democratic Front (UDF)[1] rally of some 9000 people at a stadium in Soweto, where they had assembled to honour the award of the Nobel Peace Prize to Bishop Tutu. Mandela declared that he would not give any undertakings to the government while he and his people were not free, and while his wife Winnie was in banishment in Brandfort. He called on the government to renounce violence, to unban the ANC, to permit political activity, to free political prisoners, to allow those in exile to return, and to dismantle apartheid. In short he rejected P. W. Botha's offer, and when he was finally released on 11 February 1990 it was unconditional.

My interest in prisoners over many years, which resulted in improvements in their physical conditions, also created a continuing bond between ex-prisoners and myself, despite differences in our political philosophy or their disapproval of my opposition to sanctions and disinvestment. Over-riding this was the fact that I had cared about them when they were imprisoned, had made that care a special cause and had campaigned for their release. I once said jocularly that I could organise a Robben Island Old Boys Club (in fact it exists, as I found on visits to Lusaka and Harare). Whenever I encounter ex-prisoner exiles, they greet me warmly, and when I fail to recognise some of them, they remind me that I visited them on Robben Island. Steve Tshwete, formerly a high-ranking member of Umkhonto we Sizwe (Spear of the Nation), the ANC's armed wing, and now head of the special sports committee of the ANC, had an affectionate hug for me when I met him at the Five Freedoms Forum Conference in Lusaka in 1989. He recalled later that, on saying goodbye in Lusaka, my last remark to him was 'No damn bombs between now and September!' (the date of the impending general election). There were none.

As for Nelson Mandela, the bond we formed long before he became the world's most famous political prisoner endured throughout his long years in jail and continues now that he has his freedom – although we disagree on a number of issues, such as sanctions and the continuing link between the ANC and the South African Communist Party. When I visited him at Victor Verster Prison in July 1989, six months before his release, he asked me to autograph a book I had brought him. I did so, and he in turn autographed *Fear No Evil* by Natan Scharansky, the Russian dissident, which I had lent him. The book is one of my prized possessions. The autograph reads: 'For Helen – None can do more than her duty on earth. The countless tributes you received on your retirement from Parliament show that you acquitted yourself beyond words. You will always be in our thoughts. Meanwhile we send you our very best wishes. From Nelson – Victor Verster Prison, P/B X6005, Paarl South 7624.' It is dated July 1989. When I retired from Parliament in 1989, he wrote me a letter from that prison which was read out at my final Report-Back meeting to my Houghton constituents:

Dear Helen
The consistency with which you defended the basic values of freedom and the rule of law over the last three decades has earned you the admiration of many South Africans.
A wide gap still exists between the mass democratic movement and your party with regard to the method of attaining those values. But your commitment to a non-racial democracy in a united South Africa has won you many friends in the extra-parliamentary movement.

Allow me to hope that you will continue to enjoy good health for
years to come, that in the days that lie ahead your voice will be heard
throughout the country, free from the constraints which parliamentary
convention impose.

Fondest regards and best wishes to you and your family.

Sincerely,
Nelson

Nelson's wife Winnie was another prominent victim of the
apartheid system and the government's vicious reprisals against its
opponents.

When Winnie Mandela was found guilty in the Johannesburg
Supreme Court on 13 May 1991 of kidnapping and of being an
accessory to the assault on four young Black boys, I phoned her
lawyer, my friend George Bizos, and offered to give evidence in
mitigation before sentence was passed. My offer was graciously
refused, as the defence was simply going to appeal and was not
intending to ask for mercy. Winnie was sentenced to six years'
imprisonment.[2]

My offer was not based on sentiment, or 'sickly humanism'; it
was based on first-hand knowledge of what Winnie suffered over
the years and what turned her into an embittered woman – a victim
of the harsh apartheid system. I do not condone her actions or her
utterances, but understand what she had to endure. To remain
unaffected by her experiences would require the stuff of which
saints are made.

She had to endure more than the loneliness and misery of having
her husband incarcerated for all those years. She was detained
without trial and held in solitary confinement for seventeen
months under security regulations. She suffered the medieval
punishment of banishment, by ministerial decree, for seven long
years, when she was removed from her house in Soweto and sent
to live in the dreary Black township in Brandfort, a miserable one-
horse town near Bloemfontein in the Orange Free State. The
Blacks there spoke Tswana and the Whites Afrikaans – neither of
which was Winnie's mother tongue. To all intents and purposes
Winnie was isolated, far from her Soweto friends and family,
except for her younger daughter, Zinzi, who was with her for part
of those years, and an assortment of bodyguards. She was
constantly harassed by the security police during her banishment.

I visited her three times in Brandfort. This entailed flying to Bloemfontein, hiring a car and driving myself the thirty-two miles to Brandfort on a lonely road winding across the veld. I had one uneasy return journey dogged by a man I thought I recognised as belonging to the security police, when it occurred to me how easy it would be for him to run me off the road.

My first visit was in August 1977. I had had words with Jimmy Kruger, Minister of Justice, over the treatment meted out to Winnie, and told him I intended to see for myself the conditions under which she was living. Winnie and Zinzi lived in the township – a few miles out of town – in a tiny three-room house, with no ceiling, no inside doors, no indoor plumbing, one cold water tap. There was no telephone in the house, and Winnie or someone from her household would station themselves at certain times of the day in the public telephone booth in Brandfort lest there be a call for her from someone who knew the routine. As Winnie was under house arrest, she was allowed no visitors at home, where she was confined from 6 p. m. to 7 a. m. each day. On my first visit, I met her at the office of her attorney in Brandfort, who conveniently had taken to the hills for the morning. I then went to her house with Zinzi while Winnie drove around the block in her little Volkswagen, closely followed by a captain of the security police. It was ludicrous.

Quite by coincidence, no doubt, on my subsequent two visits, the security police arrived at her house. Winnie and I always laughed about it because we would sit there talking quite openly. Her views were known. My views were known. On one such occasion, the security police went rummaging around the tiny living room, taking books from the bookcase and pictures off the wall, and then went into her bedroom and came out with a bedspread. I said, 'What are you taking that for?' No reply from the grim policeman. Then I realised that it was knitted in the African National Congress colours – black, green and gold; it was a subversive bedspread. So it was confiscated. US Congressmen read about this incident in an article I wrote for the *Washington Post*, and they arranged for a quilt from Indiana to be sent to Cape Town to replace the filched article. A staff member of the US consulate presented this to me and I delivered it to Winnie in Brandfort, much to her delight.

My third and final visit was at the end of August 1980, after addressing a meeting in Bloemfontein at the University of the Orange Free State. I had expected to be stoned to death at this verkrampte [narrow-minded] institution, but instead the students gave me a very cordial reception. I was then driven to Brandfort to visit Winnie at her home, as the local magistrate had given his permission. We chatted for about three-quarters of an hour in her miserable little house, which was freezing cold. Then there was a knock at the door and in walked two creeps, who identified themselves as security police; they told Winnie she was contravening her restriction order by having a visitor, and threatened to arrest her if she did not get me out within five minutes. I protested and said I had a permit, which I showed them. 'Out of order,' said creep number one. I said to Winnie, 'Let's go, we have really said all we want to say and I don't want you to get into trouble.' So we stood and chatted outside her house for a few minutes, and then we started walking back to the town, as my driver had not yet returned. The creeps offered me a lift and I told them I would prefer to walk with Mrs Mandela. I checked with the lawyer back in the town, and confirmed that he had obtained permission for me to visit Winnie. When I got home I phoned the Minister of Police, Louis le Grange, and complained bitterly. He replied that he had been told what had happened and that technically the permit was not in order, as it was I, and not the restricted person, who had initiated the request. I attacked him for hiding behind such trivia, but he refused to rebuke the security police. I said later in Parliament that the authorities were behaving idiotically; they persecuted Winnie at every turn, and as a result provided her with an excellent public relations service, free, gratis and for nothing.

At one stage during her banishment, Winnie was informed that her house in Soweto was going to be taken over permanently by the Bantu Administration Board and allocated to someone else. (Previously the Board had billeted a policeman in the house until she was allowed to return.) She phoned me frantically, and I managed to stop that spiteful plan, but it added to her anxiety. The police later said she could live and work in Mamelodi, the Black township near Pretoria where she had been offered employment. She declined, on Nelson's instructions. His view was that only a return to Soweto was acceptable – nowhere else. In 1984 her house in Brandfort was vandalised and set on fire when she was in Johannesburg consulting a doctor. Thereafter she refused to return to Brandfort and reoccupied her Soweto home, despite the banishment order.

In 1984 I shared with Winnie an award for human rights from two Scandinavian newspapers, one Danish and one Swedish – *Politiken* and *Dagens Nyeter* [Daily News]. Her elder daughter, Zenani, and her husband came to collect the award on her behalf, as Winnie was refused a passport. Both Zenani and Musi, her husband, who is a member of the Swazi royal family, were very friendly but I met with a lot of hostility from ANC exiles who came to witness the ceremony. They made it clear that they did not regard a White liberal from South Africa (especially one who was an MP) as an ally in the struggle for liberation. We liberals were becoming a truly endangered species: for many years under attack from the right, we were now attacked by the left as well, especially by bitter exiles. But not by old allies and friends like Winnie who, despite differences in policy, always warmly acknowledged the efforts I had made on her behalf and for Nelson and his colleagues.

On one occasion, however, Winnie let me down badly. In 1985 I had obtained permission for Lord Bethell, a member of the European Parliament, to visit Nelson at Pollsmoor. Bethell intended to campaign for his release, and had already begun to do so with an excellent article for the London *Daily Mail*. I also arranged for Bethell to see Winnie in Johannesburg. However, having originally agreed to see him, Winnie decided she was going to take umbrage because he had permission to see Nelson, whereas, as she put it, her own relatives had not been allowed to see him. What she really meant was, if the government wouldn't allow Nelson to meet Teddy Kennedy, who was on a South African jaunt at the time, she was not going to agree to see Bethell. I was particularly mad at her because I had given her full information about the visit far in advance and she had readily agreed to see him. Winnie can be difficult and unpredictable.

That same year she and I visited some Soweto schools, and I saw for myself how disturbing it was for the pupils to have armed men from the defence force wandering around the school grounds and confronting the children at every turn, fingers on triggers. Winnie and I were 'detained' for questioning at Orlando High School by an embarrassed young sergeant, who said he had orders to hold us until a security policeman arrived. I put on my sternest parliamentary manner when the security policeman arrived and we were released at once. However, what was especially interesting to me was Winnie's total ignorance of the excellent work being done by the African Self-Help Organisation which looked after some 5000 pre-school children in thirty-six creches scattered throughout Soweto. It was apparently a revelation to Winnie to see the excellent work being done by a group of White women who sought no publicity whatsoever and who provided an immense service to the Black community by enabling women to take jobs knowing that their children are being properly cared for in their absence.

If I ever wondered what Winnie truly felt about me, my doubts were resolved when she was asked about me during a BBC interview with Sue MacGregor for the BBC *Women's World* in 1986.

Sue to Winnie: How important to you has been the support of the Whites in South Africa who are sympathetic to your cause, and I am thinking in particular of people like Helen Suzman, who I think you have got to know quite well over the years?

Winnie: We have grown to know each other very well over the years. Of course we disagree a lot, we don't see things the same way, most of them as a matter of fact. Our politics are at times totally against each other's views and we have had to accept the fact that there will be those times when we really speak past each other. As human beings, I value her as a person and I value, like all my people do, her role. Had it not been for her, I doubt if there would have ever been any opposition to South Africa's racist regime. And of course during the earlier years, when it was extremely difficult for Black opposition to voice itself, she occupied the position of being a spokesman for all the non-voters in this country. She went to prisons, she went to Robben Island during those earlier years when life in Robben Island was extremely difficult, when our husbands and our leaders' lives were made extremely difficult by the state, she highlighted those conditions and had it not been for her lone voice in Parliament those years, the rest of the world would never have known what was going on in this country.

Sue to me: What is your relationship with Winnie Mandela? I know you have known her on and off, although it hasn't been easy because she has been under various political restrictions for many years. Are you good friends, the two of you?

Me: It's true we don't always agree with each other's views. But Winnie and I are good friends. We like each other, I think, and I get a feeling of great warmth when I see her. I certainly have great admiration for her courage and the way in which she withstood more than twenty years of loneliness while Nelson was imprisoned. I think she is sometimes reckless and sometimes says things emotionally which she herself may regret.

Sue: You say one of the things you have in common is you are both fairly tough.

Me: She is tough; she has had to be. She has had to be much tougher than I have been – I have never been put in prison and I have never been banned. And I certainly haven't had a husband imprisoned all those years. And you need a very special kind of fortitude to withstand that type of punishment. I have had abuse and so did she, I have had hard work that I have had to carry out, but nothing compared to the problems that Winnie has had to face.

Over the past couple of years Winnie has probably been facing her most trying time – the appeal against the six-year prison sentence hung over her, she and Nelson have separated, there have been allegations of corruption, the ANC hierarchy has become hostile and has forced her to resign her official positions in the organisations. Although she retains the support of many young Black radicals, an uncertain future confronts Winnie Mandela.

10

Back in Business:
Opposition Politics – Prog Style, 1975–7

By 1974 another general election was due. I informed Colin Eglin that if the Progressive Party did not win any seats other than Houghton, I would resign. Apart from the enormous strain of being the sole representative of the party in Parliament, I felt that the effort and financial cost of keeping a party functioning which could win only one seat after thirteen years of struggle, was excessive. Perhaps we Progs should accept the fact that the electorate rejected us and that the party had no future.

In that election the United Party nominated a total fraud to oppose me. No well-known person had agreed to stand against me in Houghton. Marais Steyn, Transvaal leader of the party and Graaff's right-hand man (who subsequently crossed the floor and became a minister in the National Party) insisted that I be opposed. He knew nobody could beat me (my majority had increased at every general election since 1961), but a contest in Houghton would prevent all our skilled workers from offering their services elsewhere, and would reduce my availability to appear on platforms in support of Progressive candidates. So at the last moment, a nondescript man was produced at the nomination court as the United Party candidate in Houghton, a Mr B. Senekal, who told the press he was employed by the United Party to obtain adverts for *Die Volkstem*, their Afrikaans-language newspaper. But Senekal's election manifesto also claimed he was a civil engineer with a degree from Wits University.

My antennae twitched: what would a highly qualified man be doing scrounging adverts for a rag like *Die Volkstem*? It seemed decidedly fishy. I phoned the convocation office at Wits and asked for verification that the graduation records contained the name of a B. Senekal. The clerk refused to give the information, saying that only university staff members had access to their records. So I contacted my friend John Dugard, the Law professor who had often advised me on legislation on constitutional matters, and asked him to check out Senekal. He reported back that there was no such name in the convocation card index of the names of graduates. I told Max Borkum of my discovery and was all for exposing Senekal to the press as a fraud. Max said I should not do so; there might be a mistake in the convocation records, and it wasn't worth taking a chance since our canvass showed me well ahead. But as the United Party hierarchy must have been aware of the fraudulent claim, disclosure would have had a spin-off to the Progressive Party's advantage in other constituencies. So I pursued the matter. Off I went to the university to enlist the help of the Vice-Chancellor, another friend and Progressive Party supporter, Professor G. R. Bozzoli. Together we scrutinised the civil engineers' graduation programmes which listed the names of every student who had graduated, whether present or *in absentia*. We knew Senekal's age and we started by assuming he was a child genius who had graduated at eighteen; then probably moving closer to reality we assessed him as either dull and backward or a late developer who had obtained his degree at forty. There was no Senekal on any civil engineering graduation programme spanning more than twenty years.

Bozzoli wrote to Senekal asking him to produce proof that he was, as he claimed, a Wits graduate. Senekal promptly went to ground. I contacted the *Rand Daily Mail* which was wary of printing the story without giving Senekal the opportunity to refute it. But he had disappeared, and did not emerge until well into election day when it was too late to publish anything.

On 24 April 1974 the unexpected happened: the Progressive Party won not only Houghton but five additional seats in the general election. The solo years had ended.

Election night 1974 was the most exciting night of my life – politically, that is!

We knew we had once again won my seat at Houghton. During the count, done as usual in a school hall, my rising pile of ballots showed early on that I had a majority; and that my fellow candidate for the Provincial Council, the enthusiastic and able Dr Selma Browde, who had done a great job as the sole representative of the Progressive Party in the Johannesburg City Council, would also win. While we were busy with the count, the window opened at the end of the classroom and a head came through. It belonged to one of our supporters who shouted, 'We've won Jo'burg North!' I said, 'I don't believe it.' He said, 'I tell you, we've won Jo'burg North.'

Selma and I threw our arms around each other, cried 'Hooray!' and waltzed up and down the schoolroom, to the horror of our opponents, who were shaken to the core by this first ominous election result.

One by one the other results came in. Flash – another Progressive Party win in Orange Grove, and flash – a win for the Progressive Party in Parktown; three wins apart from Houghton –such rejoicing! After my win and Selma's were confirmed, we all repaired to the campaign tent which had been erected on a school playing-field in the Houghton constituency. The other successful Johannesburg candidates, and hundreds of their campaign workers, came streaming in. Loud cheers roused my slumbering constituents, as the thrilling news came over the radio that the Progressive Party had won two more Cape Town seats, including the all-important seat of Colin Eglin, who had become the leader of the party in 1971 when Jannie Steytler retired from politics.

Colin had lost his Pinelands seat in the 1961 débâcle. His re-election as MP in 1974 was for a different seat – Sea Point, a densely populated flatland in Cape Town with many Jewish constituents. Colin, a Methodist, became very familiar with barmitzvahs and yarmulkas. I was deeply relieved when Colin won his seat on that historic occasion in 1974, because I had been accused of being the reason for his narrowly failing to win Sea Point in the previous election in 1970. I had spoken in his support at his final pre-election meeting in the constituency. The large hall was packed with hundreds of enthusiastic supporters. At question time I was asked if the Progressive Party would unban the Communist Party, which been banned since 1950. I said, 'Yes – the Progressive Party does not believe in banning.' Then I added, 'However, should the Progressive Party come to power, any political party or person preaching or practising violence will feel the full force of the law.' Unfortunately that part of my reply received little prominence the next morning in the *Cape Times*. The headline read: 'Progressive Party Will Unban Communist Party.' Colin's United Party opponent, who held right-wing attitudes, had the headline blown up on large posters which he plastered over every polling station in the Sea Point constituency on election day. Colin lost his seat by 232 votes, and I was blamed. (The irony is that one of State President de Klerk's first moves in launching his 'New South Africa' nearly twenty years later, was to unban the South African Communist Party as well as the African National Congress and the Pan-Africanist Congress.)

Colin faked his age during the Second World War, so as to enlist in the South African army when he was sixteen years old, and saw active service in Italy. On one occasion when a Nat MP had the impudence to accuse him of being unpatriotic, it pleased me very much to remind the House of Colin's army service when South Africa was fighting the Nazis – while some members of the National Party were languishing in internment for sabotaging the war effort.

Colin is a huge man with hands like hams. When he returned to Parliament in 1974, we shared a front bench. I cowered in the far corner, expecting to be struck unconscious any moment because he delivered his speeches with frequent chopping motions of those large paws. National Party MPs on the other side of the House would watch this scenario with fascination and hope. I don't believe I ever heard Colin make a speech – in or out of the House in either English or Afrikaans – that wasn't first class. He is a political animal through and through, with a thorough grasp of issues, great perception, and a talent for analysing cause and effect. He can, however, be abrasive to both friends and foes, but his debating skill and useful contributions in the House and in select committees are appreciated by his opponents in Parliament. It was only his own party that underrated him.

★

Apart from Colin Eglin, the other Progresive Party winners in 1974 were all new boys – and what a wealth of talent they brough to the party in Parliament.

The star acquisition was Dr Frederik Van Zyl Slabbert, an Afrikaner and a former sociology professor at Wits and Stellenbosch Universities, with more than his fair share of charisma. He also has a very good brain, is an excellent speaker in both languages, with the ability to express himself in attention-catching phrases – a headline in every speech. 'Van', as he is affectionately known to many, relates to people with ease and grace.

Shortly after the 1974 election, the Progressive Party won an additional seat at a by-election in Cape Town, thus bringing another bright spark to join the team: Dr Alex Boraine, a former moderator of the Methodist Church in South Africa. Apart from possessing an engaging personality, Alex is a polished speaker. I flew to Cape Town to help him in the by-election, which entailed five meetings in six days, plus phone canvassing in dulcet tones for hours each day. All six Prog MPs were there to help, so it was a great team effort; and Alex, who worked hardest of all, deserved his victory.

So now we were seven, à la A. A. Milne.

I couldn't help feeling cynically amused at the ambitious plans to employ three full-time researchers as well as the necessary additional typists. In the solo years I was expected to cope with all the portfolios with only Jackie Beck and Barbara Mouat to help me.

I took the new MPs into the House and introduced them to the Secretary of Parliament, J. J. H. Victor, who was very affable and took them into the Chamber to show them the seats they would probably be occupying and the offices where they would churn out all those brilliant speeches. It was rather touching to see those big chaps, all about six foot and more, looking like a lot of kids on their first day at school.

When I walked into the House at the next opening of Parliament to take the oath with the six other Progressive MPs, a Nat member called out, 'There comes Mrs Rosenkewitz.' (A woman who'd had sextuplets in Cape Town a few months before.)

We were back in business!

★

The election of Dr Selma Browde as provincial councillor for Houghton relieved me of a great deal of additional responsibility in local government matters. And, of course, the presence of other Progressives in Parliament meant a profound change for the better for me. It was impossible, I told my constituents at my Report-Back meeting that year, to describe the pleasure, after all those solitary years, of having friends with me in the House – to talk to, to laugh with, consult with, have a drink with, even to argue with –not to mention the 'hear-hears' when I sat down after making a speech instead of a hostile silence or unpleasant comments.

The success of the Progs in 1974 had its effect on the leader of the official opposition, Sir De Villiers Graaff. He took a new line in supporting trade union rights for Blacks, which he had formerly opposed. And he actually accepted that the logical consequence of repealing job reservation would be that some Whites might have to work under the direction of non-Whites, a concept he had previously firmly rejected. I wondered how much of Graaff's new attitude had come about because there was now no such animal as a safe United Party seat. I told my constituents that the United Party appeared 'to have undergone a sort of metamorphosis – a sex change one might say – they have almost become men'.

Disgust with the United Party's collaboration in the Schlebusch Commission and its feeble acquiescence in the government's destruction of due process played a large part in the Prog victories, aided by the strong criticism of the United Party by the English-language press.

Attempts to reduce White opposition seem to have rendered the Government oblivious to the increasing intensity of Black resistance which exploded soon afterwards, in 1976 – the watershed year.

I was in the United States when the Soweto riots took place on 16 June 1976. Indeed on the very day that I was to receive an honorary doctorate at Harvard University, the *Boston Globe* carried a dramatic front-page photograph of a young Black man carrying the body of a youth in his arms. It was Hector Petersen, the first fatality of the Soweto unrest. The police had shot him dead during the protest march of school children that day.

It was with some trepidation that I stepped forward to receive the honorary degree, expecting a hostile reception from the vast assembly in the Harvard yard. Instead I received a standing ovation. When I returned home, Minister of Justice Jimmy Kruger could not resist commenting, 'And where was the Honourable Member for Houghton when all the trouble began in Soweto? She was in America receiving a degree from some obscure university.'

My first reaction to news of the Soweto unrest had been to catch the next plane home. But on phoning Colin Eglin I was reminded that I wasn't the only Prog in the House who could respond to the crisis. I was advised to fulfil my remaining commitments in the United States. The American Jewish Committee in Philadelphia was to confer a human rights award on me, and I had appointments with members of the State Department, members of Congress and of the Senate in Washington. When I was approached by the media in the United States for comment on the tragic happenings in Soweto, I could express only utter dismay but no surprise. After all, had we not warned over and over again that violent confrontation was inevitable unless conditions were improved in the Black urban areas?

The attempt to impose Afrikaans – perceived by Blacks as the language of the oppressor – as a medium of instruction in Soweto schools was the ostensible cause of the uprising. In fact, anything could have sparked it off. It was very difficult indeed to make people overseas, either in the US or in the UK, understand the arrogance and intransigence of the National Party government. In any normal democratic country a government knows it can be slung out of power, and therefore reacts to public opinion and respects opposition views. Not so in South Africa. The government had been in power by then for over twenty-eight years and enjoyed substantial majority support of the all-White electorate. Sheer arrogance thus led them to brush aside all our warnings. We were dubbed agitators and ignored.

In Parliament the year before the Soweto unrest, I had warned the Minister of Bantu Administration, M. C. Botha, that I believed we were reaching a crisis situation in Soweto with its huge, seething, sullen population living in hopelessly overcrowded conditions, with few modern amenities. During the 1976 session, my colleague, René de Villiers, twice warned the Deputy Minister of Bantu Affairs, Andries Treurnicht, of ominous rumblings in Soweto. René read a telegram from the South African Institute of Race Relations warning of serious repercussions if Treurnicht went ahead with this highly unpopular step. The warning was ignored and Soweto erupted.

One of the most astonishing sequels to the disturbances in Soweto and elsewhere was the absence of any reaction from the Bantu Administration Department; from the Minister responsible, M. C. Botha; from his deputy, Treurnicht, and from other responsible officials. Allowing the language medium issue to escalate into full-scale civil unrest, which lasted two years and cost at least 700 lives, had disastrous effects on race relations, and on the South African economy. The officials all took to the hills leaving the Minister of Police to carry the can. The whole neglectful, inefficient bunch in the Bantu Administration Department, from the Minister down, should have been kicked out. Treurnicht in fact stayed put as Deputy Minister, became a Cabinet Minister in 1979, but resigned from the National Party in 1982 after a stormy showdown in the caucus over power-sharing and formed his far-right Conservative Party. He angrily denied my accusation that he had been partly responsible for the 1976 catastrophe. (The government made this accusation against him only after he had left them.)

I moved the reduction of the salaries of M. C. Botha and Andries Treurnicht, not only for having ignored all the warnings of imminent trouble in Soweto but because they had paid only one visit to Soweto between 16 June, when the unrest broke out, and the end of 1976. My motion was not carried, of course, but ministers and deputy ministers were, as usual, most displeased by the adverse publicity they received as a result.

In August 1976 the situation in Soweto was still very dicey. Almost every day was marked by some sort of march, with the inevitable violent police reaction. After my return from the United States I had several meetings with civic leaders from the township, all of them adults. The young Blacks did not want to know and that was a bad sign. It looked as if things had gone too far for White liberals to play any role other than continuing to put pressure on the government to do something which might give some hope to Blacks. The editors of some of the Afrikaans papers, such as *Die Transvaler, Beeld* and *Rapport*, published strongly critical leading articles calling for a rethink of policy on urban Blacks. There was however no immediate response from the government, whose first concern was to restore law and order. They seemed wholly unperturbed by the fact that about 50,000 high school students were boycotting schools and that there was a distinct possibility that the primary school children in Soweto would follow suit by the end of the month. There were mind-boggling dangers in allowing over 250,000 youngsters to wander the streets all day with absolutely nothing to do but look for trouble.

Young Blacks displayed a growing intransigence which was frightening. The expected radicalisation had taken place and they rejected all Whites. Their motto was 'Liberation before Education', and it was to result in a generation of functionally illiterate people doomed to a life of low-paid unskilled jobs (or no jobs at all). It was hard to see how the Soweto deadlock could be broken. The police said they would continue with raids and arrests as long as the pupils refused to return to school, and the pupils said they would not go back to school as long as the police continued to raid. I saw Kruger about this, but did not expect any flexibility from that quarter. Meanwhile I was besieged by phone calls from desperate parents whose children had been picked up and were being held they knew not where. Some of them had slipped across the borders into Swaziland or Botswana; others simply fled into the veld. There was total chaos in the townships. I spent hours on the telephone – to hospitals, police stations and even to the mortuary – trying to trace the whereabouts of missing children.

I was busy with all sorts of unsatisfactory meetings and interviews about the ongoing crisis. Every day, somewhere or other, there were confrontations with the police and the burning down of schools. Worst of all, the Internal Security Act was used widely and people involved with Black student activities were picked up – how many no one knew, or under what particular law, or where they were held. It was a spooky feeling, worse than ever before because the police were totally arrogant about using these powers and refused to give any information. Public reaction was minimal; the protest marches and City Hall meetings of the 1960s were not repeated. Everybody was punchdrunk and scared of being accused of inciting the Blacks.

My Report-Back to my constituents on the Soweto unrest emphasised the significant role played by Black youth. I warned that unless moderate Blacks could achieve some positive results soon, they would be pushed aside by far more militant people. The days of patient submission were over. Another factor I felt we would ignore at our peril was the threat of industrial unrest. South Africa simply could not afford to have industry turned into a battlefield; the economy was far too vulnerable to withstand internal strife, what with the lack of foreign investment capital, increased disinvestment by foreign companies, and sanctions.

Part of the government's tactics in handling the aftermath of the 1976 Soweto riots was to use the preventive detention powers of the Internal Security Act. They detained about 136 prominent Blacks, many of them the very people young Blacks trusted and whom the government should have been consulting about defusing the continuing unrest in Soweto and elsewhere. Instead, they locked up these people. In November 1977 I got permission to visit four of the men in preventive detention at Modder B prison on the East Rand, including my old friends Percy Qobozo, editor of the *Sowetan* newspaper, and Dr Nthato Motlana, a civic leader and physician. I saw them one at a time for half an hour each, and they were delighted to be visited by someone other than a near relative. They had a radio given to them by a sympathetic businessman and were not in solitary confinement. But they had been imprisoned without trial. I brought them books and a large meat pie – still hot – from a local bakery. The warder asked suspiciously what was in it, so I suggested he stick his finger into it. I was allowed to deliver the pie.

The government completely misjudged the situation. They thought a quick, tough purge would do the trick – arrest, detention, police action – and then the townships would settle down into their old submissive pattern. What happened instead was that a real spirit of resistance emerged among the young Blacks in Soweto. I had no doubt, as I told my constituents, that this attitude would not only persist but would grow, and at increasing speed, unless real and fundamental changes were introduced to improve materially the whole quality of life of urban Blacks.

I told Parliament it was significant that during the urban and campus riots in the United States during the worst five years in the 1960s, when more than two million Americans took to the streets to protest against the Vietnam war and about civil rights issues, fewer than 200 people were killed. But in the two years following the Soweto unrest of 1976, about 700 people were killed; it seemed to me therefore that the methods employed by the riot police needed severe overhauling.

The 1976 Soweto uprising had some further side-effects, as one overworked woman at the US consulate could bear witness. Apart from the numerous people who were contemplating leaving the country as a result, she had to cope with an additional spate of would-be 'medical' emigrants who were devastated by the news that a curtain would come down in October when the United States government was expected to remove doctors from the priority list of immigrants and to introduce a much tougher qualifying examination.

Appropriately enough, the name of the woman handling all these applications at the US consulate was Mrs Flood, and when I asked her to tell me the criteria for acceptable immigrants she rattled off a list. People who had 'first-degree relatives who were US citizens', she said, 'walked in'. Those who had special qualifications wanted by the US walked in. Those who had obtained jobs in America and were able to produce proof that no Americans wanted those particular jobs, walked in. Those who were elderly and had sufficient funds to ensure that they were not going to become a charge on the state, they walked in too. Political refugees also walked in. 'Oh,' I interjected, 'that's great, Mrs Flood, that lets me in!' 'Oh no, Mrs Suzman,' she replied, 'you've gotta be Black.'

In May 1976 we had won yet another seat at a by-election in Durban North. Later that year the Progressive Party merged with Harry Schwarz's Reform Party and was renamed the Progressive

Reform Party. The following year, after being joined by other former United Party members, we became the Progressive Federal Party. I had some difficulty about finding myself in the same caucus as Harry Schwarz; we had fought each other bitterly when he was in the United Party and I was in the Progressive Party. We continued to confront each other with hostility, although we were now in the same party. I was often irritated by his angry outbursts in the caucus when he did not get his own way, and was embarrassed by his hawkish attitude towards the South African Defence Force. He in turn strongly disapproved of my frequent attacks on the South African Police. As his front bench was adjacent to mine, I could hear clearly a disapproving hum – like a large mosquito – when I was speaking on this subject.

The 1978 congress of the Progressive Federal Party in Durban marked the high point of our hostility. I spoke in favour of a national convention which would include all players across the political spectrum. Schwarz moved an amendment to exclude all persons convicted of crimes of treason or sabotage. That of course would have excluded all the Rivonia trialists including Nelson Mandela. Schwarz was enjoying considerable acclaim at the congress, as he had acquitted himself well on financial matters during the past session of Parliament, and his amendment carried the day. I was deeply upset and contemplated resigning from the party. Only the fact that Congress had changed its outdated qualified franchise policy to universal adult franchise, deterred me from doing so, as I considered this to be the most important issue. I stayed in the party, but relations between Harry Schwarz and me were very strained for some time thereafter. They improved only in 1986 when Van Zyl Slabbert resigned from Parliament and the Progressive Federal Party. Harry Schwarz and I were the two most outraged members of the caucus, and our other differences faded into insignificance as a result. We developed a mutual respect.

He was an extremely able MP with a good financial brain, and a hard worker who could devastate National Party members in Parliament, especially Ministers of Finance, who feared his vigorous attacks. Like me, he could be unpleasant both in and out of the House. Harry retired from politics in 1991 to become the

South African ambassador to the US, where he has filled the post with flair and competence.

The merger with the Reform Party affected our relationship with students at the liberal English-medium universities. In 1977 I spoke at a mass meeting of students at the Great Hall at Wits, and it was jam-packed despite impending exams. I was furious with the secretary of NUSAS who spoke after me and advised students to ignore the White elections and boycott the ballot box. That might have been all very well if he had an alternative, but it was just the usual radical reason for doing nothing. He evidently didn't realise that if the Nats had an overwhelming victory on 30 November, what they were presently doing would look like a school picnic compared with what they would do thereafter. I wrote to the NUSAS president asking if the secretary's statement to 2000 students was official policy and told him that if it was I would resign as an honorary vice-president of the organisation. If it were not, I asked him to repudiate publicly the secretary's advice. He did not do so, but he assured me that NUSAS had not taken any such resolution. It did, however, within the next ten years, by which time I had been deposed as honorary vice-president, with not a word of thanks for my past efforts on behalf of the students when they were under siege at the Schlebusch Commission hearings and under attack by the police on campus. I felt this to be a sad reflection on what became of the close relationship between us in earlier years – a rejection of shared liberal values, now replaced by radicalism.

In February 1977 I gave evidence to the Cillie Commission, which had been appointed to enquire into the Soweto riots of the previous year. It was not nearly as awesome as I thought it would be. The formidable Dr Percy Yutar, who was leading evidence for the state, was positively ingratiating, while Judge P. M. Cillie was charm itself.

There were many leading questions, for example: 'How do you account for the fact that some of the worst riots occurred in the United States after the Civil Rights legislation was introduced?' (Vietnam was ignored of course.) Then there was that good old chestnut: 'Is it not a fact that South African Blacks are better off

9a 1983: Celebration of the 30th anniversary of my becoming an MP. Photographed with members of the Progressive Federal Party caucus, past and present.

9b 1984: Mosie's 80th birthday. Celebrated at 'Blue Haze' with Patty and Francie.

9c 1985: With my grandchildren, Danny and Josie Jowell, in England.

10a Addressing the crowd at the mass funeral of victims of police shootings in Alexandra townships in 1986.

10b Molly Black-burn, MPC, in Angola in 1984.

10c With Black Sash observers, taking statements from residents of Moutse who had been kidnapped and assaulted by vigilantes.

10d Talking to residents of Oukasie who were threatened with forced removal.

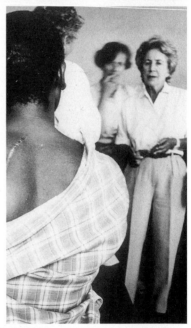

11a China: with Colin Eglin and James Selfe at the Great Wall, 1987.

11b Israel: with Bella Apzug in Jerusalem at the Women's Protest Stand against the proposal to change the Law of Return, 1988.

12 With Winnie Mandela at my home. This picture was notoriously pirated and used on the front page of several pro-Nationalist newspapers to discredit me immediately prior to the 1987 election. The altered caption read: 'With our match-boxes and our necklaces we will liberate our country'.

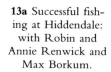

13a Successful fishing at Hiddendale: with Robin and Annie Renwick and Max Borkum.

13b With Colin Eglin, on the way to our discussions with President P W Botha, to plead for the fate of the Sharpeville Six in 1988.

13c With my colleagues Zach de Beer and (*left*) Ray Swart.

14a With Chief Buthelezi at a party in Cape Town to commemorate my 21st session in Parliament.

14b With Alan Paton at a book launch in Johannesburg in 1986. He dedicated his book, *Save the Beloved Country*, to me.

14c With Harry Oppenheimer, who presented me with a copy of the Festschrift in 1989.

14d With Margaret Thatcher, photographed outside No. 10 Downing Street, 28 September 1989.

15a Oxford University, 1973: with Harold Macmillan, Chancellor, and Sir John Maud, then Master of University College and previously British Ambassador to South Africa.

15b Warwick University, 1990: with my actress niece Janet Suzman.

15c Outside Buckingham Palace, after the conferment of the DBE, 31 October 1989. Great occasion, terrible hat!

16 Visiting Nelson Mandela at his home in Soweto, shortly after his release, in February 1990, from 27 years in prison.

than their brethren in the rest of Africa?' The evidence I submitted simply summarised all that I had been saying in Parliament for many years about the hopelessness of the quality of life among Black people, and the lack of civil rights such as the franchise.

I had thought that I should visit Soweto again before giving evidence, so I asked Ina Perlman, then working at the Institute of Race Relations and now director of Operation Hunger, to arrange for the required permit to enter the township. I went to Soweto with Ina and Sophie Thema, a reporter on the black newspaper, the *World*, accompanied by a photographer. Despite the fact that there had been book burning the day before at several schools, we encountered nary a policeman, no one asked to see my permit, and I received a great welcome from the pupils at the two high schools, where the worst burnings had taken place. One entire school was assembled in the yard for me to say a few words to them, which I did, though I had my doubts about the wisdom of doing so, as the prohibition against outdoor meetings under the Riotous Assemblies Act still applied.

All hell then broke loose. *Die Transvaler* ran a front-page story which reported that I had had to flee from a school by the back gate ('Helen vlug by skool in Soweto') and that the pupils jeered at me. I threatened to report *Die Transvaler* to the Press Council unless it published a retraction forthwith and an apology on the front page for gross misrepresentation. Kruger threatened to take action against me for going to Soweto without a permit. In fact a permit had been issued but in the name of Mrs M. M. Suzman (my husband's initials). Ina Perlman said she always made applications in that way for married women – rather old-fashioned, I felt, but evidently the idiot officials did not cotton on to the fact that Mrs M. M. Suzman was Helen Suzman and informed the idiot Minister that I went in without a permit. For once I had not thrown the evidence away, and I intended to shove the permit in Kruger's face when I returned to Cape Town. Kruger also threatened to 'vervolg' [prosecute] me under the Riotous Assemblies Act, which really would have been a hoot.

I met Kruger accidentally in the lift at H. F. Verwoerd Building that week in Cape Town. I had been to see the Deputy Minister of Bantu Affairs to persuade him to stop the Bantu Administration

Board in Soweto from commandeering Winnie Mandela's house there. Kruger glared at me and, with his customary old-world charm, his reply to my good morning was, 'Ek sal jou vang' [I will catch you], which didn't upset me unduly, as I told him – the nasty little bully!

However, more serious were the sinister investigations which followed my visit to Soweto. The two Black journalists who accompanied me, Sophie and the photographer, were called in by the security police and closely cross-examined about my activities there, particularly at the school where I had addressed the students in the yard for a few minutes. Ina Perlman was also visited by the police, who were apparently seriously contemplating a prosecution under the Riotous Assemblies Act. But I heard nothing further from the authorities about my riotous assembly. They probably thought better of it.

I then awaited the result of the complaint I had lodged with the Press Council about the *Die Transvaler* article. I really did not see how the Council could not find in my favour in view of the photographs of the smiling children which the *World* photographer had taken that day, but I was not surprised to learn that the newspaper had obtained a number of questionable affidavits which it intended to produce. So I decided I had better have counsel to cross-examine. The case began badly for me because my first choice, Ernie Wentzel, had to withdraw as he was still busy with another case –that of the poet, Breyten Breytenbach. None of the other advocates I wanted was available, so I ended up with one who told me I didn't have a hope of winning. I became more miserable with every consultation I had with this man and considered handling the case myself. But there were witnesses to be cross-examined and evidence to be led, so I thought I had better keep a professional man available.

In the event, *Die Transvaler* produced no witnesses, and the judge, Oscar Galgut, said that on *prima facie* evidence the paper should not have published without trying to verify the facts. He advised them to settle by offering to publish a front-page article accepting my version of the visit. *Die Transvaler* put a small article in the bottom left-hand corner of the front page to that effect. That was not really satisfactory; it was no more than a pyrrhic victory. If my advocate had been enthusiastic, I would have insisted on a proper hearing in court. But the judge was eager for a settlement and I was unnerved by the pessimism of my counsel, so I settled. Anyway the *Rand Daily Mail* gave the case fair coverage and at least next time some Nat yelled at me in the house 'Hulle het jou uitgejag' [They chased you out], I could shut him up.

I had a more difficult task countering National Party derision after an attack from an unexpected quarter. In February 1977, a comment by Andy Young, the Black American ambassador at the United Nations, was published by several newspapers: 'Mrs Helen Suzman is the only South African I can't get along with. I can deal with cold hatred but I can't stand paternal liberalism.' I responded that I was not in South Africa when Mr Young visited the country and could only remember having met him once, at a breakfast in Washington the previous year with members of Congress. 'And evidently I am not at my best at breakfast,' I added. Of course the Nationalists used his statement in Parliament, crowing over it, and I was very angry.

Andy Young's comments infuriated a bright young advocate, Brian Doctor, who replaced Jackie Beck as my researcher for one session. He wrote a five-page letter to the US ambassador to the United Nations in which he said *inter alia*:

> Mrs Suzman's role in Parliament has had two aspects, first to oppose openly and vociferously and from a position of principle, the Nationalist Party's actions in implementing their apartheid police state, and secondly in using her position as a parliamentarian to render what assistance she can to the pitiful victims of the system.
>
> Daily she receives, year in and year out, letters and calls from desperate people who have no one else to turn to: will she please help a wife whose husband has been grabbed by the police; will she intervene with the Minister on behalf of a family thrown out of their house and 'endorsed out' of the urban areas; will she inspect and expose the ghastly hostels where migratory workers are forced to live; will she ask the Minister to give back someone's passport, so that the person can take up a scholarship or visit a dying relative; will she intervene on behalf of conscientious objectors who are being maltreated in an army prison . . . Each of these pleas is personally dealt with by a reply from Mrs Suzman . . . and it should be remembered that she helps these people without any possibility of their being able to repay her by voting for her. Most of them don't have the vote.

Brian's letter dealt also with my work inside Parliament, the wide-ranging speeches I made and the innumerable questions I put to ministers. He ended on a personal note,

> I was born after the present South African government came to power in 1948. I and people of my generation were brought up in South Africa having no experience of any other system. In so far as I have freed myself from the corroding effects of racial discrimination, it is due in no small measure to the activities of Helen Suzman. She has kept alive in South Africa, by constant reiteration of basic principles, ideas about individual human freedom, which are derived from your own country's constitution. Her educative effect on all South Africans has been enormous; if the South African government introduces any changes to the system, the credit for preparing public opinion to accept these changes will be largely hers. If you find in your dealings with the government that they are aware that what they are doing is evil, then again, much of that will be due to her. She represents South Africa's best hope for racial reconciliation and you have unjustly wronged her and the principles for which she stands.

Andy Young replied to Brian Doctor regretting that his comments 'were misinterpreted'. He said that he held me in high regard for my forthright stand on South Africa's racial problems. He added 'Mrs Suzman has taken the lead in permitting peaceful change and her determination and principles are recognised by all those who have followed her career for many years. Her courageous lonely stand in the face of bitter personal and political attacks has earned her well deserved admiration.'

He subsequently reiterated these views in the press and added, 'But American influence must be directed at those who hold power – the South African government.'

On my next visit to the US, he invited me to come and see him at his office at the United Nations, which I did; and we made up. But I thought it was very unfair of him to have made his original statement which subjected me to ridicule by Nationalist MPs. Moreover the last thing I could be accused of was 'paternal liberalism'. I have always been just as nasty to Blacks as I am to Whites, and that can be very nasty indeed! Simple justice was ever my motivation, not 'paternal liberalism'.

Some other unexpected confrontations occurred during visits to the United States. After the 1977 parliamentary session ended I went to Barnard College, part of Columbia University, New York, as a visiting lecturer. While I was there a curious pamphlet put out by 'BOSS' appeared on campus. BOSS was the acronym for the South African Bureau of State Security. My disbelieving eyes could not fathom what BOSS was doing on the campus of an American women's college. It turned out to be the Barnard Organisation of Soul Sisters, a radical Black women's student organisation which insisted on having an all-Black dormitory. The Soul Sisters' pamphlet described me as a racist and the headline was 'White Oppressor – go home'.

The professor who was to chair my meeting that evening said he was worried there might be trouble; Columbia had experienced a great deal of violence on campus during the sixties. I told him not to worry; I was used to such goings on at home. The meeting was in a huge gymnasium which was completely full. Standing at the back, bearing the 'White Oppressor' banner, were a few students and in their midst a large Black man. As I was being introduced by the nervous chairman, they marched up to the platform. Their leader announced that the Black man was from Rhodesia and demanded that he be allowed to address the meeting. I simply took the mike and said, 'This is my meeting . . . If you want your man from Rhodesia to speak, you go hire a hall and have your own meeting.' The audience responded with loud applause and the little procession turned around and left the platform. 'Gee,' said the chairman, much relieved, 'I thought they would burn the place down.'

In 1980 I again spent several weeks in the United States, during which I spoke at a seminar at the Massachusetts Institute of Technology, to the Nieman Fellows at Harvard and at Brown University at the invitation of John Kennedy junior. In New York I addressed the Foreign Policy Association and the 92nd Street Y. Mayor Ed Koch presented me with a medal at Gracie Mansion, inscribed, 'To Helen Suzman, Seeker of Truth, Champion of Liberty and Justice'. His Worship had just written and publicised a letter to P. W. Botha condemning South Africa's racial policy, so my visit was timely. However, the presentation may have been intended as a gesture to mollify hostile Blacks in New York. For my part, it had unexpected consequences, as Mayor Koch dropped the heavy brass medal on my foot, and I limped around New York for several days.

Not every contest ended in success. I twice allowed myself to be nominated for the Chancellorship of Wits University and twice I was defeated. It is likely that a split vote played a part on both occasions. When Mark Orkin approached me in 1974 to ask whether I would accept nomination, I agreed only after considerable hesitation, bearing in mind the many graduation ceremonies at which the Chancellor officiates annually. Mark had been a prominent student activist on campus and had often called on me to intervene when student protesters were confronted by police. I had strong support from several well-known Wits personalities.[1]

There were two other candidates: B. L. (Birch) Bernstein, a director of a leading mining house, Anglo Vaal, and the author Alan Paton. Alan and I had a long-distance friendship over the years; he lived near Durban and we did not meet very often but we corresponded quite frequently. I greatly admired his skill as an author: his masterpiece, *Cry the Beloved Country*, had moved me deeply when I read it in 1948. Many years later in 1987 I was honoured when Alan dedicated his book *Save the Beloved Country* to me; he had always been supportive about my parliamentary work. His editorial in the September 1973 issue of *Reality* acknowledged the honorary doctorate I received from Oxford University:

> Helen Suzman has received formal tributes from a great university for her sustained and articulate opposition to official policies in South Africa. Official South African response to this must be wry, at best; but it would be wrong to think of Mrs Suzman as not honoured in her own country, since there is probably no one so much admired and respected here among the politically conscious of all races.

As we were both high-profile people belonging to the endangered species of White South African liberals, we would clearly draw support from the same section of Convocation. Suggestions were made that one of us should withdraw, but democratic principle was against this. We were both defeated. Birch won the contest.

The second time I stood was in 1982. My opponent was A. M. (Mike) Rosholt, chairman of Barlow Rand, one of South Africa's major industrial companies and well known for his work on charitable bodies. This time I intervened on behalf of a third candidate. I was in my office in Parliament when the phone rang, well after 5.30 p. m. A brusque voice informed me that the caller was a Wits graduate named Mark Sebba and that he was calling from York University in England. He told me that he had sent a nomination form to Pollsmoor Prison, to be signed by Nelson Mandela, but that enquiries at Wits had established that the signed form had not been received by the registrar, Ken Standenmacher. Sebba instructed me to follow up the matter, to get the form signed and delivered to the registrar before midnight that night, when nominations closed. He further instructed me to withdraw my name from the contest. I told him he had monumental imperti-nence to suggest this, that I had every democratic right to stand and that I had no intention of withdrawing. However, I added that I believed Mandela also had a right to stand and I would do what I could to get the nomination form signed and delivered. I told Sebba it was unlikely I would succeed. To my utter astonishment, I not only managed to contact someone in the commanding officer's department at Pollsmoor at that late hour, but he arranged for Mandela to sign the nomination form and it was sent by special plane to Johannesburg by the Prisons Department. It was delivered to the registrar's office by a senior police officer at five minutes to midnight.

Mr Rosholt won the election.

Was it conceivable, I wondered later, that the extraordinary effort made by the prisons' officials in this highly unusual manner could have been inspired by political acumen and the realisation that Mandela and I, in competition for the votes of the liberal alumni of Wits, would cancel out each other's chances? We shall never know. But Mike Rosholt has proved an outstanding Chancellor.

In 1975 I visited Australia under the auspices of the Australian Institute of International Affairs. Under the Whitlam government the country was very anti-South African. It was going through a bad time, with sky-high inflation and rising unemployment, so that getting tough with South Africa was a useful distraction.

At my first lecture, in Canberra, I had a responsive audience, no demos and lots of questions. In fact, I was given a signal honour in Canberra, the only one, I was told, ever accorded to a non-Head of State: a luncheon by the Australian Parliament, attended by members of both Houses and hosted by the Prime Minister, Gough Whitlam. He and the leader of the opposition, Malcolm Fraser, both spoke at the function. I felt somehow that I was serving as a political football as they voiced their sentiments about South Africa, with strong condemnation from Whitlam and with Fraser uttering conciliatory remarks about how he would handle South Africa.

Whitlam referred approvingly some years later to Malcolm Fraser as 'an admirably reformed character' because his attitude to South Africa had become extremely hostile. I had some unpleasant exchanges with Fraser at international conferences regarding sanctions against South Africa. I was relieved when he did not achieve his ambition to become Commonwealth Secretary General when Shridrath (Sonny) Ramphal retired in 1990.

My subsequent meetings in Australia were well attended and all followed the same pattern. There were no interruptions during the speech, then plenty of hostile questions from students, all using the same handout from the Southern African Liberation Movement: that I was the mouthpiece of Harry Oppenheimer and the multinational corporations 'that exploit the Blacks'. I gathered that Melbourne would be pretty tough as it was said to be the seat of radicalism. I reckoned I would survive.

I did have a really hot meeting in Melbourne. The hall held 750 and was packed. There were demos outside with flags, people chanting slogans and handing out pamphlets. It was very rowdy, with police in attendance, and I had to rescue one demonstrator who was about to be arrested. There was much foot-stamping and an ANC spokesman who talked rubbish about instant revolution. He had been in Australia for seven years as a perpetual student. He was cheered and I was booed by the demonstrators, but the audience as a whole was supportive.

En route home, I spent ten days in Mauritius as the guest of the government, and I had a really torrid time at the university there. A bunch of screaming students banged on the desks and yelled 'Racist go home' for about ten minutes. 'Why don't you leave if you don't want to hear me?' I suggested. 'Others may want to.' They then walked out, leaving about sixty students who listened quietly.

A different sort of encounter took place in the Mauritius hotel at breakfast one morning. I was directed to a table occupied by a number of people readily identified by their accents as South Africans. As I sat down a deathly hush ensued and I, dismayed, thought, 'Oh dear, they've recognised me and now it will be nothing but politics at breakfast.'

Instead an aggressive female voice asked, 'Aren't you Helen Gavronsky from Germiston – I played hockey against you at school. What have you been doing since then?'

11

Opposition to Apartheid
In and Out of Parliament:
1977–87

In 1977 the United Party finally died. Its ambivalence became terminal as it teetered between a desire to move with the times and a vain hope of attracting Nationalist votes by pandering to racial prejudice. One wondered whether its members would bury the party or cremate it. In the event, they froze it out of existence at a meeting at the Johannesburg Ice Rink. They discarded its only really valuable asset – its name, long associated with General Smuts – and replaced it with the New Republic Party, under a new leader, Radcliffe Cadman, from Natal.

At a huge rally of Progressive Reform Party supporters in the Johannesburg City Hall just before the general election on 30 November 1977, I told the wildly enthusiastic audience that I had a dream (not that we would overcome, like Martin Luther King) that we would become the official opposition at the next parliamentary session. That was exactly what happened. We returned to Cape Town in January 1978 with Colin Eglin as leader and with seventeen (out of 165) parliamentary seats.

In the enlarged caucus, I shed a number of responsibilities. I retained only the portfolios in which I was particularly interested: civil rights, law and order, prisons, urban Black affairs, and women's affairs – the easy ones, as I told my constituents!

To my great delight, my old chums Zach de Beer and Ray Swart were back with us in Parliament. Zach and I had shared a backbench when we first arrived in the House in 1953. He was considered a rising star in the United Party, although he was only twenty-four years old and the youngest MP. He was an exceptionally good debater who spoke English and Afrikaans fluently, having had both as cradle languages, his father being Afrikaans and his mother Scottish. Like his father, he was a medical doctor, but politics was his abiding passion and he seemed set to reach great heights in Parliament. He was a Prog by conviction, however, and left the United Party in the 1959 upheaval and lost his seat in the 1961 election. He joined a leading advertising agency, a job at which he excelled, but then Zach would have done well at anything he chose as a career. Later he joined the Anglo American Corporation, whose chairman, Harry Oppenheimer, had recognised Zach's ability early on when he was a fellow MP.

Ray Swart, another original Prog of 1959 vintage, was a Natal member with an Afrikaans name who was totally anglicised. In fact, he is a confirmed monarchist and often had to undergo a fair amount of leg-pulling about this in republican South Africa. But Ray is a true liberal, absolutely uncompromising in his principles. His unequivocal speeches in Parliament and on platforms in Natal –where he was the leader of the party there until he retired in 1989 – certainly reflected his convictions. He played a vital role in keeping the Progressive Party alive and kicking in reactionary Natal during the thirteen years when it was in the wilderness.

It is a total misconception that only Afrikaners are racist in South Africa. On the contrary, some of the worst racists come from English-speaking areas like Natal and the eastern Cape, and indeed some of South Africa's finest liberals were and are Afrikaners. Ray had a difficult time combating the racial prejudice of people who voted against the Nationalists only because that party was mainly Afrikaans-speaking, and not because they disapproved of discrimination against Blacks, Coloureds and Indians.

During the 1978 session, the Minister of Foreign Affairs, R. M. (Pik) Botha, attacked Colin Eglin over an alleged breach of confidence concerning foreign policy. Negotiations about the independence of South West Africa had at that time reached a dangerous stalemate and about six weeks earlier Colin had phoned Don McHenry, US ambassador at the United Nations to find out what the Western governments were thinking about the situation.

McHenry had innocently mentioned Colin's call to the South African representative at the UN, who promptly informed Pik Botha. Botha revealed in Parliament that Colin had been to see him previously to discuss South West Africa, and he accused Colin of having betrayed a confidence. The object of Colin's call to McHenry was, of course, to obtain and not to give information. The whole incident was an obvious attempt by the government to distract attention from the Information Scandal, which at the time was receiving much coverage in the press.

It was a device which had no lasting effect in that context, but I have no doubt that it contributed to the successful campaign to replace Colin Eglin by Van Zyl Slabbert as leader of the Party, and also therefore as Leader of the Opposition. Much though I liked Van Zyl and appreciated his ability, I voted against this change. For one thing, I was not convinced that he intended to remain in Parliament. I knew that although he had allowed his name to go forward for nomination as leader of the PFP, at the same time his hat was in the ring for the vacant Vice-Chancellorship of the University of Cape Town. Moreover, I felt that Colin did not deserve such treatment from the party he had served so well for so many years. But Van Zyl obtained the support of the majority of the Federal Executive of the Party. Colin resigned as leader, and Van Zyl was unanimously elected in his place at the party congress a couple of months later.

Van Zyl was a very popular, competent and hard-working leader of the party for seven years and contributed to its good showing in 1981, when we were further entrenched as the official opposition with twenty-seven seats in the House of Assembly. The PFP even won extra seats in reactionary Natal and the eastern Cape, as well as in the Transvaal and the rest of the Cape Province.

I carried out special tasks with two young Cape Town MPs we had acquired in 1977: Ken Andrew and Tian van der Merwe. Ken and I tackled the squatter problem in Cape Town, making many depressing 6 a. m. visits to the miserable squatter camps. Tian was my deputy when I was spokesperson on the portfolio of Law and Order. His death in a motor-car accident in May 1991 was a heavy blow to the party and indeed to South Africa. Tian and I sometimes attended funerals together, generally in an effort to allay police action. The Minister or the police would issue instructions that only up to 200 people could attend but many more went than were allowed. Very often the funeral was of victims of police shooting, and since all outdoor political meetings were illegal and funerals were not, they almost invariably became protest meetings attended by huge crowds, sometimes by as many as 20,000 people. I asked irritably in Parliament, 'Were the police supposed to arrest 19,800 people?'

Indeed, mass funerals had become part of the South African way of life – huge political gatherings, reflecting the new mood of Black defiance that had marked political life since 1976. Escalating Black resistance manifested itself in mass protests, strikes, stayaways and consumer boycotts. It is no exaggeration to say that during the following ten years South Africa lurched from crisis to crisis, starting with the Soweto unrest in 1976–8, and continuing with violent confrontations between police and Blacks elsewhere. From 1984 the government repeatedly proclaimed a state of emergency and the regulations always included indemnity to police and officials for any actions taken in the course of their duty – an open invitation to abuse their power.

The 1979 session of Parliament was dominated by one issue – the Information Scandal – which had started during the previous session with revelations that the Department of Information had used taxpayers' money to establish a pro-government English-language newspaper. The minister, Dr Connie Mulder, denied this in Parliament, a denial which was to cost him dear. Furthermore the department under its chief, Dr Eschel Rhoodie, had attempted, again with taxpayers' money, to purchase the *Washington Times* in the United States and to gain control of South African Associated Newspapers, the influential anti-government morning group.

This was thwarted by the prompt action of public-spirited men including Max Borkum and Gordon Waddell, Prog MP, who between them raised funds to prevent the takeover. The pebble which the Auditor General cast into that pool caused ripples that spread far and wide. Together with the courageous and remarkable investigative journalism by Kitt Katzin of the *Sunday Express* and by news reporters on the *Rand Daily Mail*, plus the resolute disclosures of Judge Anton Mostert, the repercussions of the scandal led directly to the downfall of two leading politicians: Prime Minister John Vorster and the Minister of Information, Connie Mulder. It resulted also in the disgrace of leading figures in the civil service, a major Cabinet reshuffle, bitter infighting in the National Party caucus and interminable rows in Parliament.

As a result of the revelations, the Erasmus Commission was appointed to enquire into irregularities connected with the former Department of Information. One of its lighter by-products was a batch of malapropisms and mixed metaphors. Here are some examples. A civil servant makes 'a clean breast of it like a lanced boil'. The Minister of Finance explains that he could not be expected to search for a black cat in a dark room when he had no knowledge of the cat. Witnesses spin cocoons; a pupa becomes a fly in the ointment and then applies the brakes; and there is a germ-infested apple. But I think Judge Erasmus himself takes the biscuit for describing a global trip as 'a trip around the bulb', and something being 'like duck's water off his back'. The description of 'a man who had a finger in every tart' was also attributed to him, but is doubtless apocryphal.

Of course, in most Western countries, the government would have resigned immediately the Information Scandal broke. Joint Cabinet responsibility should surely have been accepted, instead of the government's feeble excuse that 'they did not know'. Indeed this was all the more reason for them to resign, because they should have known. It is difficult to imagine any other government surviving a situation where the Minister of Defence permitted millions of rands allocated by a trusting Parliament to a Defence Secret Projects Fund to be passed to the Department of Information to use for its own secret projects. It is difficult to imagine any other government surviving a situation where the Minister of Finance signed an authorisation for the expenditure of some R15 million for 150 such projects, and deliberately avoided knowing what those projects were. And all this, of course, was taxpayers' money. The *Citizen*, a blatantly pro-Nationalist English-language newspaper, was financed from this slush fund to the tune of R32 million. Vorster's 'punishment' was to be appointed to the highest office in the land, State President. Dr Mulder was allowed to stand in Vorster's place for election as Prime Minister, although by then the entire Cabinet knew about his machinations.

Perhaps the most cynical of the government's actions was the way it forced through Parliament the Information Service of South Africa Special Account Act, which enabled the Minister of Foreign Affairs to approve, *ex post facto,* irregular and unauthorised contracts entered into by the former department. In other words, the taxpayers could kiss goodbye to the R32 million of their money still unaccounted for. The government also tried to pass a Bill entitled 'The Advocate General Bill', which would have put an end to any form of investigative journalism in South Africa. But to their credit, government-supporting newspapers joined with opposition papers in strongly criticising the measure, and the National Press Union, representing the boards of all the newspapers and various other important associations, rallied to protect the freedom of the press, such as it was.

Controversial clauses affecting the press were dropped, but the final measure still severely restricted the public's right to know. Only the most limited coverage of unrest areas and police activity was possible. I was convinced that if the South African public had been shown the ugly scenes of police shooting at unarmed demonstrators, the sjambokking (whipping with leather thongs) of students on campuses, the teargassing inside schools and churches, and later the 'Trojan Horse' incident where police popped up from the back of a lorry and shot at demonstrators in a Cape Town Black township, there would have been a great wave of revulsion. Just as in the United States the sight on television of Bull Connor with his dogs and his hoses spurred the American civil rights movement in the sixties, so too, I believe, the revolting scenes of police excesses in the townships and on the campuses would have provoked strong public reaction in South Africa.

During the 1979 recess I learned that suspicion had been cast on me as a security risk, and that the government had been tampering with my mail. My daughter Francie had long been complaining that my letters to her in London were taking an unconscionable time. She said she suspected that the mail-box up our street, where

I always posted my letters, was being searched for my mail. She proved to be right. That I had been under the attention of DONS (the Department of National Security, formerly BOSS, the Bureau of State Security) became evident at the beginning of the year when a defector, Arthur McGiven, surfaced in England. He handed a number of documents to the *Observer* newspaper, including letters written by me and to me, which were among those published. I obtained copies, and there was no doubt that they emanated from BOSS reports. The documents carried the code name 'Operation Knoopsgat' (Buttonhole) in a Bronverslag (Source Report) lodged in a file where I was identified as number W/V 24596 ['wit vrou' – white woman], by party affiliation, by occupation, by constituency and by more numbers – J42/32/200 ('J' meaning Johannesburg or Jewish?). I was livid at this disclosure and announced to the press that I intended to raise the matter in Parliament at the earliest opportunity. I did so in the No Confidence debate shortly after the session began.

I charged the government with illegally tampering with my mail and tapping my phone. I said that instead of having its ear to the ground and informing the Cabinet, for example, that serious unrest was brewing in Soweto in 1976, the government had its ear to my telephone. 'Perhaps the one comforting thought I got out of this whole disgusting affair,' I added, 'was that over the years when the government was tapping my telephone, it must certainly have heard some home truths from me about themselves, often couched in good Anglo Saxon terms.'[1] I said the government was guilty of the grossest abuse of power, and the grossest invasion of the privacy of persons and of organisations that had not the slightest connection with subversion. I accused them of abusing the powers given to them under the relevant section of the Post Office Act of 1972.

I produced in Parliament four pieces of evidence taken from the document 'Knoopsgat W/V 24596' by McGiven and printed in the *Observer*. One was a letter to me from an American professor containing the dangerously subversive information that he and his wife would be visiting South Africa and discussing plans for me to visit the US later that year. The second was a letter from me to the director of the J. F. Kennedy School of Government at Harvard

University. Third was a letter from me to the director, confirming my visit to Harvard later that year; the fourth was a letter from Winston Churchill, MP (grandson of Sir Winston), also published in the *Observer*. I said that the safeguards put into Section 118A of the Post Office Act were not worth the paper they were written on. I asked for a Select Committee to investigate what had clearly been a gross breach of parliamentary privilege.

Prime Minister Botha said in reply:

> If you want to sup with the devil you need a long spoon. If you want to communicate with the devil, use his postal facilities or allow him to use your postal facilities or your letterheads . . . The Honourable Member must not push me too far or I shall tell her who writes on her letterheads, and who writes her name on the back of the envelope and signs his own name to the letter. The Honourable Member is a vicious little cat when she is wronged, but I say to her, 'choose your friends better'. Things were written about secret meetings on her letterheads, and her name was put to wrong use on the back of that envelope by a person who, according to our information, is a member of a foreign intelligence service[2] [later revealed as a reference to the US Central Intelligence Agency].

I could not imagine who this mysterious 'devil' could be. Finally it dawned on me that 'the secret agent' was Robert Rotberg, then a professor at the Massachusetts Institute of Technology, who had, with my permission, used one of my lettercards when he was my house guest, on which he wrote to his wife and daughters in Boston. All my lettercards contained my name and address stamped on the back, and when the DONS investigators intercepted the lettercard sent by Rotberg, with my name on the back and a different signature within, dark suspicions arose. This, apparently, was all they could produce after what had obviously been a frantic search in the files of W/V 24596, after I had said I would raise the matter in Parliament. I told the Prime Minister it was not my friends I should choose more carefully, but my enemies.

Botha made it clear that he had no intention of appointing the Select Committee I had demanded and refused to answer a question from me. I called out, 'You are a coward', and was ordered by the Speaker, J. J. Loots, to withdraw the remark. I refused to do so and was told to leave the House for the rest of the day's sitting, which I did – the second and last time in my thirty- six years as an MP that I was chucked out of the debating chamber.

My next step was to table a Private Member's Motion asking for the appointment of a Select Committee. The debate took place shortly afterwards. In my introductory speech, I reminded the House that when a Member of Parliament is sworn in, he or she takes an oath of loyalty to the Republic. In effect the Prime Minister had accused me of treason and I claimed the right to be exonerated. In the meantime I had written to Rotberg and had asked him to send me (by messenger and not through the post!) a copy of the letter sent by him from my house in January 1979. When I received it, I found it contained the totally innocuous statement that he and I had seen some secret films at a friend's house in Johannesburg. I had already revealed this, and said the whole thing 'was one huge giggle', and that Rotberg was 'as much a member of the CIA as is the Minister of Tourism and Statistics who is glaring at me from across the House'.[3] The 'secret films' Rotberg had referred to rather melodramatically were videos such as *Last Grave at Dimbaza* which had been shown legally, albeit privately, all over South Africa, and had been seen by hundreds of people.

What concerned me was who had given the instruction to intercept my mail: 'Whodunnit?', I asked in Parliament. To be legal such an instruction had to be in writing, from the Minister of Post and Telegraphs or from a person to whom he had delegated such authority or via any minister who was a member of the National Security Council. My question met with no reply in the House. The Postmaster General accosted me in the Lobby and denied that he had had anything to do with the interception of my mail – a denial I accepted unreservedly. I wound up my peroration by wondering how many people had been detained or banned under the same flimsy evidence as that produced in this dirty trick, which was therefore no giggle after all. I was ably supported in the debate by my PFP colleagues, but of course my demand for a Select Committee was rejected.

Instead the government changed the law to make it easier in future to tamper with the mail of anyone on the list of the security services. However, since my mail seemed thereafter to reach its destination rather more swiftly than before, I assumed that file W/V 24596 had been sent to the shredder and that they stopped tampering with my mail. What I should have done, of course, was to sue the government for illegal interception of my mail. We had clearly won the debate in Parliament, and I construed the government refusal to appoint a Select Committee as an admission of defeat, despite the fact that National Party MPs would have constituted the majority on the committee. I did consult an eminent lawyer, who agreed I would win my case, but suggested I had better drop it for, he said, one never knows 'what these people can cook up'. I think I made a serious mistake in accepting his advice, and I have regretted it ever since.

In 1980 the Cillie Commission which enquired into the 1976 Soweto riots produced its report. Despite its tardy appearance, the report was of considerable value in that it analysed the causes of the unrest and contained an unmistakable indictment of government policy. Of course, it told most of us who had studied race relations in South Africa nothing we had not known for years: that Pass Laws and inferior education, low wages and inadequate housing and transport, had contributed greatly to the unrest in 1976 and 1977, and that the threat to introduce Afrikaans as a language of instruction in the Black schools was just the catalyst.

I took issue with the commission for its exoneration of the police. I simply could not reconcile the enormous number of people killed by police action – 114 in the first six days and a total of 445 in the months covered by the report (which incidentally did not cover the entire duration of the unrest) – with the police purportedly intent on using the minimum of force and keeping the death rate down.

When asked why no special riot equipment had been initially provided to the police so as to reduce casualties, Jimmy Kruger, then Minister of Police, gave the unforgettable reply:

> To have our policemen running around like knights of the Middle Ages, heavily armoured with coats of mail and visors and goodness knows what else – policemen in such garb pursuing fleet-footed little Bantu all over the veld – is something I can hardly imagine. Not only would it be ridiculous, it is also completely unnecessary.[4]

During the debate on the Cillie Report, a ridiculous incident took place. I was finishing my speech when my waist slip dropped to my feet. No one would have known about it, as my desk screened me from view, if I hadn't said 'Oh God' rather audibly and sat down and afterwards told one of my colleagues what had happened. Of course my gossipy colleague could not resist telling John Scott, who wrote a satirical article on Parliament every day for the *Cape Times*. The way it came out in next day's issue one would have thought I was standing in full view of the House with my slip around my feet, and that I had been unable to finish my speech. Actually, my time had expired and I had to sit down anyway. John offered to write an explanatory note when I complained to him, but I decided it wasn't worth the fuss, especially as I had recovered my sense of humour by then, after receiving a sympathetic note, with a safety pin attached, from one Nationalist MP and a pair of braces from Minister le Grange, the Minister of Police and Law and Order (the latter portfolio was added in 1982).

The reaction to the Cillie Report from the Minister of Co-operation and Development, Dr Piet Koornhof, was to warn the opposition not to raise expectations among Blacks which could not be realised. He made what he called 'a very friendly request' to Members opposite and to the news media not to indulge in this dangerous practice. This was from the man who had assured audiences at Palm Springs, California, and in Washington DC, from the safe distance of 9000 miles from his caucus, that his government would not rest until racial discrimination had disappeared from the statute book and from everyday life in South Africa, and until the Pass Laws were abolished.

I must say that the Minister of Co-operation and Development was an engaging chap. He was a cartoonist's delight, with his large ears at right angles to his head and his Cyrano de Bergerac nose. He had a disarming way of laughing at his own jokes and at himself, especially when he was the subject of the impersonations of South Africa's premier satirist, Pieter-Dirk Uys. Koornhof had a long and chequered career before becoming South African ambassador to the United States in 1985. He was a Rhodes scholar and wrote a thesis while at Oxford condemning the migratory labour system and its effects on Nkandla, a small village in the Black homeland of KwaZulu. The influence of the dreaming spires did not last long.

On his return to South Africa, Koornhof became the secretary of the Broederbond. I was informed a couple of years ago by Wynand Malan, a former Democratic Party MP who is also a Broeder, that the organisation had now become much more moderate and was devising a democratic constitution for the 'New South Africa'. I replied: 'And why not – since it has achieved everything it set out to do. It can afford to be moderate. It has ensured Afrikaner domination over the entire South Africa.'

Koornhof graduated from his position as secretary of the Broederbond to one of the most important Cabinet posts in South Africa, controlling the lives of millions of Black people. It was in this capacity that he and I had sharp exchanges in Parliament, especially concerning the inhumanity of depriving Black squatters of the elementary requirement of shelter by destroying their shacks on the Cape Flats in mid-winter, particularly during the early eighties.

Koornhof's euphemistically entitled portfolio had been through several name changes over the years: from Department of Native Affairs to Department of Bantu Administration and Development (in Verwoerd's day), to Department of Plural Relations and Development, to Department of Co-operation and Development. (A current joke when the department was called 'Plural Relations and Development' was that Bushman rock art should be renamed Rural Plural Murals.)

In August 1981, during the post-election session, there was considerable public agitation against the government's ruthless treatment of the squatters at Nyanga on the Cape Flats. A protest meeting was held in St George's Cathedral, a short distance from Parliament. I was called out of the House by one of the protesters, who told me that they intended marching to Parliament to present a petition to the Minister of Police, Louis le Grange.

I realised that there was going to be trouble when the procession formed outside the cathedral. A large contingent of police had arrived with vans and dogs; the colonel in charge had announced that the procession would be illegal, as demonstrations within a certain radius of Parliament were prohibited. I went into the cathedral and was allowed to advise the assembled throng of the likely consequences of a procession. Before leaving the House, I had obtained permission from the Minister of Police to take the two main speakers with me to Parliament to present the petition to him. I suggested that the rest of the gathering disperse in pairs and so avoid arrest, as had been agreed between the colonel and me.

I accompanied the two speakers from the cathedral to the gates of the parliamentary gardens. The constable there had locked the gates and stood inside with his large alsatian dog. I said, 'You can't keep me out – I am a Member of Parliament.' He said, 'You can go in, but not the other two.' I pointed to the Minister standing large as life nearby and he signalled his consent. The constable unlocked the gates and we walked into the gardens. The dog began growling in a menacing way. Mindful of Barbara Woodhouse, whose television lessons on canine discipline I had followed with keen interest, I raised my hand and said firmly, 'Sit'. The dog sat. Even the constable smiled. The Minister accepted the petition and the crowd left the cathedral two by two, unmolested by the police.

Minister le Grange gave me no credit, however, for preventing an ugly incident when the cathedral protest was discussed in Parliament that afternoon. Nor did he leap to my defence when I was wrongly accused by his colleagues of taking part in an unlawful procession. The heated argument that ensued proved irresistible to P. W. Botha, who snarled at me, 'You try to break the law and you will see what happens to you.' And I snarled back: 'I'm not frightened of you. I never have been and I never will be. I think nothing of you . . . You have been trying to bully me for twenty-eight years and you have not yet succeeded.'[5]

There is only one accurate way to describe P. W. Botha: an irascible bully. Nothing demonstrated that more vividly than the humiliating dressing-down he gave on television to the Reverend Allan Hendrickse, leader of the Labour Party in the Coloured House of Representatives (set up as part of the tri-cameral Parliament in 1983), for taking a dip in the ocean at a 'Whites–only' beach in Port Elizabeth. He must later have regretted this outburst, for never again did he get any co-operation from Hendrickse, who used procedural tactics to prevent Botha postponing the 1989 general election for the White House of Assembly. He did this by blocking the required amendment to the Constitution.

During the 1980s I took up several cases of forced or threatened removals. In 1982 I went with Ann Bernstein, a keen young party member,[6] to Bothashoek in the northern Transvaal, forty miles from Pietersburg, the nearest 'growth point'. On my return I wrote an article on our travels for the *Sunday Times*.

En route to Bothashoek, from Seshego, the township in Lebowa into which the Pietersburg Blacks were removed (entailing the breakdown of existing houses and the rebuilding of others, all presumably in the interests of the 'White-by-night' policy), we passed the 'betterment' area of Chuene. Just what is better about it, escaped me. It is no different from any of the other resettlement areas. Nobody grows anything because there is no easily available water, though it overlooks the Chuene Dam.

The contrast between such places, occupied by Blacks, and the White farms in the Republic, sometimes just on the other side of the road, is stark indeed. Lush green fields of sprouting crops, sparkling jets of spray irrigation on the White side, and desolate, bare red land on the other. 'You can't eat the vote,' someone once said to me. True, but you don't get to eat unless you have the vote . . . for it means loans from the Land Bank and co-operative societies to look after farmers' interests, subsidies and water. And the right to move off the land and into the cities, if you so choose.

Lenyenye, not too far from Tzaneen, accommodates the people removed from there when the Black township was shifted into the homeland. Among the 8000 people who now live in this bleak and dusty place are farm labourers who used to live on the White farms in the district. Their lot has worsened, for they have lost the wages-in-kind that used to augment their low pay. They and their families now exist on the meagre cash wages . . . 'a rand a day, if they are lucky', I was told, paid by the local farmers who collect them in trucks and transport them to the farms daily.

The only bright spot we could find in Lenyenye was at the clinic run by Dr Mamphela Ramphele, one of those remarkable Black women that South Africa produces. She was Steve Biko's close friend and mother of his child. Banned and banished to the northern Transvaal five years ago, she has run a medical and community service for the people of the district on a shoestring. Originally she received assistance to build the clinic from a sympathetic mining house and from church funds. Now, however, she is battling to find the money to meet the evergrowing demands made on her. Despite her miserable surroundings, and the fact that her banning order was recently extended for a further two years, Dr Ramphele radiates energy and good humour.[7]

Everywhere in the 'resettlement' areas the same dreary picture presented itself – poverty-stricken communities of old men, women and children. Conspicuous by their absence were the young able-bodied men, except for a few youths hanging around with nothing to do and with no hope of finding employment in those dismal and remote areas. The remainder of the men were away in the towns as migrant workers, seeking a livelihood, sometimes legally as contract workers but very often illegally, running the gauntlet of the police in the cities. I concluded my article in the *Sunday Times*:

> The impression I gained on my visit to these resettlement areas in the Transvaal merely fortified what I felt when I visited other such areas in Natal and in the Ciskei. The word 'resettlement' is a total misnomer. What the policy really means, in the vast majority of cases, is destruction of family life, of the community as a whole, and of the opportunity to earn a living. The whole policy of removals, of uprooting hundreds of thousands of people, is a disgrace to a so-called civilised country.

Equally depressing were the areas threatened with removal, the doomed 'Black spots' which were often inhabited by well-settled communities engaged in farming. These people were consumed with anxiety because they knew they were in danger of being uprooted and dumped into areas already overcrowded with impoverished people. Invariably, they were pushed into nearby 'independent' Bantustans, which meant that they lost their South African citizenship, thus making jobs even more difficult to find.

The Mathopestad community in the western Transvaal, consisting of about 2000 people, was one such example. Some twenty-two families had acquired the land by purchase in 1910 and their descendants had been there since. Together with Sheena Duncan, then president of the Black Sash, and two American friends who were staying with me at the time in Johannesburg – the late Barbara Watson, who became US ambassador to Sri Lanka, and her sister Grace, who is on the staff of the Department of Education in

Washington – I visited the little village, which was surrounded by fertile fields and pasture where cattle and sheep were grazing. We had a long and interesting talk with the leaders of the community. They told us they had deposed their chief, as he was collaborating with the government on the proposed removal to Onderstepoort, about forty-eight miles away. They claimed that the chief had been offered the farmhouse on the land where they were to be resettled.

Armed police accosted us after we left Mathopestad. They ordered us to follow them to the police station at the nearby dorp of Boons, to await the arrival of a policeman from the security branch who (they said) wished to question us on the purpose of our visit. The informer network had obviously alerted the local police to our presence in Mathopestad.

I left my bemused American visitors in the car while Sheena and I waited impatiently inside the charge office. Having ascertained that we were not under arrest, I told the officer that I would give the security policeman ten minutes to arrive. When he did not show up within that time, off we went and lunched at nearby Sun City, the Las Vegas of Southern Africa, in Bophuthatswana. We then visited Onderstepoort, the official destination of the Mathopestad people, with its rows of tin toilets, a primary school building and nothing else but barren land. I heard nothing further about the incident, except to learn later that the deposed chief (and probable informer) had been poisoned soon after by persons unknown. When I complained to the Minister of Police about the police action, he said they were just doing their duty to ensure we were not dangerous agitators.

Mathopestad has since been reprieved and its community continues with its peaceful pastoral and agricultural activities, no longer under the threat of removal.

The saga of the Black community at Driefontein in the Transvaal contains both tragedy and restitution. For over twenty years the people resisted attempts to remove them into KaNgwane and KwaZulu from the land they had owned since 1912, despite promises of adequate compensation for schools, houses, clinics and other facilities. Their fate appeared sealed when the government approved a plan to build a dam which would encroach on their land, but they continued to resist removal.

Their leader, Saul Mkhize, was shot dead in a confrontation with the police at a peaceful protest meeting at Driefontein in 1983. I knew Saul Mkhize well, as he had visited me at my home several times. He was a dignified man, very formal, always in his Sunday best and wearing a hat. I was devastated when I was phoned one morning and a voice said, 'They have shot Saul.' The policeman who killed Saul was charged with murder, but was acquitted. The family instituted a civil action and the Minister settled just before the case commenced. The family received R38,000 (£23,700)[8] in compensation. In August 1985 the community was informed that it would be allowed to remain at Driefontein.

The people of Mogopa had a long and very stressful battle to return to the lands from which they were forcibly evicted some years ago, and transferred to a dry and inhospitable area which they never considered their home. After persistent appeals to ministers, in which I was involved, and after numerous court cases initiated by the Black Sash and conducted by the Legal Resources Centre, the excellent organisation that handles public interest cases without charge, the Mogopa people were finally allowed to return to one of the two farms on which their ancestral homes were situated. The other farm, which was the main source of crop production, remained in the government's hands and was leased to White farmers for grazing purposes. The official explanation for this partial restitution was, cynically, because less than half the community originally removed had returned to Mogopa. Having no option, the rest of the community had settled elsewhere since the forced removal in 1984, but this should not have invalidated their claim to the entire land area once owned by the Mogopa people. The government's action in this – the highly sensitive issue of land appropriation – undermined confidence in the announced intentions to redress the wrongs of forced removals.

The Oukasie people were also threatened with forced removal. I visited Oukasie at the request of the residents in 1986 in order to assess the situation. They were a longstanding community which lived within walking distance of the little Afrikaans-speaking town of Brits in the Transvaal, where many of them were employed. Largely because the far-right Conservative Party was gaining control in that constituency, efforts were made to persuade the government to remove the Oukasie community to the newly established township of Lehlabile, some twelve miles from Brits, on the border of the 'independent' Black state of Bophuthatswana. This gave rise to the suspicion and fear among the Oukasie people that the area where they were to be moved was shortly going to be incorporated into Bophuthatswana, which would have meant losing their South African citizenship. The removal also meant, of course, for those who worked in Brits, a daily journey of about twelve miles each way to and from work.

Although there was much opposition to the proposed removal, some people moved voluntarily to escape police harassment. Some were attracted by the school and the clinic, and by other facilities such as reticulated water and flush toilets, which had been provided on each stand in the new 'resettlement' area. But the bulk of the community stood firm and resisted removal. They approached the Legal Resources Centre for advice and assistance, and I went to Oukasie with a lawyer from the Centre to meet the civil leaders and to see the township. It was obvious to me that although living conditions at Oukasie were hardly ideal, it was by no means a squatter camp as had been alleged in Parliament, since the community had been settled there since 1930.

The Legal Resources Centre carried out a feasibility study which showed there was no reason whatever why Oukasie could not be upgraded *in situ* at reasonable cost. Despite all this evidence, the government insisted that it intended to remove these people, hoping thereby to regain the support of the local Whites at the next election. The Oukasie story has a happy ending; eventually the township was allowed to remain, as a consequence of the reform moves in the 'New South Africa' after 1990.

In 1983 Ray Swart introduced a motion on behalf of the Progressive Federal Party protesting against the uprooting of Black communities. We called upon the government to abandon all future plans for forced removals. Ray pointed out that the seventy-five consolidation plans for KwaZulu would entail the further removal of some 300,000 people, and if 'Black spot' removals were added, some half a million more would be moved into the already impoverished and overcrowded KwaZulu

homeland. Errol Moorcroft, another Prog MP, who was
thoroughly familiar with the dismal conditions in the eastern Cape
and the Ciskei, gave a detailed analysis of the effects of removals
into resettlement areas on hundreds of thousands of people and of
the despair of those awaiting removal, such as the 32,000 who were
living in Duncan Village bordering on East London. He also
mentioned that some 660,000 other Blacks on farms and in 'Black
spots' in the eastern Cape were under threat of removal.

I dealt with the areas I was familiar with – those in the Transvaal
– and I stressed yet again the tragic consequences of forced
removals.

> There is hunger, sickness, despair and a deep sense of grievance,
> particularly on the part of people who are waiting to be removed,
> people who have occupied their land for decades . . . I refuse to call
> them resettlement areas. They do not resettle, they disrupt, they break
> up communities . . . They are given three days' rations. I want to know
> what happens on the fourth day . . . I appeal to the government to call
> an immediate halt to all plans for removals of all sorts.[9]

Our pleas were ignored. All in all, it is estimated that some
three million people were forcibly removed. This tragic saga is told
in detail by the Surplus Peoples' Project – a massive survey
conducted by a number of individuals and organisations in Cape
Town and also in the researches of TRAC, the Transvaal Rural
Action Committee, originally part of the Black Sash. When the
history of South Africa and of the National Party regime is written,
the ruthless disregard for human suffering caused by forced
removals will be one of the worst blots on the government's dismal
record.

Closely linked to the whole issue of forced removals was the
treatment meted out to the squatters in the western Cape. These
people were essentially refugees from poverty: the poverty in the
Transkei and Ciskei, so-called independent homelands, where the
land is desperately overcrowded and overstocked with cattle and
goats, and where there are very few jobs. They came to Cape
Town to seek a livelihood. Many, in fact, had been there for over
twenty years, usually illegally, as Cape Town fell within the area
declared in the mid-fifties to be a Coloured Labour Preference

Area. This meant that it was wellnigh impossible for Blacks to enter legally into Cape Town or any other town in the western Cape falling within this area, except as contract labourers. They could only take other jobs legally by producing a certificate from the Coloured Affairs Department stating that no Coloured person was available. Many thousands of Blacks spent their entire working lives dodging the police, or being arrested and jailed, and were then 'endorsed out' of the urban area and sent back to the Ciskei or Transkei. As there were no jobs available there, they returned to Cape Town where there was no accommodation, except single-sex hostels for contract workers. Inevitably, huge sprawling squatter camps developed in Cape Town and its environs. People erected pitiful shelters made of wattle branches and plastic sheets.

Night after night, the police and Bantu Administration Board officials moved in and tore down the shelters, leaving men, women and children exposed to the freezing rain and wind in the wet Cape winters. Many a morning my colleague Ken Andrew and I drove out to the shanty towns at dawn, having been alerted to a raid, in an attempt to curb police action. Week after week this ugly charade was played out. Year after year my colleagues and I raised the issue of the desperate shortage of accommodation for Blacks in the area, with special reference to Crossroads, some nine miles from Cape Town, where about 80,000 people lived under primitive conditions in home-made shacks of corrugated iron and wood.

We finally extracted an announcement from Piet Koornhof, Minister of Co-operation and Development, that a new township for Blacks was being laid out at Khayelitsha, some eighteen miles from Cape Town, where it was intended that the people from Crossroads would move. Blacks would also be moved, however, from the long-established Cape Town townships of Nyanga, Langa and Guguletu – the condition insisted on by local Nat MPs before they would agree to a new township for Blacks in the Cape. Khayelitsha was being rapidly prepared for the people who would live there. Bush was cleared and roads laid out; there was even a mobile post office for the inhabitants of the ten iron structures erected as temporary housing. That was in 1983.

But however much of a slum it was, Crossroads was where the

people wanted to stay, mainly because of its proximity to the city and to jobs. Moreover, it had evolved into a community, although much harassed by warlords who demanded payment for each site and a monthly levy per family. They used threats, intimidation and violence to enforce their mafia-like operations. In 1985 Crossroads erupted, because of a rumour that a squad of Black men from the Transvaal was being brought in to effect the forcible removal of the people from Crossroads to Khayelitsha. A major riot took place. The Crossroads people put up barricades and set fire to any vehicle entering the area.

Five Prog MPs, including myself, went to see what was happening. We found ourselves in the *mêlée*, watching the crowd heaving stones at the police, who were firing back at them. It was a very ugly scene, and we were perturbed to find that the new Minister of Co-operation and Development, Dr Gerrit Viljoen, whom we had warned to expect serious trouble at Crossroads, was apparently unaware of the crisis. We saw him the following day and put several issues to him. We warned that there would be a bloodbath and that he had to fulfil some of the promises to improve Crossroads made by his predecessor, Koornhof. More particularly, transport should be subsidised, since the present cost of R1.65 each way from Khayelitsha to Cape Town was totally excessive for casual labourers who were lucky to earn R10 a day. And of course the crucial issue was to legalise the presence of those who had come to Cape Town many years before from the Transkei and Ciskei and who had never been allowed to register as legal residents.

Ray Swart, in a debate on a matter of urgent public importance, correctly described Crossroads as 'a legacy of the failed Coloured Labour Preference Area scheme'. A Conservative Party MP said, 'The time has come for the South African Police to be given the green light to enforce the laws of this country, and they must not have to bend the enforcement of these laws in specific circumstances for political purposes.' My reply was that there could be only one interpretation of what he had said, and that was 'to give the police the green light to shoot people and that is absolutely disgusting'. I added:

Nothing had been learned from the lessons of Sharpeville and Soweto. When my colleagues and I went to Crossroads when the rioting was in full spate, what did we see? We saw police, absolutely unprotected, standing in the street, shooting at crowds who were throwing stones at them. Of the 18 people who were killed, 3 were under the age of 12, of the 228 who were injured, 11 were under the age of 12, 17 were injured by rubber bullets, including an 11-year old child whose jawbone was fractured by a rubber bullet.[10]

I then brandished a rubber bullet – a lethal weapon indeed, three inches long, one and a half inches in diameter. Some Nationalist MPs were clearly taken aback at the sight of this menacing missile, but one interjected: 'A rubber bullet is a lot softer than the stones which were thrown at peace-loving citizens of this country'[11] – quite ignoring the velocity factor involved when a rubber bullet was fired from a gun.

Later that year, I was invited to visit the police training centre at Maleoskop in the northern Transvaal to see for myself the type of riot-control training given to the police. During the course of the morning, I was asked if I would like to fire a rubber bullet and I foolishly agreed to do so. As I raised the gun, I saw a television camera trained on me and I knew the picture of Mrs Suzman trying out this lethal weapon would be shown to astonished citizens that evening on the television news. And of course it was. I received a number of reproachful letters from liberals, and had to reassure them I had not transferred my sympathies to the riot police.

As for Crossroads and the Cape Town townships, some concessions were made. Today more than half a million Blacks live at Khayelitsha, mostly in abysmal conditions, but they are no longer harassed by Pass Laws. Graffiti on a wall in Cape Town sums up the situation: 'The rich get richer, and the poor get Khayelitsha!'

Civil disturbances were not limited to South Africa itself, but also took place in the so-called independent Black states and other neighbouring territories. Thus I had reason to say some very hard things about Lennox Sebe, Chief Minister of Ciskei. This arose out of a boycott of the buses, owned by a Ciskeian firm, which served the Black township, Mdantsane, on the border of the city of East London, in the eastern Cape. Mdantsane had been declared part of the Ciskei, much to the fury of the inhabitants, most of whom worked in East London. The bus fares went up, the people started using the trains, and Sebe sent his police toughs to beat up those who refused to use the buses. Hundreds were detained and trade unionists were locked up.

During the 1983 debate on Law and Order, I said that one of the many indictments against the South African government would be that they had subjected hundreds of thousands of people to the vicious rule of Sebe. This was published in the newspapers, and I received a letter from Sebe expressing his dismay, and saying, 'Come and see for yourself. I guarantee you safe passage in my country!' In fact, I *had* seen for myself a year or two earlier when several of us went by minibus on a personally conducted tour led by Prog MP Errol Moorcroft through the Ciskei, visiting resettlement areas where Blacks had been dumped.

Nevertheless I accepted Sebe's invitation, and later that year several of us again visited the Ciskei. We received VIP treatment; two helicopters awaited us at East London airport and we were whirled around for two days, bucketing in a high wind, from one end of the Ciskei to the other. One of the passengers became so sick that we had to land and let him off in a field. We saw a great many projects: irrigation schemes and industries, all existing because of vastly uneconomic incentive schemes, like low rail tariffs, tax exemptions and wage subsidies from the South African government. There was a huge foundry making heavy mining parts, which were shipped directly to America. Dimbaza, which had been the subject of so much adverse publicity, had become a showplace, with factories, schools, shops and a clinic. At Mdantsane there was an enormous clothing factory employing 3000 women, making blouses which were exported to the US and could be bought, the manager told me, at Macy's in New York. Of course, it was the low wages that made these extraordinary arrangements feasible. The South African government, or rather the taxpayers, paid the total wages bill, which was up to R110 per month per worker, for seven years. But what would happen when the subsidies were removed, we wondered? Investors in for a quick profit would get out and these uneconomic industries would collapse. Of course all this stemmed from Influx Control which restricted Blacks from entering and getting jobs in the Republic's established industrial areas.

Other homelands had other problems. A few years later, in 1986, I received an urgent call from a Lutheran priest in Pretoria about the tension in Moutse, then part of the non-independent Lebowa territory, but about to be transferred to KwaNdebele, which was destined to become independent. This was yet another example of high-handedness by the government, and there appeared to be no hope that it would reverse the decision. Moutse was to be incorporated into KwaNdebele and placed under the jurisdiction of Chief Minister Skhozana of KwaNdebele, a shady character who, according to rumour, had his eye on all the liquor store licences in the area and ran a mafia operation. I knew about Moutse, as I had been involved ever since receiving a deputation of its leading citizens. On their behalf, I had approached a series of government officials and ministers, but without success. I warned that the treatment of these people was a recipe for disaster, and sadly I was right. I decided to see for myself, and drove out there with some Black Sash women, a 3–4 hour journey from Johannesburg. All we heard there were tales of death, destruction and savage treatment of dissidents. The Moutse affair was an outrage.

Eventually, through the Black Sash, the Moutse grievances were referred to the Legal Resources Centre, which went to court. The court found that the incorporation was illegal, because Parliament had not first given its consent. The government tried to change the law, but in 1990 conceded, as part of the reform programme, that Moutse would remain part of Lebowa.

There were also many problems beyond our borders. The end of the Portuguese regime in Mozambique in 1974 had been followed by a devastating civil war. An attempt to end it was made by an enforced political settlement ten years later, and in March 1984 I travelled to Nkomati on the Mozambique–South African border to witness the signing of the Accord between President Machel of Mozambique and President Botha of South Africa.

I wrote to my daughters in March 1984:

Big deal. En route there I sat next to the Chief of Police, who gave me a glib spiel about the need to win the hearts and minds of the people, and said that South Africa could not just use force in these circumstances. I was reminded of the famous saying of President Johnson, 'When you've got 'em by the balls, the hearts and minds follow soon after.' This I think was exactly what was happening to Mozambique. It was on its knees – to use another part of the anatomy. It has been destabilised by South Africa which supported the rebel movement Renamo in its guerrilla tactics: Renamo keeps cutting the railway line, blowing up the hydroelectric installation of Cabora Bassa and terrorising the villagers. So now Machel had no option but to accede to South Africa's demand not to allow the ANC to operate from Mozambique.

Anyway, anything that goes for peace in Southern Africa was, I supposed, to be welcomed, so I set off together with Van Zyl, Colin and three other PFP colleagues to witness the great ceremony . . . all carried out with military precision. We travelled by plane, bus and train and finally reached the banks of the Komati River. It was as hot as hell, and we sat for over two hours in the blazing sun under a sort of gauze canopy, watching the ceremony. There were guards of honour from the South African Army and the Mozambique Defence Force and the men kept keeling over at regular intervals, but other than that nothing untoward happened. It seemed to me looking around and seeing all the military personnel present, that the only way anyone could have done anything to disrupt the proceedings would have been to have disguised himself as a crocodile and swum up the Komati River to the site of the signing of the Accord with a time bomb in his mouth.

Later that year, I extended my 'see for yourself' practice to the western wartorn side of southern Africa. We boarded a sinister-looking Shackleton plane on a two-day official visit to the operational area on the Namibia–Angola border. We were a motley group from all parties, accompanied by top brass from the army, headed by General Constand Viljoen and a bevy of brigadiers who came along as escorts. It was well organised and the army did its best to show us they were doing their job.

We started off at Katima Mulilo, the farthermost corner of the Eastern Caprivi, where it meets with Zambia, Angola and Namibia, and spent the night at the base camp. A VIP bungalow was allocated to Molly Blackburn, PFP member of the Provincial Council and me. We were looked after very tenderly by a female colonel and plied with much food and drink. There was a braaivleis [barbecue] every night and we were up at 5.30 each morning. The next day we moved on from base to base, starting with Wenela, where the South African marines patrolled up and down the Okavango River, the border between Angola and Namibia. We went on to Mpacha Air Force Base, and to Omega, where South Africa had a Bushman camp, using hundreds of these little men as trackers against SWAPO infiltrators from Angola. They were paid the unusually high wage of R500 a month each. There was nothing to spend the money on, so apparently there are great boxes of bank notes cunningly concealed all over the place, probably being devoured by white ants. What on earth would happen to these Bushmen, originally refugees from Angola, if and when the war ever ended, nobody seemed to know. On being asked this question at one of the briefing meetings, the officer commanding that area gazed into the distance and said, 'We will not let them down.' (I understand they are now billeted in a remote area in the northern Cape.)

I asked about atrocities allegedly committed by the armed forces, and the answer was 'Well, they took place, but if reported, were investigated, and if offenders were found guilty, they were punished.' The top brass said they heartily disapproved of such atrocities and indeed that their policy was just the opposite, as they believed they must win over the local population. Just how true and how successful this would be, remained to be seen. I was convinced that in an election, SWAPO would win. Numbers must tell – 52 per cent of the population were Ovambos; there are only about 80,000 Whites out of a total of a million people, and the other eight or nine ethnic groups are relatively small.

Our next stop was Oshakati, the Ovamboland military head-quarters, a very big base indeed. Molly, the lady colonel and I were covered in clouds of dust on every journey, as we travelled either in a combi minibus or in an open vehicle known as a Samel.

Later in 1984 I went on another visit to Mozambique, this time to Maputo at the invitation of the Journalists Association of Mozambique. I took Colin Eglin and Ray Swart with me. I had a sad, nostalgic feeling when we arrived at the Polana Hotel, remembering holiday visits there many years before. The Polana was a poor shadow of its former grand self. The rooms were shabby, with worn carpets; the food was awful. The city was run down and the shops were empty. Everywhere there were food queues. Despite all, there was a spirit of optimism and everybody believed that since South Africa had signed the Nkomati Peace Accord, the economy would get going again, if only the MNR (Renamo) could be eliminated. People were hopeful that tourism would return, that the port of Maputo would once again function as a major import and export outlet, that the railway would resume its former important role in southern Africa and that the mines in South Africa would employ more labour from Mozambique.

To me the best thing about Mozambique was its totally non-racial society. Many White Portuguese who had supported Frelimo now occupied key jobs in the administration. But being a Marxist state, it was of course bureaucratic to its fingertips, which was not for the likes of me – more than enough of that at home!

No one is in any doubt that South Africa supported Renamo before the Accord. Some contend that this support still continues on unofficial levels, and the location of the huge ammunition caches which have kept the bandits going have not been revealed. Mozambique's recovery has been tragically slow, as the depredations of Renamo continue. Hundreds of thousands of refugees have fled into neighbouring countries. To reach South Africa these desperate people walked great distances through the Kruger National Park (game reserve) and had to penetrate an electrified fence which they call the 'snake'. Many died en route. Those who survive the physical dangers are confronted with the ever-present possibility of being sent back as illegal immigrants.

Despite the Nkomati Accord, the civil war in Mozambique raged on with a death toll of some 600,000 people during the sixteen years it lasted. It is to be hoped that the Peace Accord signed in Rome in October 1992 between President Chissano and Renamo leader Alfonso Dhlakama will eventually bring peace to the sorely tried people of Mozambique. Up to the present, this hope has not been fulfilled.

12

Three Martyrs:
Sobukwe; Biko; Aggett

Robert Sobukwe was born in 1924 in Graaff Reinet, a small town in the Karoo, a semi-desert area in the eastern Cape. He was the youngest child in a large Methodist family, and attended a missionary school where he completed a three-year teachers' training course. He then went to Fort Hare University College where he took a BA degree. Thereafter he taught at a town in the Transvaal and was National Secretary of the Youth League of the ANC. He was later appointed an assistant in the Department of Bantu Languages at Witwatersrand University, and acquired an Honours degree.

By 1958 a serious split had developed in the ANC. The Africanist Movement, which objected to White communist influence within the ANC and to too much co-operation with other racial groups, broke away. Six months later the Pan-Africanist Congress (PAC) was formed with Robert Sobukwe as its president; its main aim was to rally the African people into one united front on the basis of African nationalism. It pledged to fight for the overthrow of White domination: its slogan was 'Service, Sacrifice, Suffering'. On 21 March 1960 the defiance campaign against the Pass Laws was launched by the PAC. It was to take the form of a non-violent protest, with Blacks handing in their passes at police stations, demanding arrest and refusing bail. At Sharpeville, as I have related, the confrontation between the police and a crowd of some 6000 Blacks resulted in 69 deaths and more than 180 injured. Mass demonstrations and violence followed throughout the country.

Sobukwe and twenty-two other leading PAC members were arrested and charged under the 1952 Act passed to break an earlier defiance campaign. Sobukwe was sentenced to three years' imprisonment, while the others received sentences ranging from eighteen months to two years. A state of emergency was declared, and the ANC and PAC were banned.

In 1963 a law was introduced aimed specifically at Sobukwe. Section 4 of the General Laws Amendment Act empowered the Minister of Justice to impose additional terms of imprisonment after a prisoner had served his sentence. Introducing the law Vorster explained:

> I want to tell Honourable Members why we are inserting this clause. We may find it necessary. Sobukwe will have served his sentence on 3 May. He was the leader of the PAC and I can tell Honourable Members there has been no change in him during the time he has not been in our midst. If the government comes to the conclusion that it would be failing in its duty to the peaceful citizenry if it were to set this man free, this clause will be used to keep him there longer. For here we are dealing with a person – let me say this – who has a strong magnetic personality, a person who can organise, a person who feels that he has a vocation to perform this task, well knowing what methods will be applied.[1]

Robert Sobukwe was the only person that law was used against during the six years it was in operation; it became known as the Sobukwe Clause. (When the government finally decided to release Sobukwe from Robben Island in 1972, that law was suspended.)

As with Nelson Mandela, I did not meet Sobukwe until I visited him on Robben Island. By then he was well into an additional six-year term of imprisonment. I found him living in a small, isolated cottage on the island in the sole company of a taciturn White warder with whom he could not communicate. He was not allowed contact with any of the other prisoners, although there were at that stage many educated political prisoners on the island, such as Mandela, Sisulu and others with whom he might have found common cause. Sobukwe had books to read, supplied to him mainly by his friend Benjamin Pogrund, deputy editor of the *Rand Daily Mail*, and he also had a radio. He told me that as there was no one to talk to he felt he was forgetting how to express himself.

I raised Sobukwe's case every year in Parliament, but to little avail. The government said his wife and children would be allowed to spend a fortnight twice a year with him on the Island, hardly adequate compensation for the freedom to which he was entitled, having served his initial sentence. In 1972 he was finally released, but was immediately banned and restricted to Kimberley, which was not his home town, and while he was there, he obtained a law degree. He was not permitted to leave the district.

The next time I saw Sobukwe was at Groote Schuur Hospital in Cape Town where he had been admitted suffering from terminal cancer. I was accompanied by my friend, Moira Henderson, who had looked after Sobukwe and his family during those years. She was in charge of the Dependants' Conference, an organisation financed by the South African Council of Churches, which had acquired a house in Cape Town where the families of prisoners on Robben Island and elsewhere could stay when they came to visit their relatives.

It was our last meeting. His calm, thoughtful appraisal of the political situation was remarkable coming from a man who had been so ruthlessly treated by the government, and who clearly did not have long to live. Our conversation ranged over many subjects; he showed no extremism, only sadness and intense dismay about the deterioration of race relations in our country. I was struck by his quiet dignity and his lack of bitterness about a wasted life which he knew was nearing its end. Perhaps he also knew that although he could be banned, his ideas could not be banned and would live on in the minds of young Blacks. He died in Kimberley a few months later.

On 12 March 1978 Moira and I attended Sobukwe's funeral at his birth place Graaff Reinet. Sobukwe's wife, Veronica, had asked if I would deliver an address at the funeral; I agreed to do so and spent some time preparing it. Benjy Pogrund and his wife Ann were also there; they were close personal friends of Sobukwe, had looked after him devotedly during his years in prison, written to him regularly and sent him parcels. They had also cared for him in his last illness. Benjy had also been asked to speak at the funeral.

When we arrived at Graaff Reinet, we were told that the young Black PAC members had taken over the arrangements and had decided they did not want any Whites to give the funeral addresses. This was part of the rejection by young politicised Blacks of White liberals, and I accepted it; it was something I had been expecting for years. I just said, 'OK, if that's what they want. That's fine with me.' Understandably, Benjy was extremely upset; he had prepared a long and heartfelt address about his revered friend.

The funeral was held at the agricultural show grounds just outside the town, with a platform in the middle of the grounds for the family and special guests. Since I was not going to be allowed to deliver my speech, I took a place on the stands with the general public. There I sat in an isolated little group of Whites among a huge crowd of Blacks, when one of the Black priests, who had been on the platform, came across the field to us. He beckoned to me and said, 'We'd like you to come on to the platform, Mrs Suzman.'

'Well, are you absolutely sure about that?' I asked. 'Because I'm perfectly happy to stay here.'

'No, no,' he said, 'we really would like you to come on to the platform, and there's room for one other.'

'You come with me,' I said to Moira. So off we went across the field, on to the platform, where we found ourselves seated together with the Pogrunds and a number of other people, White and Black.

There were several ambassadors who had come to Graaff Reinet for the funeral of this high-profile man, and I noticed that among the people on the platform was Gatsha Buthelezi, Chief Minister of KwaZulu. As we sat waiting, there was a sudden sound of chanting and a procession marched along behind the field. It consisted of a large number of Blacks bearing Sobukwe's coffin, singing as they came. Funerals are always very big emotional events in the Black community in South Africa, and as I have said – since outdoor meetings other than sporting events and funerals were banned – they inevitably became political protest meetings which continued for hours. As a result, many went to the funerals of people they did not know. Sobukwe was a public figure, so his funeral drew a large crowd from all over the country. Bus-load after bus-load of people came to this remote little country town to pay their last respects.

The procession came on to the field, and the coffin was laid at Mrs Sobukwe's feet on the platform. Then the bearers caught sight of Buthelezi, and almost immediately there was uproar. They started yelling, 'Gatsha out, Gatsha out, Gatsha out!' It became very nasty, because they began advancing towards the platform. The moving throng took not the slightest notice of us; the American ambassador was hustled off the stage by his aides, who did not want him involved in any fracas. The Transkeian representative and members of the Coloured Representative Council were ejected, all in disfavour with the PAC as was Buthelezi, dubbed 'collaborators' with the Nationalist government. There was a very ugly scene. Gatsha left hastily with his aide, who fired one shot into the air. The funeral service was then allowed to begin and continued for five hours under a blazing sun. There were no police in sight; they sensibly kept a low profile. Buthelezi was deeply offended when a press report about this humiliating incident implied that I had written off his leadership in the urban areas. What I had in fact said was that militant young Black radicals in the cities were antagonistic towards him because he was working within the system. The *Argus* of 24 April 1980 carried a headline, 'Inkatha Chief in Slashing Attack on White Liberals'. It reported Buthelezi's remarks in the KwaZulu Assembly about me, Alan Paton and other 'super liberals', who he said 'were determined as ever to do the thinking for "us Kaffirs" '.

I wrote to him to express my indignation at this unjustifiable attack, and had a very long reply in which he accused me of being negative towards him, of making anti-Buthelezi remarks at home and abroad, and of sharing platforms with those who denigrated him. He also said that I had personally contributed to an image of the PFP's being more identified with Black Consciousness protest politics than with Inkatha's constituency politics – none of which was true.

One cannot help wondering what the situation in South Africa would have been like today if Robert Sobukwe had been able to use his considerable talents and ability during the challenging years of the seventies instead of being forced into the twilight existence of a banned person. Released from prison, he was banned under the Suppression of Communism Act – though not only had he never encouraged or advocated communism, but he had broken away from the oldest African political movement on the continent, the ANC, because, *inter alia*, he felt it was falling under the influence of communists. Furthermore, it was only after he was sent to prison and his organisation banned and forced into exile, that the PAC abandoned the policy of non-violence, as Robert Sobukwe had previously advocated.

Even after his death, certain restrictions still obtained. It was forbidden to quote anything he had said or written when he was alive. The silencing of this man thus continued beyond the grave.

★

The vacuum in Black leadership in the sixties caused by the imprisonment of Nelson Mandela and the banning of Robert Sobukwe was filled by a young man who founded the Black Consciousness movement.

Stephen Bantu Biko was born in King William's Town in the eastern Cape in 1946. He matriculated at a Catholic mission school in Natal and began medical studies at the University of Natal in 1966, but his political activities led to low grades and exclusion from medical school. By then he had become a full-time organiser for the South African Students Organisation (SASO), a breakaway body from the multiracial National Union of South African Students (NUSAS). He also organised the Black Community Programmes. In 1973, he was banned and restricted to the King William's Town magisterial district. Among the projects sponsored by the Black Community Programme of which Biko was now the director, was a health programme, the Zanempilo Clinic run by Dr Mamphela Ramphele – one of the few Black women doctors in South Africa – Biko's close friend and mother of his child. As I have stated, Dr Ramphele was later banned and restricted to Tzaneen, a remote area in the northern Transvaal, hundreds of miles from King William's Town.

I never met Steve Biko. Donald Woods, my good friend from his days as a parliamentary correspondent, had a close relationship with him. He thought it absurd that Biko and I did not know each other since I was the only MP elected on a policy which rejected race discrimination, and Biko was an acknowledged Black leader. Donald arranged for us to meet, but it was not to be.

Steve Biko and a friend, a Coloured man, Peter Jones, were stopped en route to Cape Town by car. Both were detained on 18 August 1977 under Section 6 of the Terrorism Act, which gave the police powers to hold people in solitary confinement indefinitely. Biko was held at the Walmer police station in Port Elizabeth. On 6 September he was taken by the security police to a building in Port Elizabeth, interrogated by ten security police officers for forty-eight hours, and returned to the police cells after a couple of days in the prison hospital. Biko never emerged from detention. He was transferred to Pretoria Central Prison over 750 miles away, in the back of a Land Rover. He died in the prison hospital on 12 September 1977, aged thirty.

A few days later, I received a phone call from an old friend, Dr Jonathan Gluckman, an eminent pathologist called in by the lawyers acting for the Biko family. On their instructions, John had performed a postmortem on Biko. His words were stark and shocking; 'Helen,' he said, 'they murdered him.'

I attended a few sessions of the Biko inquest, which began on 14 November 1977, in Pretoria in the Old Synagogue, which had been converted into a court. Sydney Kentridge was the advocate appearing for the family. I particularly remember his cross-examination of one of the security policemen who was part of the interrogating team when Biko was murdered. Kentridge asked him whether he had thought Biko was shamming illness when he had found him lying in a pool of urine. The young policeman simply looked straight at the magistrate and said in Afrikaans, 'Ja, jou Edele, ek het so gedink.' [Yes, your honour, I did think so.] Kentridge then asked: 'And when you found Biko sitting fully clothed in a bathtub full of water, did you still think he was shamming?' Again he replied: 'Ja, jou Edele, ek het so gedink.' And when Kentridge finally asked, 'And tell me, now that Biko is dead, do you still think he was shamming?' the policeman answered yet again: 'Ja, jou Edele, ek het so gedink.' It was an unforgettable scene.

Steve Biko's funeral was an enormous event, held at his birthplace, King William's Town, on 25 September 1977. I went with two of my Prog colleagues, Alex Boraine and Zach de Beer. The ceremony took place in a football stadium on the outskirts of the town. We were escorted to a stand where a number of diplomats were already seated. We sat down on the lowest rung of the stand as the grounds gradually filled with people who arrived on buses throughout the morning. They stood on the field because it had rained the night before and the ground was sodden. As a result we couldn't see anything that was happening on the platform because it was in the middle of the field, with only a slightly raised dais. So I said to Zach, 'This is ridiculous. We haven't come all this way just to look at the backs of people. Let's work our way up to the front, so that we can see what's going on.'

So we started pushing our way through the huge crowd, with no problems at first. It was only when we got near the front, where the field was much more tightly packed with people, that my polite request – 'Excuse me, may we get through?' – met with resistance. A young Black man standing nearby objected, in a very hostile voice: 'No, you may not. We don't want you Whites here.' So I turned to hm and said, 'Look, we didn't come here to fight with you. We came here to pay our respects to Steve Biko. Would you please let us through?' 'Certainly not,' he said, 'you go and talk to Vorster, and you go and talk to Jimmy Kruger, we don't need you to come here and talk to us.' He then said a few words in Xhosa, which I did not understand, but they were obviously, 'Don't let them through', because the crowd just closed in around us.

We could hardly move. I got very angry, and turned and said, 'Look here. I didn't come all this way to fight with you. I'm Helen Suzman, and I've come here to pay my respects to Steve Biko.'

'Who did you say you are?' he asked.

'I'm Helen Suzman.'

'You prove that!' I opened my handbag – with great difficulty, because my elbows were pinned to my sides by then – and extracted a credit card which had my name on it (plastic money has many uses!). He looked at it and he said, 'Mrs Suzman, I beg your pardon. You may certainly go through.' He said another few words in Xhosa, and the crowd parted like the Red Sea, and Zach and I walked through to the platform. Zach said, 'Well, now I've seen everything.'

When we reached the front, we were asked to go on the platform, but no sooner had we climbed on it than it collapsed. However, it was not a bad fall – only a few feet. We sat there in pouring rain and watched the entire impressive ceremony. All in all, it was an amazing morning, with the vast crowd of about 20,000 Blacks singing their heads off. Many of the songs were in Xhosa and, according to an interpreter, included phrases like 'Kruger is a dog. Vorster is a dog.'

A few months later when I faced Kruger, Minister of Justice, Prisons and Police, in Parliament I insisted that the blame and responsibility for Biko's death lay fairly and squarely at his feet.[2] The inquest showed that Biko had died as a result of being struck on the head, causing extensive brain damage. However, the Chief Magistrate, M. J. Prins, refused to attribute blame: 'The available evidence does not prove that the death was brought about by any act of omission involving or amounting to an offence on the part of any person.' I infuriated government Members by saying that I wanted to place on record my utter astonishment at the findings of the inquest into Biko's death.

There followed an exchange between a Nat Member and me:

'Have you read it all?'

'Yes,' I said, 'I have read the entire court report from page one to the end.'

'Do you accept the findings as correct?'

'No,' I said, 'I do not accept those findings. And I do not believe that any reasonable person who has read the court record would accept those findings. Indeed Sir David Napley, the eminent lawyer brought out from England by the Association of Law Societies of South Africa as an independent observer at the Biko inquest, also makes it very clear in his report that he does not accept the findings.'

I continued:

I was extremely surprised at the fact that the magistrate gave no motivation for his findings and simply in a matter of minutes handed down his findings on a matter which had been the subject of a most exhaustive enquiry in his court for two full weeks. But now, whatever the outcome of the inquest and the findings on Steve Biko, one thing is absolutely certain, and that is that nobody is under any illusions any more about the sort of treatment which is meted out to the unfortunate people held in detention in solitary confinement by the security police under Section 6 of the dreaded Terrorism Act.

'That is a shocking remark,' said the Member. I replied:

> What is shocking is the way Steve Biko was treated. What is shocking is the callous and inhuman treatment that was handed out to a man, helpless, in solitary confinement, in the hands of the security police. He was kept naked for days on end, he was kept in handcuffs and in leg irons, manacled by one leg to an iron grille in security headquarters. And later when the man was already gravely ill, he was conveyed 750 miles in the back of a van, unconscious and naked, lying on a mat with just a blanket to cover him and delivered to the prison hospital in Pretoria. I want to know what justification there could be for meting out such treatment to this man, even if he was supposedly shamming illness. He shammed so successfully that he was dead in less than forty-eight hours after he left Port Elizabeth.[3]

I asked what sort of condonation came from the top for all and any kind of conduct by the security branch. I said that the colonel in charge of this case (Colonel Goosen), had the gall to tell the inquest court, when asked specifically to name the statutory authority allowing him to keep a man in chains, that his branch of the police did not work under the statutes.

I then dealt with Kruger himself, quoting first the hunger strike story, about which the Minister had issued an official statement. He was reported by the South African Press Association (SAPA) as saying on 12 September: 'Mr Biko, the honorary president of the Black People's Convention, died in detention in Pretoria last night after being on a hunger strike.' Then on 14 September, in his speech to the National Party congress in Pretoria, he made the notorious remark: 'Dit laat my koud' [It leaves me cold], which for sheer callousness outdoes Marie-Antoinette's 'Let them eat cake'. He also shared a tasteless little joke with one of the delegates about its being a man's democratic right to starve himself to death. However, two days later, Kruger changed his entire story, because he had by then been given some preliminary post-mortem findings. Prime Minister Vorster had probably ticked Kruger off for his misleading statement at the congress two days earlier, when he asserted that a hunger strike caused Biko's death. Kruger later denied that he had said this, although every newspaper in the country had interpreted his statement as meaning just that.

Kruger had also said to the press that 'Heads may roll' – presumably security police heads. He said he was not protecting anybody. I asked him what heads had rolled, what had he done about the security policemen who had made a number of inaccurate statements under oath? What had he done about the security policemen who clearly did not obey their own regulations? Would he tell us how it was that the security police could overrule medical instructions about prisoners? Would he tell us why the next of kin had not been informed when Biko became ill? Had Colonel Goosen been given the high jump? Had any other security policemen who thought they were a law unto themselves been given the high jump and how many heads in the security branch had rolled as a result of the disgusting revelations at the inquest?

I said Kruger should be declared a disaster area, and that he was totally unsuitable to hold the portfolios of Justice and Police and should be chucked out. Later in the session, I moved the reduction of his salary, the ultimate censure on a minister, with the usual unsuccessful result.

Although Kruger started the session in a rather subdued mood, he was a good recoverer and by the end of the session was his usual hectoring self, informing us that he was sick and tired of the Biko affair and that as far as he was concerned, he had uttered his last word on the subject. I said it was a pity he had ever uttered his first words on the subject ('It leaves me cold') when news of Biko's death became public. I also told him that, like Macbeth, he could cry 'Hence, horrible shadow!' but that the ghost of Biko, like that of Banquo, would not so easily disappear, and would haunt South Africa for a long time to come.

Finally I asked him to tell us what had happened to Peter Jones, the man arrested with Biko on 18 August. 'Where is he, why is he not being charged? More important, how is he?'[4] There was no reply to my question. (Peter Jones was eventually released, unharmed, but banned and restricted to Somerset West near Cape Town. I managed to get him a job there subsequently.)

Despite the findings of the magistrate at the inquest in 1978, the Biko family was awarded an out-of-court settlement of R65,000,

(£36,400), surely a tacit admission of the state's responsibility for the death of a young man who was in good health when taken into police custody and who was dead soon after he was interrogated. Shortly afterwards Donald Woods was banned. The restrictions made it impossible for him to continue to write or to remain editor of the East London *Daily Dispatch*, and his passionate articles denouncing the appalling manner of Biko's death could no longer be published. Donald, his wife Wendy and their five children left South Africa in a dramatic escape. His story and Biko's were the inspiration for Richard Attenborough's moving film, *Cry Freedom*.

The two doctors who attended Biko during his detention, both district surgeons, deserve special dishonourable mention for the shameful way they treated their patient. Drs Ivor Lang and Benjamin Tucker took instructions from the security police, and accepted their version that Biko was shamming. They failed to insist that he be transferred to a hospital, where treatment might have saved his life. Dr Lang issued a misleading medical certificate and falsified the bed–letter (patient's record attached to the bed). They should have been disciplined by the South African Medical and Dental Council as soon as their unprofessional conduct became known at the inquest. Instead the disciplinary committee decided, more than two and half years after Biko's death, that there was no *prima facie* case against the two doctors.

In November 1984 a group of six prominent doctors and academics took the matter to court, and the South African Medical and Dental Council was compelled by court order to review and set aside the disciplinary committee's decision and to hold an enquiry. Eight months later, Dr Tucker was found guilty on ten counts of misconduct. He was suspended from the medical register for three months, the sentence suspended for two years. Dr Lang was found guilty on eight counts of improper conduct. He was cautioned and discharged.[5]

Dr Phillip Tobias, head of the Department of Anatomy at Wits, who was one of the six crusading doctors, commented that irreparable harm had been done abroad to the image of the South African medical profession by the eight-year delay in enquiring into the professional conduct of Drs Lang and Tucker. I said that the sentences handed down were superficial and astonishing, in view of the fact that the doctors had been found guilty of disgraceful conduct. In October 1985 the full South African Medical and Dental Council of South Africa ordered Dr Tucker struck off the medical register.

Six years later – fourteen years after the death of Steve Biko – Dr Tucker presented the council with an affidavit in support of his application to be restored to the medical roll. In it he said that the shame of his misconduct had forced him to live almost as a recluse since he had been struck off. 'I have largely withdrawn from public and social life,' he said. 'Any contact outside my usual circle of family and friends invariably results in my part in the death of the late Mr Biko being raised again and the old wounds being reopened.' He said he had been unemployed since his name was struck from the register. 'I cannot stress too much the humiliation and constant abuse which my family and I have suffered since the inquest into the death of the late Mr Biko.' In the affidavit Dr Tucker disclosed that he had become 'too closely identified with the interest of the organs of the state, especially the police force', and that this prevented him from acting with the 'fearless independence' required of a medical practitioner. The affidavit went on to say: 'I have suffered for many years under the weight of the knowledge that my part in the late Mr Biko's death has caused well-nigh irreparable harm to the medical profession and my country, but this is a load which I have come to accept in the recognition of my failure.' The South African Medical and Dental Council agreed to restore Dr Benjamin Tucker's name to the medical register, on payment of R100.

★

On 3 February 1982, the Minister of Police, le Grange, told Parliament that 'Detainees in police cells or in prison are being detained under the most favourable conditions possible. All reasonable precautions are being taken to prevent any of them being injured in some way or from committing suicide.' He went on to say that 'during the past two and a half years there has not been a serious case of this nature and everything possible is being done to prevent anything irresponsible happening to these people while they are in detention.'[6] The following day I asked whether he could give us 'the categorical assurance that methods of interrogation that had been declared to be in breach of Article 3 of the European Convention of Human Rights by the European Court of Human Rights were not being used on detainees in South Africa?'[7] I said those methods included standing for long periods of time, hooding, subjection to noise, deprivation of sleep and of food and drink. I added a further method – the use of electric shock. I did not get this categorical assurance; all the Minister would say was, 'Carry on. I am listening to you.'

However, within forty-eight hours the Minister's original statement was nullified by the tragic death of Dr Neil Aggett while in detention at police headquarters in John Vorster Square, Johannesburg. On 5 February at 1.30 a. m., he was found hanged in his cell.

Neil Aggett was born in Kenya and came to South Africa at an early age with his parents. He qualified as a doctor at the University of Cape Town, and thereafter became involved in trade union activities and workmen's compensation cases, serving as medical adviser to the Black Food and Canning Workers' Union. He was arrested and detained under Section 6 of the Terrorism Act on 27 November 1981.

I was contacted by the sister of a detainee in the same section of John Vorster Square as Aggett. She phoned me to say she had some very important information for me and would motor to Cape Town to give me a letter. There was a good deal of cloak-and-dagger business about all of this, and we met at night in the centre of Cape Town where she handed me a letter from her brother which had been smuggled out of John Vorster police headquarters. It was a little bigger than a postage stamp, and I needed a magnifying glass to read the minute handwriting. The detainee claimed that he had seen Aggett being badly mistreated – kept naked, being made to stand for hours, and being beaten.

Within the next two weeks, a special debate was arranged to discuss the Report of the Rabie Commission, which had been appointed 'to examine the necessity, adequacy, fairness and efficacy of laws affecting the Internal Security of the Republic'. I took this opportunity to expose the Aggett case.

I concentrated on the section which dealt with the impact of the security laws on detention without trial. I gave scant praise to the report for its recommendations, which I felt brought little relief or protection to the unfortunate people so detained. I criticised strongly the fact that the Commission had made but a passing reference to death in detention, although at that time there had been more than fourteen such deaths. (This number increased to seventy-three by the time the detention laws were radically amended in 1991.) Why, I asked in the debate, had the Commission failed to find the answer to the question so pertinently put by Lawyers for Human Rights: 'What makes death preferable to detention?' How was it possible that the Commission failed to examine the two factors which dominated the lives of detainees – solitary confinement and methods of interrogation? Why was there no mention of the dread effects of solitary confinement? The Minister of Justice told us that he put people into solitary confinement so that they could 'cool off'. I said that some go off their heads in solitary confinement and quoted numerous articles about its effects. I went on to say that I hoped nobody was going to stick to that ridiculous statement made by Jimmy Kruger, 'Well, of course they commit suicide. They are given their instructions by the Communist Party: rather die than betray the Party.' I asked him:

> If there is no torture, and you allege there is no torture, why can they not just keep quiet? They do not have to commit suicide rather than betray the Party. So either there is torture and they commit suicide not to betray the Party, or it doesn't make sense to me.[8]

I received no answer.

I then quoted le Grange's earlier statement that all reasonable precautions were taken to prevent a detainee from coming to harm; and yet within forty-eight hours of this assurance a detainee was found hanged in his cell. 'Solitary confinement might well be part of the answer to the question of why death is preferable to detention,' I said. The rest of the answer, in my view was to be found in the methods of interrogation used by the Security Police. The Rabie Commission apparently did not investigate this.

I asked whether the Rabie Commission had talked to any single detainee or ex-detainee to find out how they were being treated and went on:

> While I am on the subject of techniques of interrogation, perhaps the Honourable Minister of Police can now answer the question I put to him on 4 February. 'Can he give the House a categorical assurance that inhuman and degrading methods of interrogation of detainees under Section 6 are not used by the security police on detainees?'

'Yes, I can give that assurance,' the Minister of Police replied. I said,

> I want the Honourable Prime Minister and Honourable Members on the other side of this House to hear. Say that louder. Well this time the Minister says 'yes'. But the Rabie Commission neither confirms nor denies allegations of ill-treatment of detainees. It ignores this issue despite the fact that in a number of cases . . . evidence was given by detainees that they were beaten, kept standing for long periods, deprived of sleep, forced to do exercises over long periods, and that evidence was accepted by the courts and confessions by those detainees were excluded. Not one of the officers concerned in those security cases has been disciplined – in fact some of them have even been promoted.

And I then asked the Minister to verify a case that had come to my notice:

> An allegation was made to me. [It] reads as follows: 'I saw him being interrogated by approximately six guys. Some left and three remained. He was standing all the time. Later he was still standing, except he was naked. He was made to do push-ups, a substantial number. He was hit either with a belt or with a rolled-up newspaper while doing them. Then he had to get up and run on the spot, arms outstretched in front of him. Every so often he was made to lift his legs up high while running, and all this was interspersed with more push-ups. All the while he was being interrogated, the hitting with the newspaper went on all the time, especially if his arms sagged. He was sweating profusely, and when once he nearly fell over a chair with exhaustion, he was further harassed. When he got dressed after twelve o'clock, he was pushed around even then.' The man who was allegedly subjected to this inhuman and degrading treatment was Dr Neil Aggett at John Vorster Square. I ask the Minister to investigate the truth of this allegation.

'I can tell the Honourable Member at this stage, with the knowledge at my disposal, that that can definitely not be true,' said the Minister. 'I will, however, go into the matter, but that can definitely not be true.'

'I am glad to have the Honourable Minister's assurance,' I said.

'What did you read from?' he asked.

'This comes out of jail quite clearly. It comes from another detainee.' Calls came from Members to mention his name.

'Whatever the findings of the postmortem and whatever the findings of the inquest on Dr Neil Aggett, I want to say that it was Section 6 of the Terrorism Act that killed Neil Aggett.'

As a parting shot I added:

> Sir, I want to finish with a quotation from James Madison: 'You must first enable the government to control the governed and in the next place you must oblige it to control itself.' I do not think I can find a more apt quotation for the Nationalist government than that.

Over the next couple of days all hell broke loose in Parliament. My speech appeared in the press in Cape Town and elsewhere in South Africa on the same afternoon I had made it. I had taken the precaution of handing a copy of it to Peter Sullivan, parliamentary correspondent of the Argus Group evening press.

'Are you sure you are going to say this?' he asked.

'Well,' I said, 'unless I drop dead between now and when I get up to speak in Parliament, I am going to say exactly that.' Peter took the chance that I would not drop dead and published the speech before I had made it.

The infuriated Ministers of Police and of Justice accused me of fabricating the letter I had produced in Parliament; of being totally unfair because I had not informed them that I was going to raise the matter; and of ignoring the Speaker's ruling that the Aggett case was *sub judice*. If the speech had not already been published in full in the evening newspapers, I have no doubt that they would have persuaded the Speaker to have it struck from the Hansard record. As it was, the matter was public property.

I was reprimanded severely by the Speaker for having subverted his ruling by not mentioning the name of the person to whom I was referring until the end of my speech. Thus he did not know that I was referring to a matter which he had ruled *sub judice*. I was told that I had ignored the rules of Parliament and that an experienced

Member like myself should have known better. The Minister of Police said that in using the letter I had made absolutely unfair, scurrilous and 'disgraceful accusations'.[9] He challenged me to reveal my source, and I said I would if I was assured that the person would not be victimised.

But perhaps the most extraordinary contribution to the debate was made by Adriaan Vlok, a National Party Member who later became Minister of Law and Order. He said he could not understand my concern about the loneliness of detainees: 'In the same breath she says they are interrogated for hours. I want to ask her – in that case when are they lonely?'[10]

I cannot say that the accusations made by government members in this debate in any way disturbed me, and I had no qualms about subverting the rules of Parliament in this instance. What did disturb me was the fact that a young man, twenty-eight years of age, had hanged himself in the police cells while he was being detained under Section 6 of the Terrorism Act.

Neil Aggett's funeral service was a remarkable event. According to the Johannesburg evening paper, the *Star*, it was attended by fifteen hundred people, who spilled out of St Mary's Cathedral into the streets of Johannesburg. Most of the people were Black trade unionists who had come to pay their respects to the man who had championed their cause. I was present and observed the remarkable love and respect with which Aggett had been regarded. A union official paid a moving tribute to him. I was relieved that the police kept a very low profile at this funeral, and made no attempt to stop the procession which formed after the service, when his coffin was carried on the shoulders of mourners the entire eight miles to West Park Cemetery, where he was buried.

Several months later I attended part of the Aggett inquest, which lasted forty-three days. I sat in court and heard George Bizos, counsel for the Aggett family, argue that his suicide was induced by ill-treatment at the hands of the security police. After calling ten former detainees to testify about Aggett's treatment under interrogation, he singled out two security policemen and demanded that they be charged with culpable homicide. Having considered the evidence, the Magistrate, P. A. J. Kotze, ruled that death was not brought about by any act or omission on the part of the police.

What a travesty of justice it turned out to be! The magistrate dismissed the evidence of all the witnesses on the Aggett side – most of them ex-detainees – and accepted all the police evidence as gospel. Indeed he gave the police more than their counsel had asked for, and completely exonerated them from any blame whatsoever for Aggett's death.

Morice Smithers, the detainee whose letter had been smuggled out of jail and given to me by his sister, was present and gave evidence. He had since been released; and I thought it was particularly courageous of him to come forward, as there was nothing to stop the police from rearresting him, putting him into detention again and treating him as badly as they had treated Aggett. In fact a two-year banning order was served on him in court.

Neil Aggett's parents thanked me for having raised their son's case in Parliament. They had spent about R87,000 (£51,500) on the case. The rest of the enormous costs were met by church bodies, private donors and by sympathetic trade unions. There was no restitution.

Robert Sobukwe, Steve Biko and Neil Aggett were but three of the many tragic victims of apartheid.

13

The Tri-cameral Parliament –
A Flawed Constitution and its Wake

Nineteen eighty-three saw the introduction of the most important Bill to come before Parliament for a long time: a Bill which embodied a new Constitution for South Africa. It was generally agreed that the Westminster system of government had not proved suitable for South Africa's heterogeneous population, but in the parliamentary opposition only the New Republic Party was prepared to accept the government's Constitution Bill which proposed an alternative tri-cameral Parliament – a White House of Assembly, a Coloured House of Representatives, and an Indian House of Delegates.

The Progressive Federal Party and the Conservative Party were both totally opposed to the new Bill, though for completely different reasons. We objected to the exclusion of Blacks, who were more than seventy per cent of the population, whereas the Conservative Party objected to the participation of Coloureds and Indians.

We had further reservations: the Bill lacked legitimacy, since it was created without proper consultation with all sections of the population; the proposed Coloured and Indian chambers could legislate only in relation to so-called 'Own Affairs', such as education, welfare and health of their respective communities. No fundamental changes to any 'general' law could be introduced in their chambers. That meant that the Group Areas Act, the Separate Amenities Act, the education acts, and the Population Registration Act – all cornerstones of apartheid – would remain outside their jurisdiction.

Furthermore, we objected to the absence of checks and balances to curb the very wide powers the President would exercise: no court could over-ride any decision he made. He could refer disputes between the three Houses concerning general matters to a President's Council controlled by the National Party.

Finally, despite the flowery preamble to the Constitution which talked of 'respecting human dignity and the rights and liberties of all in our midst', there was no Bill of Rights to protect civil liberties. All the existing measures giving arbitrary powers such as banning and detention without trial were retained.

The proposals for the new Constitution were put to a referendum of the White electorate. The PFP advised a 'No' vote and I addressed eighteen public meetings in our countrywide campaign against the Constitution. We emphasised that rejecting the proposals did not mean that we wanted the status quo to continue; there was a third option, and that was to press for real reform so that a true democracy could emerge where all adult citizens would have the vote and would participate in a parliamentary system.

Many supporters of the Progressive Federal Party did not agree. They considered it to be 'a step in the right direction' and believed that the government had a secret agenda which would ultimately include the Black population, probably in a fourth house. We were also undermined by the support given to the government's proposals by two influential opposition English-language newspapers, the *Sunday Times* and the *Financial Mail*, while the *Star* advised its readers to abstain from voting. ('The Editor's Indecision is Final' read a notice in the *Star* office!)

To our dismay the government won the referendum by a two-thirds majority in November 1983. The Progressive Federal Party accepted the result and we decided to occupy our seats in the new Parliament. We felt that not to do so would have been an abdication of our responsibilities as the official opposition.

Although the new Constitution was supposed to replace the Westminster system, it retained its worst features – the high degree of centralised power and the 'winner take all' electoral system – and omitted the best – universal adult franchise under the rule of law. We felt, too, that a Constitution devised in the 1980s should be an instrument to promote unity, whereas what was proposed was totally divisive. It divided the Whites (and it certainly split Afrikaner nationalism from top to bottom, maybe a plus factor), and it rent asunder the Coloured and Indian communities on the issue of participation in the new tri-cameral system.

The Constitution Bill was not a recipe for a peaceful South Africa in the future. It increased polarisation and conflict. It consolidated Black, Coloured and Indian opposition. Perhaps the one positive result of the ludicrous tri-cameral parliamentary system was that in the debates on 'general affairs' in the Great Hall of the People (so dubbed by the PFP) in which members of all three Houses participated, there was an eyeball-to-eyeball confrontation between the government MPs and the Indian and Coloured MPs, who described in lurid detail exactly what they had felt when their parents, or they themselves, had been dispossessed of their homes and businesses under the Group Areas Act. There is no doubt that many of the National Party Members were shamed by these firsthand accounts from the victims of their policy of race discrimination and racial oppression.

I had a case in my own constituency, Houghton, which I used in Parliament as yet another example of the nastiness of the Group Areas Act. A woman phoned me and said she was an Indian whose family had bought a house in my constituency. They were ordered by inspectors of the Group Areas Board to leave, as Houghton was a White group area and neighbours had objected. I advised her to apply for a permit and promised to support her application, which I did. The night following her phone call, a man phoned to say he lived in my constituency and wanted my help. I asked him what his problem was. He said that Indians had moved in next door to him.

'Really?' I said, 'do they throw empty beer cans into your garden?'

'No,' he said.

'Do they have vicious dogs that attack your children?'

'No,' he said.

I then asked whether his neighbours played their radio very loudly at night, to which he answered 'No.' So I asked again, 'Then what is your problem?'

'I've told you,' he said, 'they are Indians.'

'And I tell you, sir, that you are a racist. And I must also tell you that I have agreed to support your neighbour's application to remain where she is.'

Unfortunately this story did not have a happy ending, for the permit was not granted and the Indian family had to move or face prosecution. Since the repeal of the Group Areas Act, however, they can now own and occupy a house in Houghton and if their neighbour does not like having Indians next door, he and not they would have to move. (Nelson Mandela now occupies a house in Houghton. I told him that my one regret at no longer being an MP was that I could not be his parliamentary representative.)

A direct outcome of the proposed Constitution was the formation in 1983 of the United Democratic Front (UDF), consisting of between 300 and 400 organisations, among them civic associations in the townships, church groups, left-wing trade unions belonging to the Congress of South African Trade Unions (COSATU), student groups such as the Congress of South African Students and the Transvaal and Natal Indian Congress.

At a giant rally held at Mitchell's Plain, the Coloured township outside Cape Town, the UDF adopted a charter similar to the 1955 Freedom Charter of the ANC.

The UDF was a powerful ally of the ANC, which was at that time banned and in exile. Its avowed intention was to oppose the participation of Coloured and Indian people in the elections for the House of Representatives and the House of Delegates in the tri-cameral Parliament, and of Blacks in the election of the Black Local Authorities. The latter had been presented by the Minister of Bantu Adminstration as a substitute for the parliamentary franchise – a foolish ploy which Black activists rejected with contempt. There were very low polls for these elections.

The UDF set about making the Black Local Authorities ungovernable. Rent boycotts were organised in the Black townships, sporadic trade boycotts, strikes and stayaways took place. Violence erupted, starting in Natal and spreading to the PWV area (Pretoria, Witwatersrand, Vereeniging) in the Transvaal.

Two trials involving the UDF made legal history in South Africa. The first was the Maritzburg treason trial in 1985 in which members of the UDF were tried and acquitted, their counsel, Advocate Ismail Mahomed, having demolished the state's case in record time. (Ismail Mahomed was appointed a judge in 1991. He was one of two chairpersons at CODESA, of which more later.)

The second case was the Delmas trial which was one of the longest and most costly trials ever to take place in South Africa; it lasted approximately three years. It was named after a small town on the East Rand, about fifty miles from Johannesburg, where it was held, in order to make it difficult for people to attend demonstrations, or for relatives and friends to be present at the hearings or to visit the accused, none of whom had been granted bail and who were kept locked up in the local jail.

There were twenty-two accused, all UDF activists. The charges were treason, terrorism, subversion, murder and advancing the aims of an unlawful organisation (the ANC). Eleven were acquitted fairly early in the trial.

I attended the trial on two occasions, escorted by David Dison, lawyer for the accused. On my second visit in 1986 I was accompanied by my grandson Daniel. At the lunch break, I went to speak to a couple of the accused: 'Terror' Lekota (so named because he was an aggressive football player) and Popo Molefe, both of whom, to Danny's obvious pleasure, greeted me warmly, pleased that I had driven out a second time to observe the trial.

I also attended the final court sitting in November 1988 in Pretoria, where the trial had been transferred, to hear the verdict. The eleven accused were found guilty either of terrorism or treason. All received prison sentences which in some cases were suspended. No bail was allowed to the others.

The case had been heard by a judge and two assessors (trial by jury was abolished in South Africa in 1969). During the trial, the judge ordered the recusal of one of the assessors (Professor Willem Joubert) as he had informed the judge that he had added his signature in the campaign to obtain a million signatures to a declaration of support for the UDF.

When the case of the eleven came before the Appeal Court in November 1989, the dismissal of Professor Joubert was declared invalid and the convictions and sentences of all eleven accused were set aside. Popo Molefe and 'Terror' Lekota were free men again and today have important positions in the ANC, which, unbanned and out of exile, rendered the UDF obsolete.

Soon after the first tri-cameral Parliament convened in Cape Town in September 1984, there was widespread unrest, culminating in violent confrontations between protestors and police. At Sebokeng, south of Johannesburg, a mass protest against rent increases introduced by the local town council (which had been elected on a tiny minority poll) ended in the shooting of thirty-nine Blacks by the police. There was continuing unrest thereafter – strikes, stayaways and consumer boycotts by the Black population, compounded by horrific violence which cost many thousands of lives over the ensuing seven years.

During the 1985 parliamentary session a tragic incident occurred at Langa, a Black township in Uitenhage in the eastern Cape. On 21 March the police shot dead twenty people and wounded twenty-seven, who were among a crowd of several thousand marching from Langa towards KwaNobuhle, a township on the other side of Uitenhage, to attend the funeral of victims of police shootings a few days before. The funerals had originally been scheduled to take place the weekend before, but in an attempt to reduce attendance the magistrate postponed the date for which permission was granted to 21 March, a weekday. When it dawned on the magistrate that that date was the twenty-fifth anniversary of the Sharpeville massacre of 1960, the funerals were again cancelled. But the people in Langa had not been informed of the cancellations, so they set off in buses, taxis and cars for KwaNobuhle. The police stopped the vehicles and made the passengers alight. The people then started to march and were confronted by police in a Casspir (an armoured vehicle).

At the instigation of Molly Blackburn, an indefatigable Black Sash worker and a PFP provincial councillor, who had total credibility in the Black community in the eastern Cape (and who was tragically killed later in a car accident), six PFP MPs, of whom I was one, immediately went to Uitenhage to ascertain what had happened that day. After speaking to a number of eye-witnesses, we came back with impressions very different from the account given in Parliament by le Grange, the Minister of Law and Order.

He insisted that the police had no option but to fire on the crowd of several thousand hostile Black people, armed with sticks, stones and petrol bombs with which they had attacked a police vehicle, and who were on their way to attack the Whites in the town of Uitenhage. What was worse, after going to Uitenhage himself three days later, the Minister returned and repeated that same erroneous statement in Parliament.

The government announced the appointment of a judicial commission of enquiry into the tragic affair, under the chairmanship of Judge D. D. V. Kannemeyer, a senior judge in the eastern Cape. We decided not to wait for the commission to report and to raise the matter in Parliament at the earliest opportunity.

Fortuitously, the weekend immediately before the debate, I had travelled to Johannesburg and found myself sitting on the plane next to Geoff Budlender, a senior member of the Legal Resources Centre (to which I often turned for assistance on difficult legal problems). I said it seemed very possible that the government would try to prevent the debate on the grounds that as a commission of enquiry had been appointed, the Uitenhage matter was *sub judice*. Geoff said he remembered that there had been a court ruling that commission proceedings did not carry the same *sub judice* restrictions as court cases, and he later gave me the reference. When I returned to Parliament I was able to convey the relevant details to our Chief Whip, Advocate Brian Bamford. He in turn advised the then Speaker, J. W. Greeff, a very fair-minded man. Sure enough, when the debate started and we attempted to make our case, the Minister of Justice leapt to his feet and demanded that the matter be ruled *sub judice* by the Speaker. However, the Speaker had made his decision and was able to quote the actual court ruling.

The following day, State President Botha came into the debate and made a statement on the security situation, in which he appealed to Members not to discuss the Uitenhage affair any further. He said, 'I suggest to Parliament that the judicious course would be for Parliament not to address this matter in any fashion until we have at our disposal the commission's report.'[1] Immediately after Botha sat down, I came into the debate and said that although I had listened with great interest to what he had to say, we could not accede to his request. There was no doubt that discussion on the events at Uitenhage would continue outside the House, despite what the State President had said.

I contended that Parliament could not abdicate its responsibility and tackled the Minister of Law and Order about his original statement in the House, and for repeating that misleading statement after he had returned from Uitenhage. I asked whether he had bothered to talk to any Black people present at the scene of the shootings on the twenty-first of March, other than Black policemen. Had he talked to any of the ordinary residents of the township of Langa, or did he get only a police version? The residents had a very different view from the police version, which he had accepted without question. A Nationalist Member asked, 'Did you talk to the police?' I said that we had tried – and tried very hard. We not only phoned the Minister the day before we left, but asked him to inform the police that we were coming to Uitenhage, because we particularly wanted to hear their side of the story as well as the story of the Black residents. The police had refused to talk to us, and refused us permission to go into the township unless we went under their escort.

I reminded the House that the Minister had reported to Parliament as follows: a police unit of nineteen men in a police vehicle told the leader of the march that it was illegal and that they should go back, but that these instructions were ignored; a warning shot was fired into the ground, the police were suddenly surrounded and pelted with stones, sticks and other missiles. The police were informed that the crowd intended to attack the White people in Uitenhage. However, the Minister's report had not mentioned that the 'police vehicle' was in fact a Casspir:

A vehicle is defined in the dictionary as a wheeled conveyance, and therefore it could have been a bicycle, but in fact this particular wheeled conveyance was an armour-plated vehicle which sticks, stones and bricks and even petrol bombs were highly unlikely to affect, even if they were used against the vehicle. The affidavits that we obtained told a very different story. They told us that it was an unarmed crowd being transported in taxis and combis to attend a funeral in the township of KwaNobuhle on the other side of Uitenhage. They were told by the police to get out of the vehicles and when they started to walk, they were not allowed to go any further. Nor does one take a taxi when one is planning to invade a town in order to attack the residents.[2]

I wanted to know what had happened to all the riot control training which I had observed at the Maleoskop police base a couple of weeks before. I also wanted to know about the adamant statement of General Coetzee, the Chief Commissioner of Police, that standing police orders were that minimum force was to be used in crowd control, and that fire power should be used only as a last resort after sneeze gas, rubber bullets, birdshot and buckshot had been used. And yet, according to the police's own version, fire power was used as a first resort in Uitenhage. What possible explanation could there be for this?

There were many interjections from the Minister and attempts to persuade the Speaker to rule me out of order, but I was well protected by him. He said, 'The words being used by the Honourable Member for Houghton at present constitute criticism on public information already published'; he repeated the ruling that he had given and asked me to continue. At which stage I told the Minister to sit down, saying he had already made a fool of himself, and I recorded the strongest objection to the way those who were wounded by the police at Uitenhage had been treated – they were immediately placed under arrest, with armed guards at the hospital. Nobody had taken the trouble to seek out their relatives to inform them about those who had died or been wounded. I asked, 'What sort of behaviour is this in a "civilised" country?'

It astonished me that the local magistrate had shown such a dismal lack of understanding about the importance to Blacks of funeral arrangements. I repeated the plea I had often made in the House: 'Keep the police away from funerals, especially those of people who have been killed by the police. Their very presence is like a red rag to a bull.' I told the House I had attended three very large funerals – those of Robert Sobukwe, Steve Biko and Neil Aggett. Thousands of people were present at these emotion-charged events; at all of them the police were sensible enough to keep a low profile, and there were no confrontations. Finally, I expressed the hope that we had learned something from the tragic events at Uitenhage.

One sequel to this debate was that Speaker Greeff was transferred from Parliament to the President's Council, where he became chairman. Was this because Greeff had defied P. W. Botha, I wondered?

I was very disappointed in the Kannemeyer Report when it finally appeared; it was inconclusive. Although it criticised senior members of the police for not issuing the standard riot control equipment at Uitenhage, it said that it could not determine at which level this decision was taken. While it condemned the confused chain of command and the fact that officers were no longer adhering to proven methods of riot control, it exonerated the lieutenant in charge of the Casspir, who gave the order to fire, saying that he was faced with an 'awesome decision'. The judge did not attribute the blame for the tragic incident to any one person.

The fact that thirty-five out of the forty-seven people shot, were shot in the back, he described as 'disquieting'. That seemed a masterly understatement. Indeed the Minister himself condemned the police in the eastern Cape more strongly than Judge Kanne-meyer did, for he said in an interview that they had flagrantly disregarded clear instructions. The Kannemeyer Report let the Minister off the hook and he refused to resign.

Nevertheless when the Law and Order Vote was discussed, about a month later, I strongly criticised the Minister for not curbing police excesses. Having ascertained from a constable at the entrance to Parliament what his annual salary was, I moved an amendment to reduce the Minister's salary by R69,600, which amount would 'leave the Minister with the salary of a constable'.[3] He was not pleased.

Within a year of the Uitenhage massacre came the ghastly news that Molly Blackburn and Brian Bishop, husband of Di, our able and energetic PFP member of the Provincial Council, had been killed in a head-on car crash on their way back to Port Elizabeth after visiting a Black township in Oudtshoorn, where the residents were threatened with removal.

Foul play, of course, was the first thought in everyone's mind, but I thought this improbable. Who could have known exactly where their car would be on the road from Oudtshoorn at 8.30 p. m. or have recognised it in the dark? Moreover, the driver of the other car would have had to be a kamikaze, for he was also killed in the collision. But of course there was much speculation, because there were so many unsolved hit squad murders. Many anti-government activists had been assassinated over the years, and none of the assassins had been brought to justice. There were strong suspicions that the security police were involved in plots to eliminate the 'enemies of the state'. Molly's husband and brother went to visit the parents of the driver of the other car and to make enquiries in the township. They found he was totally non-political. One inexplicable fact they unearthed, however, was that although the driver was known to be teetotal, a considerable amount of alcohol was detected at the postmortem.

I attended the funeral service for Molly which was held in a large church in Port Elizabeth. It was incredible – there were thousands of Blacks, inside and outside the church and, as frequently happened, the event was turned into a huge political rally with all the ushers wearing the ANC colours. It was very moving and a great tribute to the work Molly had done for the Black community, especially during the Uitenhage crisis.

On the thirty-second anniversary of my becoming an MP, in March 1985, twenty-one years after I had moved my first Private Member's Motion on civil liberties, I again moved a Private Member's Motion with the same basic aim: that South Africa should return to the rule of law. It was a very sad reflection on the political history of South Africa that it was necessary to reintroduce such a motion.

My speech covered much the same ground as the 1964 speech, but went a good deal further, because conditions had changed for the worse – more stringent security laws, more deaths in detention, widespread use of Section 6 of the Terrorism Act, the tidal wave of unrest throughout South Africa, and the concentrated campaigns in the United States and elsewhere for punitive actions against South Africa because of the absence of 'due process' and the apartheid policy.

There was another difference: in the 1964 debate not a single MP supported me or even spoke to the Motion; in 1985 I had the wholehearted support of the Progressive Federal Party caucus of twenty-seven – the entire official opposition. Strong back-up speeches were made by two of my colleagues. Even a Nationalist MP, Leon Wessels, paid me an unexpected compliment:

> My positive remarks about the Honourable Member for Houghton are, in truth, meant sincerely. In a certain sense she is a noteworthy political opponent of this government. Over the years she has persevered, she has taken a consistent stand in this House, she has participated in the democratic processes of this country and has fought the government tooth and nail. I think that is remarkable and we on this side wish to give her credit for that.[4]

The Minister of Law and Order, le Grange, however, was less complimentary. While congratulating me on having been in the House for thirty-two years, he added, 'It is hard on a man to endure it all these years. . . . Go to Northern Ireland if you think you will be happy there. We will give you an exit permit.'

I had a curious, ambivalent relationship with le Grange. Inside the debating chamber, especially after he took over the portfolios of Police and Law and Order, we had many hostile exchanges. On a personal level I got on much better with him than I had done with his predecessors, Vorster and Kruger.

On my one visit to the Soviet Union in June 1982, I could not resist sending a postcard to le Grange. It read: 'There is plenty of law and order here – I am coming home.' It was addressed to 'Dear Comrade Louis', and I signed it 'Kind regards, Comrade Helen'. Le Grange claimed he never received it, so it is either languishing in the rusty files of the KGB or in the hands of the South African security police.

When le Grange became Speaker, he was always courteous to me and often stopped me in the Lobby for a chat. He wrote to congratulate me in 1989 when I was awarded the DBE: 'You are certainly a worthy recipient of the particular honour and I am proud to know that a Member of our Parliament has distinguished herself in this manner.'

After I had retired, I heard from Colin Eglin that Speaker le Grange had agreed to allocate wall-space in Parliament for my portrait. I wrote to thank him, and as he was then in hospital recovering from heart surgery, I also wished him a speedy recovery. He wrote back thanking me for my good wishes and added, 'You will appreciate my disappointment at not being able to be present at your "unveiling" especially as it was my privilege to take the initial decision whether you would be allowed to be "hanged" in the corridors of Parliament.'

He told a journalist that every time he passed my portrait, I seemed to be looking down and saying, 'I told you so'. This of course was after the reform speech of State President de Klerk in February 1990.

Louis le Grange died in 1991, of a heart attack.

In August 1985 there was much anticipation about a speech Botha was to deliver at the National Party congress in Durban. Rumour had it that it would be an enlightened speech promising far-reaching reform: the so-called 'Rubicon speech'. He had recently made a number of atypical statements where he used expressions such as 'adjust or die'. Also, he had actually visited Soweto, had discussions with homelands leaders and had held an historic meeting with some 200 businessmen at the Carlton Hotel in Johannesburg in November, when he said things to reassure them and sent them home bright-eyed and bushy-tailed. Our expectations of fundamental reform, however, were soon dashed. The speech Botha delivered was very different from the original draft.

A copy of the draft of the undelivered speech reveals that it contained fundamental values totally foreign to accepted Nationalist philosophy. Instead of espousing domination and separate development, the speech proclaimed,

> We must prosper or perish together. The inalienable human rights of life, liberty and the pursuit of happiness must therefore be enjoyed by all if any of us is to benefit from them . . . The over-riding common denominator is our mutual interest in each other's freedoms and well-being. Our peace and prosperity is indivisible. Therefore the only way forward is through co-operation and co-responsibility . . . The views and aspirations of all must be heard. This is why these aspirations must be accommodated by a process of negotiation . . . The government now accepts the principle that all our population groups must be jointly responsible for decision-making at all levels of government in matters of common concern without domination by any one population group over another.

The speech went on to make conciliatory comments about the possibility of releasing Nelson Mandela and his fellow prisoners and to assert that 'violence is tragic and unnecessary. The government is addressing legitimate grievances: it is abolishing discrimination based on colour or race and it is promoting constitutional development with a view to meeting the needs and aspirations of all our communities.

'Today, we are crossing the Rubicon,' proclaimed the draft speech.

Had that speech been delivered, the course of history in South Africa over the ensuing five years may well have been very different. But Botha faltered on the banks of the Rubicon, deterred, it is said, by right-wingers in his Cabinet and probably by his own basic sentiments.

Instead, Botha told the NP congress that he 'was not prepared to lead White South Africans and other minority groups on a road to abdication and suicide'. He made a sideswipe at the press and at enemies from abroad and lauded the government's efforts to stimulate Black economic enterprises, misquoted the speech Mandela made at his trial, and castigated revolutionaries. Although he used the 'over-riding common denominator' contained in the original speech and talked of the 'indivisibility of peace and prosperity' he made no mention of joint decision-making. In short, the much anticipated Rubicon speech turned out to be the usual finger-wagging Botha performance, as well as a mixture of thinly disguised threats, conciliatory remarks and self-laudatory comments.

It is interesting to speculate what the effect would have been had the original speech been delivered. Certainly it is likely that the hostility of the outside world would have diminished and South Africa might well have been spared the punitive economic measures such as the strictures on bank loans and the sanctions imposed by the United States the following year.

The last few years of the Botha regime marked instead the hardening of the government's attitude towards dissent. In the mid-eighties the Civil Co-operation Bureau (CCB) was set up – a shadowy organisation with no accountability whatsoever. It was a unit which operated under the auspices of the South African Defence Force's Special Projects Fund and its objective was the elimination of apartheid's enemies at home and abroad. Many unsolved political assassinations have been attributed to the CCB.

★

My last direct contact with P. W. Botha was in 1988 when Colin
Eglin and I went on a deputation to ask him for clemency for six
people sentenced to death. They – the so-called Sharpeville Six –
had been charged with the murder of the Black mayor of
Sharpeville township, and had been found guilty of common
purpose murder.

As we entered Tuynhuis (the State President's official town
office) Colin, knowing of my ongoing feud with Botha, said to
me, 'Behave yourself – the lives of six people are at stake.' I did.
David Welsh, Professor of Politics at the University of Cape
Town, had reminded me about a speech made by Dr Malan during
the Second World War, as leader of the opposition, when he
pleaded for the lives of two men, van Blerk and Visser, who
belonged to a subversive organisation, the Ossewabrandwag [Ox-
wagon watch]. They had been sentenced to death for placing a
bomb in a post office as part of a campaign to sabotage the war
effort. I knew that Malan's persuasive words had been effective in
the van Blerk/Visser case, and I used his speech in support of our
plea. Perhaps many years later these words helped to save the
lives of the Sharpeville Six. Our plea for clemency was backed by
all the Western diplomats in South Africa on behalf of their
governments.

Botha granted a reprieve at the eleventh hour. As a *quid pro quo*,
he also granted reprieve to two White policemen who had been
sentenced to death for murder. (Eventually all the Sharpeville Six
were released.)

Paradoxically, it was during Botha's ten year regime that the
dismantling of the apartheid structure began in Parliament.
Whether Botha was aware that these changes would herald the
beginning of the end of the entire apartheid system, one cannot be
sure. I refer to the repeal of job reservation in industry and the legal
recognition of Black trade unions in 1979, giving Blacks the right
to strike after procedures laid down by the Industrial Conciliation
Act had been carried out; the repeal of Section 16 of the Immorality
Act (which prohibited sex across the colour line, outside marriage);
and of the Prohibition of Mixed Marriages Act in 1985; the

recognition of the permanency of the Black urban population by the granting of 99-year leasehold, and then freehold tenure, instead of one-month tenancy of houses in the townships. Most important of all was the repeal of the Pass Laws and Influx Control in June 1986, which relieved millions of South African Blacks of impoverishing restrictions on their mobility and of the threat of arrest and imprisonment for the 'crime' of looking for jobs in the urban areas without the necessary permits. More than two million Blacks had been arrested in the past ten years, bedevilling the relationship between the police and the Black community.

The Pass Laws had become impossible to implement against the irresistible tide of Black urbanisation and the increased pressure of Black resistance. Why, I asked the House, had it taken the government forty years to appreciate the disastrous mistake it had made in creating this unstable society?

During the debate I received an unexpected accolade from a Nat MP, Albert Nothnagel:

> As a quite ordinary South African parliamentarian – this might sound very liberal to many people and quite off the rails too – and as one person to another I should like to tell the Honourable Member for Houghton frankly this evening that as far as these measures are concerned, measures in regard to which she, without any assistance, took up the cudgels in this House for many years, she had a better insight into the problems and could see further than many other people in South Africa. I want to add that although she does lash out at us at times, taking us to task in a manner which we feel is very unfair to the National Party, for example in regard to security legislation, I hardly think there will ever again be anyone in the history of this country who could do as much for human rights as she has done.[5]

Whether these remarks were responsible for Nothnagel's being removed from Parliament soon after and sent to The Hague as South Africa's ambassador, I do not know!

The irony was that few Black leaders were inclined to say a kind word for the government when the Pass Laws were finally abolished, although the lives of millions of Black South Africans would be materially improved. Hardly any recognition of these meaningful changes was given either at home by those who had always vociferously protested against the Pass Laws, or abroad by South Africa-watchers. This was due to the timing (or rather, the mistiming) of the repeal of the Acts of Parliament. The debates took place in the midst of strong public opposition to the introduction of two security Bills tightening the Internal Security Act and the Public Safety Act, and coincided with the reintroduction of the stringent emergency regulations, followed by a massive spate of detentions.

At the beginning of 1986 the PFP had suffered a shattering blow. Van Zyl Slabbert, leader of the party, came to see me in Johannesburg shortly before the session started. He told me that he intended to resign at the end of that session.

I begged him not to go public, hoping he might change his mind in the interim. But at the end of the first week of the session, he sent for me and said, 'I just want to tell you I intend announcing my resignation from Parliament this afternoon in the course of my reply to the No Confidence debate.' I was appalled that the leader of the official opposition would contemplate undermining his party in so drastic a fashion at the very beginning of a session. And I told him so. He replied that there was never a good time to resign. I said, 'But you have chosen the very worst time' and begged him to reconsider. He said he had stuck it out for seven years. I replied nastily, 'Don't talk to *me* about seven years!' To which Van Zyl replied, 'But you have a built-in survival kit second to none.' He added that he believed extra-parliamentary politics to be more meaningful to the country. I left his office in a state of despair and sat next to him on our front bench while he made his wind-up speech in the No Confidence debate, hoping against hope he would conclude without any resignation announcement. But it came, with stunning impact, right at the end of his speech.

The party now had a major crisis on its hands. A week later, a PFP Whip and close friend and confidant of Van Zyl, Dr Alex Boraine, another very competent MP, after first canvassing the idea of becoming leader in Van Zyl's place, also decided to resign. He joined Van Zyl, who shortly afterwards formed an extra-parliamentary organisation, the Institute for a Democratic Alternative for South Africa – commonly known as Idasa. I have to admit that it has been an outstanding success, generously financed from abroad and at home. Van Zyl and Alex have been able, therefore, to arrange many conferences, in South Africa and elsewhere, at which Idasa has brought together people of opposing political factions and in different walks of life who otherwise would probably never have met. Van Zyl and I made friends again in 1989 when we found ourselves in Bermuda attending a conference on South Africa organised by the Aspen Institute, though I found it hard to forgive the way he left the party which had placed so much trust in him.

The 1986 session of Parliament saw Colin Eglin once again installed as leader of the PFP and of the official opposition. His resilience accounted for the party's maintaining its equilibrium and performing well under difficult circumstances for the remainder of the session. The effects of Van Zyl's resignation nevertheless manifested themselves in the 1987 general election. He, as leader, had declared that Parliament was irrelevant. Why then should the rank and file of the party continue to work and raise funds to keep its representatives there?

Many White students at Cape Town, Witwatersrand, Natal and Rhodes Universities – the four English-medium universities which usually supported the liberal opposition to the Nationalists – refused to work for or vote in the 1987 election. Their enthusiasm was diverted to extra-parliamentary organisations such as the UDF, and they were persuaded that they would be showing solidarity with their disenfranchised Black brethren by boycotting the elections. Indeed my own alma mater, Wits University, where I had graduated and taught many years ago, and which had awarded me an Honorary Doctorate ten years before, refused to allow me to speak on campus to present the argument for participation in the election, but permitted a three-day anti-election campaign on campus. What had happened at Wits to two cardinal democratic principles – freedom of speech and *audi alteram partem* [hear the other side] – I asked in a newspaper article.

The demise in 1985 of the *Rand Daily Mail*, our most loyal and consistent supporter, was also a major factor in the PFP's poor showing in the election. And it is likely that the neglect – deliberate or otherwise – of some 400,000 resident British to take out South African citizenship deprived the PFP of votes.

*

In my own election in Houghton in 1987, my final campaign, I ran against a National Party candidate, a Portuguese immigrant from Mozambique and a wine merchant. One of the ploys of his campaign was to try to obtain the use of a photograph of me with Winnie Mandela, taken in my home by Peter Magubane, the *Time* magazine photographer, on 31 July 1986, ten months before the election, and to change the caption. Winnie had come to see me about the presence of troops in the schools in Soweto, and Magubane accompanied her. His photograph of the two of us was published in *Time* on 4 May 1987 with the caption, 'Two Voices of Opposition – Winnie Mandela and Helen Suzman'.

My opponent asked *Time* if he could use the photograph 'for promotional purposes'. Quite what he was going to promote – wine, gin or brandy – he did not say, but the magazine refused permission. Notwithstanding this, the photograph was pirated and used on the front page of several pro-Nationalist newspapers throughout South Africa three days before the election. The caption now read, 'With our matchboxes and our necklaces we will liberate our country', which was the reckless and highly irresponsible statement made by Winnie in 1985 at a mass funeral of victims of police shooting – a remark which leading Black organisations (and I) had strongly disapproved of publicly at the time. ('Necklaces' were the burning tyres placed around the necks of Blacks suspected of collaborating with the Nationalists.) My opponent and his National Party propagandists hoped to extend guilt by association to me through the caption.

I exposed the lie at my last pre-election public meeting at Houghton, but I flatly refused to disown Winnie as a long-time friend. Houghton gave me a rousing ovation and a big majority of about 5000 votes, but it is possible that the election results of other Progressive Federal Party candidates were adversely affected by the use of that photograph. Instead of going back to Parliament with four or five additional seats as we had hoped, we lost seven to the Nats, and the PFP had to surrender its position as official opposition to the right-wing Conservative Party which won twenty-four seats to the PFP's twenty. And this was reduced shortly to seventeen, when two of our Members defected to other parties, and one became an independent.

There had of course to be a scapegoat for the disappointing results, and Colin Eglin, as leader, was the obvious target. This time his replacement was Zach de Beer.

Not being the official opposition meant we lost the first thrust in every debate, so we could no longer place the emphasis of the debate where we thought it should be; we had less speaking time allocated to us, and less representation on the parliamentary Select Committees. In short, our role in Parliament was much diminished.

This account of my years in Parliament would be incomplete without recording my efforts on behalf of women.

My first major effort on behalf of women had been in 1975, International Women's Year, in a Private Member's Motion calling upon the government to take immediate steps to remove the remaining disabilities of South African women, especially those of Black women. However, another ten years passed before any advance in women's rights took place, with the Matrimonial Property Act – thirty-one years after Bertha Solomon's Bill. Until then White, Coloured and Asian women in South Africa enjoyed (and do now) the same legal rights as men if they were sane, solvent, over the age of twenty-one years, and spinsters, widows or divorcees. However, to quote A. P. Herbert, 'should a woman enter into holy deadlock', unless she signed an antenuptial contract excluding the marital power, she was classified with minors and lunatics and was completely under the authority of her husband. He exercised the marital power and had the sole and unfettered power to administer their joint estate. Women's lack of contractual capacity in a marriage in community of property was virtually total; they had less authority than their unmarried daughters over the age of twenty-one. Community of property and of profit and loss brought benefits to the wife only on divorce or when her husband died, because then, as of right, she was able to claim or inherit half the estate.

Significant changes came about with the introduction of the 1984 Matrimonial Property Bill, which resulted from an in-depth enquiry started in 1976 by the South African Law Commission. The Commission reported in 1982 and later that year a Select

Committee was appointed, of which I was a member. I was given invaluable advice throughout the sittings by Professor June Sinclair of Wits University. The Committee presented its findings to the Minister in October 1983.

During one sitting of the Committee I overheard two National Party MPs in close discussion. Said one, in Afrikaans, 'Man, if we allow the marital power to be abolished in existing marriages, I would have to get my wife's consent if I wanted to take a new partner into my law firm.' I interrupted and said, 'You chaps don't do your homework. This amendment would not affect your professional or business affairs. But I'll tell you something – you should ask your wife, because she may know something about the proposed new partner's wife you did not know, which could be disastrous for your law firm – for example that she is an alcoholic or a spendthrift or a gossip.' The two Nationalists looked at each other and one said, 'Ja, Helen het 'n punt.' [Yes, Helen has a point.] The Select Committee eventually agreed unanimously to the abolition of the marital power in existing as well as in future marriages in community of property. It quite rightly dismissed the few memoranda which recommended retention of the marital power based on the fatuous argument that 'there cannot be two captains on the bridge'. One such memorandum came from a prestigious Johannesburg law firm. A glance at its letterhead revealed that it had sixteen captains on its bridge – all male of course.

What was ultimately passed in Parliament was an attenuated version of the original draft Bill and affected only marriages entered into after November 1984. I was shocked to the core at the Minister's justification for omitting existing marriages: the Women's Bureau, an organisation claiming to be the largest women's organisation in South Africa, had recommended against the abolition of the marital power in existing marriages. Their reason? It would be unfair to men.

Another glaring omission from the 1984 Matrimonial Property Act was the exclusion of Black marriages, for as usual Black women got the worst of two worlds. In the traditional (mostly rural) communities they were shackled by tribal laws. If married by civil rite (mostly in the urban areas), they were specifically excluded from the main advantages of marrying out of community of property as the marital power was retained by the husband. That meant that Black women had no contractual capacity *and* were denied the one positive aspect of community of property: a half share of the joint estate when the marriage was dissolved. The government's feeble excuse for the delay in including Black women was that they did not want to introduce laws without the approval of Black leaders in the homelands and in the urban areas: a fine example of sophistry, as I told the Minister, considering the thousands of laws the government had imposed on Blacks over the years without their consent.

In 1988, however, the amending Bill introduced considerable advances for Black women married by civil rite and their legal status thereafter was the same as other women. The Matrimonial Property Acts of 1984 and 1988 certainly heralded a new deal for women and this was another blow struck for gender equality in South Africa.

There is still considerable confusion regarding the conflicting claims of Black women married by civil rite and those married by customary law. Monogamous marriage is presently the only legal form of marriage fully recognised in South African law, but polygamy is still widely practised, especially in the rural areas, although on a decreasing scale. Primogeniture applies in customary law (the eldest son inherits the property if a Black man dies intestate). A man's widows have no claim on his estate, even if the deceased had a wife married by civil law as well as women he had married by customary law. The eldest son is supposed to look after the family of the deceased, but it is easy enough for him to avoid this responsibility. I knew of cases where widows were dispossessed of their belongings following the unexpected arrival of the eldest son of another wife.

Black women married by customary law fall under the guardianship of their husbands if they are living with them, and this means they are perpetual minors (except in KwaZulu). Thus they are discriminated against in three ways. First, because they are Black; second, because they are women; and third, because they are Black women. In other words the tribal set-up is against them.

Customary law differs in the various Black states and this confused position will undoubtedly continue until they are reincorporated into the Republic under the new Constitution.

My efforts to have the restrictive abortion laws liberalised met with no success. I firmly believe that women should have the right to choose whether or not to have abortions, but this is of course a highly contentious subject in many countries, fraught with religious and moral considerations. The pro-choice/pro-life conflict has been a major issue in United States politics for many years, and recently it seemed that the winning of a nomination or an election for a congressional seat, for a mayoralty or for a governorship (or even the presidency!) could depend on the candidate's attitude to abortion. (Interestingly, during all my election campaigns, I was only once asked to give my views on abortion – and the questioner was a male.)

From 1968 onwards, I had raised in Parliament, both by way of question and in the Votes, the need for reform of South Africa's abortion laws. The highly restrictive Abortion Act was passed in 1975. It followed the recommendations of a Commission of Enquiry appointed in 1973, to which, I might add, not one female member had been appointed, unlike the United Kingdom Commission on which ten out of the sixteen members were women, as I pointed out in Parliament. A National Party MP for Calodon, Dr L. A. P. A. Munnik replied, 'One need not have women on a committee in order to determine what is right or wrong. If one wanted to abolish capital punishment today surely one would not appoint a bunch of murderers to go into the matter to see whether it should be abolished.'[6]

When the Abortion Bill came up for discussion in Parliament in 1975, a number of speeches were punctuated with offensive sexist 'jokes', which totally infuriated me. The contribution from Dr E. L. Fisher, a medical doctor, and the United Party Member for Rosettenville was: 'A woman will come and say "I have been raped. I think I may be pregnant. Will you not do something for me please?" There are a lot of cases like that. Some of them were raped very easily, very easily indeed.'[7] The contribution of Dr W. L. Vosloo, Nationalist MP for Brentwood, another medical luminary, was: 'A young girl arrives at a hospital and asks for help. "I have been raped. Matron please help me." The matron then says, "Yes, come in my child. Walk this way. Go straight through to the kitchen. On the shelf you will find a lemon. Squeeze out the juice and drink it." The girl then says, "Oh matron, will it really help me?" And the matron says, "Yes, it will help remove that smile from your face." '[8] And that of Brigadier C. C. von Keyserlink the United Party Member for Umlazi was: 'The attitude of the Honourable Member for Houghton is typical of some women – they like to have their cake but they are not prepared to bake it.'[9]

Year after year during the Health Votes I moved that a new commission be appointed to investigate the workings and efficacy of the 1975 Act. I did so knowing the devastating statistics of backstreet and self-induced abortions. Special wards had to be set up in hospitals like Baragwanath in Soweto and King Edward in Durban to cope with the resulting life-threatening complications. I had no success whatever. All successive Ministers of Health proved singularly unsympathetic. Even the first female appointee to the Cabinet, Dr Rina Venter, as Minister of Health and Welfare did no more than issue a bleak statement that no change in the abortion law was contemplated 'as the public did not want it'.

The emphasis has been on family planning for Blacks and on family allowances for Whites. The question of population control was politicised years ago in South Africa when the then Minister of Bantu Affairs, M. C. Botha, issued a statement calling on every White woman to have a baby for the Republic. Blacks had good reason to laugh at this poorly disguised racist challenge.

The population explosion is a looming disaster in South Africa, but the fact that nowhere in the world has population control been successful without a liberal abortion policy is ignored by the authorities. Neither the government, the ANC, or the Democratic Party is prepared to tackle this politically sensitive subject. Only the IFP has pronounced itself in favour of pro-choice.

The Divorce Law was much improved by an amending Act in 1979 when grounds for divorce were changed from adultery or desertion to the irretrievable breakdown of the marriage. Judicial separation was abolished. The Bill was one of the rare occasions during my parliamentary career when a Nationalist Party Cabinet Minister actually congratulated me on 'making an excellent speech'. And he was none other than my fierce adversary, Justice Minister Jimmy Kruger, who had introduced this liberalisation of the divorce laws.

During the 1989 session of Parliament (my last) another interesting proposal concerning women emanated from the Law Commission. It was referred to a Joint Committee of Parliament on which I sat as one of two PFP representatives from the House of Assembly. The Law Commission had produced a draft Bill which, if adopted, would have made the rape of a woman by her husband a statutory offence, although no prosecution could be instituted without the permission of the Attorney General. Under existing law there is no such statutory offence, although assault by a husband on his wife is a common-law offence.

Some really repulsive, chauvinistic opinions were advanced in the Joint Select Committee by the male members – White, Coloured and Indian – as to a wife's 'duty' towards her husband. She was to be sexually available to him no matter what. Our efforts to persuade the Committee to accept the Law Commission's recommendations were unsuccessful, although, surprisingly enough, the two far-right Conservative Party Members of the Committee supported us. 'Rape is rape', they said with characteristic bluntness. The best we could manage, however, was an amendment to the existing situation whereby the Act lays down that in passing sentence on a guilty man, the court is required to take into consideration as an aggravating circumstance the fact that if the couple had not been married, a conviction of rape could have resulted.

Three draft Bills have been published (February 1993) and, if passed, will go some way to addressing existing gender discrimination.

The Abolition of Discrimination Against Women Draft Bill contains an important provision which abolishes the marital power in all marriages to which it still applies. The Prevention of Domestic Violence Draft Bill, if it becomes law, will make the rape of a wife by her husband a statutory offence, originally with the proviso that they no longer live together in the same home. This proviso was later omitted.

The Promotion of Equal Opportunities Draft Bill will prohibit discrimination on grounds of sex, marital status and pregnancy, and seeks to establish an Equal Opportunities Commission which will promote equality and equal opportunities between males and females.

Furthermore, in August 1992, speaking at a National Party women's conference, State President de Klerk announced that the government intended to endorse four UN conventions which aim to secure women's rights, of which the Convention on the Elimination of all Forms of Discrimination Against Women (CEDAW) is the most comprehensive. These would certainly conflict with several laws still on the statute book, mostly concerning labour.

It will be interesting to see how this question will be resolved.

14

Sanctions:
Pressure from Without

My opposition to sanctions against South Africa clouded my relationship with many people overseas and with many Blacks at home, disappointing those who expected me to be an enthusiastic supporter of punitive action against the regime I opposed over so many years. I believe I had sound economic reasons for my attitude. And as far as the academic and cultural boycott was concerned, I was convinced that contact with the outside world, rather than isolation, would be more effective in influencing public opinion in South Africa.

In 1978 I warned Parliament that the pro-sanctions lobby was fast gaining ground as a result of the government's offensive actions. Since October 1977, when the government banned eighteen organisations and outlawed Donald Woods, and Steve Biko's death in detention had hit the headlines, there was a marked stepping up of the campaign, both in the United States and elsewhere, for stronger punitive measures than the 1977 United Nations mandatory arms sanctions, and the non-mandatory oil embargo of 1978. Anti-apartheid organisations in the United States and in Europe, which had campaigned for years against investment in South Africa and which used to be laughed out of court at the annual general meetings of the companies they were targeting, were now finding far more receptive audiences. The directors of these companies in many cases threw in the sponge, deciding that the South African connection was just not worth the trouble and threat of boycotts. The influential *New York Times* supported a United Nations' declaration that South Africa was a threat to peace, and expressed the opinion that Export/Import Bank trade credits to South Africa should be ended, and that further investment should be curtailed. It also came out in support of the campus campaign for disinvestment. Indeed, there was a serious crusade developing to force United States companies to divest, and there was no doubt that this was gaining momentum and support over a very wide field.

I warned Parliament, 'The government has made the task of overseas investors much more difficult by the idiotic, precipitate and exacerbating actions which they have taken over and over again in the past few months, actions which have brought the Republic opprobrium in the headlines of the world press.'[1] Nat MPs' comments were strident: 'You do not belong here. Pack your bags and go, bitterbek [bittermouth].' Dr F. Hartzenberg, Deputy Minister of Development said, 'The Honourable Member for Houghton is in my view a typical and perfect example of an unpatriotic South African.' There were loud complaints about the use of double standards by countries criticising South Africa's racial policies while condoning oppression in other countries. I conceded that there were double standards, but since the government claimed that South Africa was a Western democracy, it was expected to behave as such.

'Are you suggesting that we do not behave like a Western democracy?' the Minister of Finance asked.

'Yes,' I replied, 'I am. We very often do not behave like a Western democracy. Detaining people without trial, having forty-four deaths in detention without trial is not behaving like a Western democracy.'

The second argument used by the government in the sanctions debate, was that the hostility aimed at South Africa was engendered by self-interest. I agreed that most countries have policies dictated by self-interest. But it was also true that South Africa provided one of those rare opportunities in politics where expediency coincided with a just cause – the removal of race discrimination. Was it not time, I asked, to give that overworked word 'patriotism' its true meaning; when your country is wrong, put it right and when your country is right, keep it right?

In 1984 I was in the United States and witnessed the landslide victory of Reagan and the Republican Party. When I was interviewed about it by a South African correspondent, I commented that no doubt the champagne corks were popping in Pretoria, misguidedly I felt, because to my mind the Democrats, in disarray, would be looking around for a rallying point. South Africa and apartheid was one obvious option.

I wasn't far wrong. The sanctions lobby in Congress became much more influential. Randall Robinson's Trans Africa organisation (a pro-ANC pro-sanctions lobby of Congress) became more vocal in its demand for punitive measures, and the hassle factor at shareholders' meetings on the issue of divestment from South Africa became more pressing. On campuses across the land, the agitation for disinvestment of university pensions and trust funds from companies with South African connections became more vehement. State and city governments denied contracts to firms doing business in or with South Africa.

My warnings fell on deaf ears, of course, and over the next ten years, every time I went overseas I saw to my dismay that there was an escalation of the campaign for punitive economic sanctions against South Africa. Other factors were also operating to reduce economic growth in the country, such as dwindling confidence in South Africa as an investment risk, which – rather than moral strictures – was the reason for Chase Manhattan Bank's refusal to roll over its loan in June 1986. Although I knew that my arguments against economic sanctions were earning me hostility at home among former allies and friends, and engendered bewilderment abroad, I felt it was absolutely essential to continue to argue. I confess, though, that there were times when I felt that since no advances had been made by the government to remove discriminatory practices, it was absurd for me to go on bashing my head against a stone wall.

Speaking on campuses or to the Council on Foreign Relations or any other organisation in the United States, and in writing articles against sanctions for influential newspapers, such as the *New York Times Magazine*, I emphasised that I understood the sincerity of the moral outrage against apartheid and discriminatory practices in South Africa. After all had I not been fighting them since my first entrance into Parliament back in 1953? But I did not believe that measures which would wreck the economy and reduce the country to chaos could improve the situation. I understood the desire for punitive action – how often had I not sat in parliament and prayed for divine retribution; but alas it soon became obvious, if one lived in South Africa, that divine retribution was not selective, and that the very people one was hoping to help would be adversely affected by punitive measures. For that reason the implementation of sanctions, which could only cause the economy to shrink and unemployment to increase, was not the answer. The population explosion – around three per cent per year in the case of Black people – meant that jobs had to be provided for 400,000 young Black people who came into the labour market each year. If these jobs could not be provided, South Africa would face an era of increased poverty, violence and crime. Moreover, South Africa's neighbouring states were more or less dependent on her for job opportunities, for electric power and for the use of ports and transport. Any action taken to affect the economy adversely would inevitably have repercussions in these states. This was why these countries, although demanding sanctions, were continuing to trade briskly with South Africa.

It was true that many Blacks in South Africa felt that economic sanctions were the only lever to pressurise the government into making changes. In addition, some Black leaders, such as Archbishop Desmond Tutu, averred that 'Blacks are suffering so much already that a little more suffering caused by unemployment would not make any difference.' I disagreed. There is no social security safety net in South Africa – no dole and no food stamps. Unemployment was a dire experience for vast numbers of workers not covered by the unemployment insurance fund. To maintain existing jobs and create more jobs was a commitment of every candidate in the US at election time. Why could this objective be disregarded in the case of South Africa? Survey after survey showed that the answer was 'No' when the question was posed, 'Do you approve of economic sanctions if your own job is in jeopardy?' The destruction of apartheid was not at issue; that was common cause. The issue was the strategy to be employed.

Certainly there was justification in the challenge by Archbishop

Tutu, that those who were against sanctions must suggest an alternative means of forcing the government to make necessary changes. My view was that it was economic growth which would empower Black workers and give their trade unions the muscle to use the only effective weapon at their disposal: industrial action. This was very different from economic sanctions because strikes, stayaways and boycotts could be abandoned or reversed when their objective had been achieved, whereas lost markets were not readily regained. When companies disinvested from South Africa, they invested elsewhere and were unlikely to rush back when the political climate had altered, as the Rhodesia-Zimbabwe experience demonstrated. Furthermore, where overseas companies had sold out to South African buyers, generally at fire-sale prices, their social responsibility programmes such as training Black employees for managerial positions, extending loans for housing, or providing educational scholarships for their children, were often reduced, as the US Sullivan Code was no longer enforceable.[2]

Sanctions was one of the few issues on which I differed from Desmond Tutu (who called me his 'dear child' though I am fourteen years older than he is!). For many years we worked together on prison cases and those involving detention without trial. I objected several times to the government's refusal to grant him a South African passport. When Tutu and I were both nominated for the Nobel Peace Prize in 1983, the press asked each of us what we thought about this. I said I didn't think either of us deserved the prize for we were simply doing our jobs. Tutu said he wouldn't mind sharing the prize with me. The following year he was the Nobel Laureate, and did not have to share it with anyone.

We had one other serious disagreement apart from sanctions: his statement to an American Jewish Committee delegation for whom I had arranged a meeting with him in October 1988, that apartheid was the equivalent of the Nazi holocaust. The delegation and I objected strongly to this assertion. (I subsequently objected to a similar statement made by Nelson Mandela.)

I cannot claim always to have convinced my audiences about the counterproductive effect of sanctions. In the UK, I lost one and won one. At the Oxford Union in a debate against Donald Woods and General Garba of Nigeria, Chett Crocker (Reagan's Under-Secretary for African Affairs and the advocate of constructive engagement) and I were defeated. At the Cambridge Union, however, I won against Bishop Trevor Huddleston.

On my visits to universities in the States I encountered surprise and disappointment because I opposed sanctions, but I was usually given a courteous hearing on the campuses, thanks to my anti-apartheid track record. Now and then, however, I was assailed by angry students, almost invariably led by Black South African exiles. This happened when I was invited to visit Wesleyan University in Connecticut as a Baldwin Fellow in 1989; the exiles organised a protest against my appearance on the campus. Pamphlets were distributed the day before I was due to speak, depicting me as a tool of the capitalist oppressors, and grossly distorting a remark I had frequently made in Parliament. I used to taunt the government for using me as 'Exhibit A for democracy' by allowing me to go abroad and criticise the apartheid regime. The pamphlets proclaimed: 'Democracy flourishes in South Africa – Helen Suzman.'

The venue on campus chosen for my meeting was too small to accommodate the large crowd which arrived, including pickets with hostile messages. There was a comical scene as audience, pickets, chairman and speaker trailed across to a larger hall in the chapel, which also proved too small; the meeting was further delayed while those outside hammered on the doors. Eventually the overflow was invited to come inside and sit behind me on the floor of the platform. I delivered my speech without interruption, fielded questions from the exiles, and gave them the benefit of my opinion regarding their gross distortions. I got a good hand from the audience.

During the 1986 session of Parliament, the visit of the Eminent Persons Group (EPG) took place. It was a seven-person committee of enquiry sent out by the Commonwealth nations after their summit meeting in the Bahamas in October 1985, and included Malcolm Fraser, former Prime Minister of Australia. The objective was to acquire firsthand knowledge of the South African situation, and to ascertain whether further sanctions should be imposed if South Africa did not announce its intention to dismantle apartheid, release Nelson Mandela and other political prisoners, unban the ANC, and end the state of emergency. Both sides should agree to the suspension of violence, to facilitate dialogue to establish a non-racial representative government. The EPG spent six months in South Africa, meeting people to the right, left and centre of the political spectrum, and a host of other organisations. The group met Mandela in prison twice.

They reached unanimous conclusions which were highly critical of the policy of the South African government, and urged various reforms. No progress was reported regarding any of the original steps the EPG had urged the government to take. Even though the state of emergency was lifted, the EPG concluded that autocratic powers remained and indeed were further strengthened during the visit of the group by stringent amendments to the Internal Security Act and the Public Safety Act. Furthermore, the EPG was understandably angered by the fact that while they were in South Africa compiling their report, the South African Air Force conducted widely condemned bombing attacks on alleged ANC bases in Maputo and on the capitals of three neighbouring Commonwealth states, Zimbabwe, Botswana and Zambia. The EPG reported that its mission was a failure and recommended that consideration be given to further punitive measures, including a ban on air links with South Africa.

I took issue with the EPG on several counts. It virtually ignored the existence of the broad middle ground in South Africa, consisting of millions of Black and White South Africans who desperately wanted the disappearance of apartheid, but who did not want a wrecked economy which would be extremely difficult to revitalise and would result in increased unemployment, poverty, crime and violence.

Moreover, the EPG barely acknowledged the existence of the White official opposition, which had unequivocally fought apartheid for decades. In a few brief phrases, it dismissed the Progressive Federal Party, despite the fact that a substantial section of the electorate had voted for the PFP in 1981 and thus for the policy advocated by EPG – the ending of apartheid and the establishment of a representative non-racial government with protection for fundamental human rights.

At a subsequent meeting with Fraser at a conference in England, I asked him why the EPG had ignored our existence. He replied that they saw no point 'in giving any credibility to people who profited from the apartheid system'. Meanwhile, I pointed out, Australia was grabbing our export market for coal, which had been closed by sanctions, resulting in the unemployment of thousands of Blacks.

The ultimate paragraph in the EPG report was untrue and naive. It said that the question before the heads of government was, 'Not whether such measures (that is sanctions) will compel change; it is already the case that their absence and Pretoria's belief that they need not be feared, defers change.' This was not true. Significant changes had begun from the end of the 1970s, because of the pressures which had built up inside South Africa, such as Black resistance and the prohibitive cost of attempting to maintain segregation in an economically integrated society. (Which is not to imply that apartheid had disappeared.)

I took issue with Fraser on another score. In an article in *The Times*, Fraser argued that the alternative to sanctions was full-scale guerrilla war from which a Marxist government would emerge which would nationalise everything in sight. Ironically enough, State President P. W. Botha used a mirror image of the same argument, that is that a transfer of power to the ANC would result in a Marxist regime, the end of free enterprise and of White survival. Fraser and many people in South Africa and overseas believed, it seemed, that a short, sharp dose of sanctions would cause the fall of the Nationalist government and its replacement by a non-racial democracy. They harboured the same misconception that Harold Wilson had about Ian Smith and UDI in Rhodesia –that it would take weeks rather than months to end the Smith regime. In the event, it took fifteen years and cost 30,000 lives.

I told my constituents at my 1986 Report-Back meeting that what with the EPG, the Commonwealth Summit, the European Community and the US Congress, I had to concede that the battle against sanctions, about which I had warned Parliament with monotonous regularity since 1978, was a lost cause. Notwithstanding the validity of the arguments about the effects on the entire economy of southern Africa, and irrespective of the sombre spectre of mass unemployment in South Africa, sanctions were upon us. I believed a long, tough haul lay ahead and the challenge was to knuckle down to the sheer hard work of political conversion, to convince the White electorate to get rid of the government which had brought South Africa to its present sorry state. They had to be told that it was not the drought, not the locusts, not the communists, but apartheid which had caused chaos at home and isolation abroad. Conversion, I said, was our one hope of avoiding both the bloodbath predicted by the EPG and the National Party government's miserable path of attrition. It was all to no avail (until the advent of State President de Klerk in 1990).

My campaign against sanctions continued throughout the eighties. I wrote articles for the *New York Times Magazine*, and in *Op Ed*, for the *Washington Post*, and for *The Times*. I gave numerous television and press interviews at home and abroad, before and after de Klerk became State President. And I continued to do so after I had retired from Parliament. In July 1991 the Johannesburg *Star* published an article of mine entitled 'Curing the Disease but Killing the Patient', which encapsulated my sentiments on sanctions.

The British ambassador, Sir Robin Renwick, was both a friend and an ally throughout his term of office in South Africa. He exercised considerable influence across the whole political spectrum, having formed close relationships with Black leaders, and having won the trust of the Nationalist Cabinet who appreciated his representing a government which steadfastly refused to impose sanctions on South Africa.

I have no doubt that it was my attitude to sanctions that accounted for Mrs Thatcher's readiness to meet me, and during her premiership, three meetings were arranged at 10 Downing Street. I found her extremely well informed and quite unshaken by the hostility her views on sanctions had engendered at Commonwealth meetings. South Africa has reason to be grateful to her for her determined stand on this issue. I personally admired her obvious intelligence and her achievement in attaining the highest political position in a country well stocked with male chauvinists.

In October 1989 a journalist interviewing me for the *Observer* asked me what the difference was between Mrs Thatcher and me since we were both against sanctions, were tough and did not falter. My reply was simple: 'Mrs Thatcher is in power. I have never been in power – quite a difference!'

Judging by her performance when she visited South Africa in 1991 after being deposed as Prime Minister, her stamina is remarkable. I spent most of one day in Johannesburg with her, visiting Soweto, Baragwanath Hospital, the offices of the British Council, and meeting people in charge of the many projects run by the consulate. She was warmly welcomed everywhere, despite the opposition to her visit by the ANC. She lunched at my house and had serious discussions with three prominent South Africans – Richard Steyn, editor of the *Star*, Murray Hofmeyr of Johannesburg Consolidated Investment (JCI) and Van Zyl Slabbert of Idasa. She went on to the Rand Afrikaans University to receive an honorary degree and to make a speech. I was with her throughout except for the visit to RAU, and was totally exhausted at the end of the evening, after a private dinner party at the Oppenheimers' during which she made another speech. Mrs Thatcher was still full of bounce. She left at dawn the next day for Natal and meetings with Chief Minister Buthelezi of KwaZulu. Two days later she was in the USSR, lending support to Mr Gorbachev. Her powers of endurance and her courage are undeniable. What she lacks is a sense of humour.

To what extent sanctions were responsible for the dismantling of apartheid is still a contentious issue. Those against sanctions, including myself, concede that they expedited the process, but also think that the claim of the pro-sanctions lobby, that their imposition was the major reason for de Klerk's about-turn, ignored many factors.

One of them was the demise of communism in the USSR and Eastern Europe which deprived the National Party government of its contention that it was the main bulwark against communism on the African continent. The justification of arbitrary measures as a defence against the 'total onslaught' of communism could no longer be used.

Another was that many major changes took place before the Anti-Apartheid Act with its widely ranging trade and other strictures was passed by the American Congress in November 1986 and before the European Community increased sanctions against South Africa.

Finally, the escalating resistance of Blacks, Coloureds and Indians is not given the credit it deserves in undermining the apartheid system.

But the argument about the efficacy or otherwise of sanctions, disinvestment and divestment is now irrelevant to the task at hand. A high price was paid in economic terms by the thousands of people who lost their jobs in the labour-intensive sectors of the economy such as agriculture and coal mining, and in an area like Port Elizabeth in the Eastern Cape where economic devastation followed divestment by the American motor companies. Recovery of the economy, creation of jobs, provision of housing and education must now be the priority consideration. And those countries, organisations and individuals which advocated punitive measures should now surely accept some responsibility to encourage investment, to stimulate economic activity and to exert their influence to rescue South Africa from the poverty and violence engulfing the country. Inheriting a wasteland will not benefit any of the people of South Africa.

15

The End of
My Parliamentary Career

In 1989 I decided not to stand for Parliament in the forthcoming September election. There were several reasons for my decision, and the first concerned the further transformation of my party.

In that year the Progressive Federal Party merged with two small opposition groups: the Independent Party led by Dr Denis Worrall, former South African ambassador to the UK, and the other, the National Democratic Movement led by Wynand Malan MP, who had defected from the Nats three years previously.

My longstanding friendship with Zach de Beer was under considerable stress over this merger. It was my firm opinion that the leadership of the new party – the Democratic Party – belonged irrefutably to him as leader of the PFP. The PFP had seventeen seats in Parliament, Malan's party three, and Worrall's none. Only the PFP had grassroots support at the time of the merger and was financially solvent; thus, its claim to the leadership of the Democratic Party was, I felt, beyond question. However, the PFP negotiators gave way and a troika was formed with shared leadership by de Beer, Malan and Worrall.

My friend Ray Swart made a similar decision. He too was infuriated by snide comments made by the newcomers who said they did not want to be 'the Progressive Party in drag', and by their determination to expunge the 'Prog image'. We believed the Prog image should be held in high regard because of its long, proud record of fighting for civil rights and against racial discrimination, at a time when our detractors had supported either the United Party, with its messy, equivocal race policy, or the Nationalists, with their ruthless disregard for the human misery they caused over many years. Ironically, some of the detractors later left the Democratic Party and joined the ANC.

Another reason for not standing for re-election in 1989 was that I had been the Member of Parliament for Houghton for thirty-six consecutive years and was rising seventy-two years of age. After P. W. Botha had left Parliament to become State President in 1984, I became the longest-serving MP in the House of Assembly. I always believed that it was a good idea to leave while people still thought I ought to stay, rather than waiting until they wondered how to get rid of me. Now was the time to make way for a younger person to represent Houghton, and I had a successor in mind who, I knew, would uphold the values I had helped to keep alive over so many years. My choice was Irene Menell, who had been the provincial councillor for the constituency for nine years and its able chairperson for many years.

The advice given by Denis Healey in his autobiography, *The Time of My Life*, that you should never resign until you know the name of your successor, proved only too apt.

In the event, after much political wrangling, she was defeated by an energetic young lawyer.

At the beginning of the 1989 session there were strong indications of fundamental change in National Party policy under the new leader, F. W. de Klerk, Minister of National Education. Botha had suffered a stroke and had reluctantly retired as leader of the party though he did not give up the State Presidency until August 1989.

My relationship with the new leader was very different from that with his predecessor. Although de Klerk was considered a member of the right wing in the National Party caucus, he always maintained a friendly and courteous attitude to me. I did not have a great deal to do with him in his capacity as Cabinet Minister, as the portfolios he handled were not my special interest. Three instances of personal contact remain in my memory, however.

The first was in June 1974, when I was invited to address a meeting of the Rapportryers Korps (Dispatch-riders Corps) – a Nationalist organisation, an offshot of the Broederbond – probably at de Klerk's suggestion, in his constituency of Vereeniging in the southern Transvaal. He introduced me in glowing terms, while making it clear that his political views and mine were very different. I remember it was a freezing night in mid-winter. The hall was unheated and we all sat in our coats throughout the proceedings. I made a strong speech advocating radical change and equal opportunity for all. I said we had the choice of facing up to the challenges of modern Africa or enduring a bitter, embattled future. I cannot claim that my oratory influenced those hardline apartheid-minded 'dispatch-riders' who were determined to maintain White domination at all costs. One day however I shall remind the State President of my prophetic words, uttered in his own bailiwick nearly twenty years ago.

The second occasion was at a lunch given by the Speaker shortly before the opening of the 1989 parliamentary session. I was included, presumably because I was the oldest inhabitant. The other guests were two Cabinet Ministers, their wives and the Chief Whip of the National Party. I was seated next to Mr de Klerk. In the course of conversation he asked me why people thought he was 'verkrampt' [reactionary]. 'Because you never make a verligte [enlightened] speech,' I replied.

The following Friday, 3 February 1989, on the first occasion he addressed Parliament in his capacity as leader of the government and as Acting State President, de Klerk made a surprisingly enlightened speech. He said it was the government's aim 'to realise full civil rights for all South Africans' and that the government 'is striving for a democratic system in which no community is dominated by another, or feels itself threatened or excluded'.[1] This uncharacteristic policy statement was not in any way due to my remark at the lunch, since the speech must already have been written, but I certainly detected a twinkle when I caught his eye as he spoke.

A third encounter was when I was about to retire from Parliament. I phoned his secretary and said I would like to come across to his office to say goodbye. She consulted him and he said I should come at once. I thought the visit would be brief; instead, we chatted for about forty minutes, mainly about the future. My final words to him were, 'Don't forget that checks and balances are necessary to prevent abuse of power by the majority.' 'Ah,' said de

Klerk, 'I see you have become a Nat.' 'Not at all,' I replied, 'you have become a Young Prog.'

On 18 May I made a speech which was in effect my farewell to my parliamentary colleagues (although not my final word in the House). I took the opportunity to welcome these indications of the 'new South Africa':

> I have to admit, without actually saying 'I told you so', that it has been a source of considerable satisfaction to me, particularly over the past ten years, to have been present in Parliament when many of the laws which I opposed when they were introduced, have been repealed or amended, years later in most cases.
>
> I have to predict today that as a result of economic forces, and increasing Black resistance and pressures which will be put upon the government by the opponents of apartheid, that many more of the laws that prop up the apartheid system will in fact be repealed in the future.

While welcoming his enlightened statement of intent, I warned de Klerk that this had now to be translated into reality. I did not consider him a starry-eyed liberal but a pragmatic, intelligent man who realised that for South Africa to flourish on the African continent, the country's interests had to be put above the interests of the National Party. This meant that he could not tailor his party's election propaganda to pander to the prejudices of the lowest common denominator in South African politics – that is, the racist. One could understand his earlier reluctance to commit himself to specific reforms, since he did not have the ultimate authority as long as the chain of command in the National Party, and indeed in the country itself, was in doubt. Not so any more however:

> As an old African saying has it: 'You should not argue with the crocodile if you are still in the water.' The State President designate, is, I believe, no longer in the water. He has both feet on the banks of the river and he is in no danger of being dragged down by the crocodile.[2] He should now go for it. He should take the gap, so to speak. He should tell us and the world what he definitely will do, as soon as he takes office, to restore peace at home and the respectability of South Africa abroad. In the meantime, he must use his power to prevent all offensive actions by the state from taking place. Deaths in detention, more blatant abrogation of due process, more hangings, more forced

removals are key provocative issues that must be avoided at all costs . . .

I concluded by saying that the past thirty-five years had been personally very rewarding:

> I respect the institution of Parliament, for, properly used, it is the premier forum of the land . . . I have had the unique experience of having a ringside seat from which to watch, and indeed to participate in, the making of over three and a half decades of South Africa's history . . . Certainly there have been times of intense frustration, and there have been times of crashing boredom, but there have also been some very interesting times. There have been many opportunities to meet people I would otherwise never have met, both at home and abroad, and thereby to make friendships which I shall always cherish. [3]

I thanked my own staff, the secretaries to Parliament, other members of the parliamentary staff, government officials, the press and my constituents.

Throughout that last session I had been trying to persuade the Speaker (Louis le Grange) to allow me to bring a motion of censure against a judge, J. J. Strydom, who had given a derisory sentence to two White farmers who had beaten a Black employee to death. At the very end of the session, having had the assistance of senior counsel at the Johannesburg Bar, I was given permission to introduce this motion and the Chief Whip of the National Party set aside a morning for Parliament to debate it. Two Conservative Party members attempted to persuade the Acting Speaker to rule my motion out of order; he declined to do so.

This was to be my last opportunity to address Parliament. I began by emphasising that only a gross perversion of the law justified my action, since like other Members, I supported the principle of the independence of the judiciary. [4] But this was indeed such a case.

Erick Sambo, a labourer employed by Jacobus Vorster on his farm, caused the death of one puppy and the maiming of another – both belonging to Vorster – by starting the motor of a tractor under which the puppies were lying, although he had been warned not to do so. Shortly after this, he fled the farm and some two months later he was found walking on the roadside by Vorster and his friend Petrus Leonard. He was abducted to the farm and there beaten by Vorster and Leonard and four farm labourers ordered by Vorster to beat him with sticks. Sambo was handcuffed around the trunk of a tree where he was left overnight. The following day he was again assaulted, then taken in a critical state to the police station, where he died shortly afterwards.

A postmortem established that the cause of death was the numerous and very severe injuries Sambo sustained while he was being assaulted. The summation of the district surgeon who performed the postmortem included descriptions of 'massiewe besering' [massive injury] and 'massiewe aanranding' [massive assault] of various parts of Sambo's body. His head, back, buttocks and liver were all brutally damaged . . .

The sentence passed on Vorster by Judge Strydom was five years' imprisonment, wholly suspended for five years on condition that the accused was not convicted of a similar offence during that period, and a fine of R3000 (£740) or twelve months' imprisonment, the fine to be paid in instalments of R250 per month.

Vorster was instructed to pay the widow of the deceased and his five dependent children the sum of R130 per month for a period of sixty months. (In fact, this money, it appeared, would not be paid to the deceased's wife, as by mistake it was ordered to be paid to his common-law wife, the woman he was living with on the farm. However, the publicity given to the case in Canada by Bill Schiller, the correspondent in South Africa of the *Toronto Star*, resulted in a considerable sum of money being collected there and delivered to the Sambo widow.)

The second accused, Leonard, was sentenced to a fine of R500 or three months' imprisonment.

I said that the entire judgement was a travesty of justice, and would adversely affect race relations in South Africa and the country's reputation abroad. It had led to unprecedented condemnation by the Johannesburg Bar Council, by the official journal of the Law Society and by an eminent senior advocate, I. A. Maisels. I added that one could but speculate on the sentence Judge Strydom would have passed had the victim been a White man and the accused two Black men.

After I had finished my speech, the Minister of Justice, Kobie Coetsee, made a number of sarcastic remarks about me and delivered a lengthy argument based on British law. He also made the extraordinary submission that the accused would suffer humiliation because he, a White man, had been sentenced to work for five years to support a Black woman. 'Vorster's ego and self esteem will undoubtedly suffer,'[5] said Coetsee, evidently thinking he had made a telling point. I had the able support of two lawyers in the Democratic Party – Harry Schwarz and Ray Swart – but the motion of censure was not carried. It was however much in keeping with my years of confrontation with the apartheid government.

It now remained for me to give my final Report-Back meeting, which took place on 26 June 1989, at the usual venue, the Houghton Primary School hall. As always, it was packed to overflowing, standing room only. The vote of thanks was proposed by my old friend and adviser, Advocate Isie Maisels, Senior Counsel – a keen supporter who had often spoken on Prog platforms.

It was a somewhat sad and emotional occasion for me, and for my old faithfuls who turned up by the score. Taking leave of the people who had supported me unwaveringly over so many hard-fought elections was not easy. The gloom was relieved by the unexpected appearance at the back of the crowded hall of the satirist Pieter-Dirk Uys, easily recognisable despite his disguise as one of his favourite victims – P. W. Botha, the recently retired State President. Pieter, an old friend and long-time supporter, pushed his way down the crowded aisle to the platform and presented me with a single chrysanthemum. Taking the micro-phone, he said plaintively in Botha's unpleasant voice, 'Why does Mrs Suzman have such nice farewell parties and mine are so awful?'

Then I spoke to my constituents for the last time. I reminded them of issues which I could claim I was the first MP to tackle, and traced other landmarks in my career. I concluded my speech with the story of dining out one night in Cape Town, and my host, trying to present me in a favourable light to his Black waiter, saying, 'Josiah, do you know this lady? She is Mrs Suzman. She spends all her time trying to help your people.' Josiah looked at me disdainfully and said, 'She waste her time.'

Well, did I waste my time? I don't think so. I think it has been a tremendous privilege to have been in Parliament, to have played a part in keeping values alive which most of us believe in, to have allowed nothing to go by default, to have had the opportunity for face-to-face confrontations with the government about its offensive actions, and especially to have been able to intercede on behalf of victims of apartheid or of police action by virtue of being a Member of Parliament.

The accolades that poured in from heads of state overseas and from South Africans in all walks of life were overwhelming. All were warm in their acknowledgment of my years of opposition to apartheid and my efforts to champion basic liberties and the rule of law. Even my erstwhile opponents in the House had good words to say about me. The press, ever supportive, published warm comments about my parliamentary career.

Especially gratifying was the announcement that the Ernest Oppenheimer Trust, the Chairman's Fund of the Anglo American Corporation and De Beers Corporation, would provide the funds to establish 'The Helen Suzman Chair of Political Economy' at Wits University. The advertisement for the post specified that 'Applicants for the Chair should have a strong record of research, publication, leadership, and should share a sympathy with the ideals expressed by Mrs Helen Suzman.' Professor Charles Simkins is the incumbent.

A handsome *Festschrift* entitled *Values Alive*, initiated by Irene Menell and edited by Dr Robin Lee, was presented to me by Harry Oppenheimer at a party held in the Oppenheimer Library.[6] The proceeds of the sale of the book were to augment the fund I had set up (with the golden handshake I received on retirement) to provide scholarships for Black, Coloured and Indian women at Wits — blatant female chauvinism, but justified, I felt, by the knowledge that if money for education was short, the male members in the family were usually favoured.

Most unexpected was the announcement made at the United Nations General Assembly on 27 September 1989 by the then Foreign and Commonwealth Secretary, the Right Honourable John Major MP:

Many brave men and women in South Africa have struggled peacefully and persistently against apartheid. If I single out Helen Suzman, it is because, for forty years, often alone in the South African Parliament, often in the face of threat and intimidation, she fought for freedom. She is in London today. I am pleased to tell the Assembly that she will be honoured by Her Majesty the Queen with one of our highest awards for all she has done in the campaign for justice. In her name, Britain will be funding a new scholarship scheme, soon bringing to 1000 the number of our annual scholarships for Black Africans.

The full details of the announcement made in London today are as follows: The Queen has been pleased to approve a recommendation by the Secretary of State for Foreign and Commonwealth Affairs that Mrs Helen Suzman, a former Member of the South African Parliament, be appointed an Honorary Dame Commander of the Most Excellent Order of the British Empire for her services in fostering relations between Britain and South Africa.

On the morning of 31 October 1989 I went to Buckingham Palace, accompanied by Mosie and Francie, to receive the award of Honorary Dame Commander of the Civil Division of the Order of the British Empire. It was, of course, a momentous occasion for me.

The Queen stood for a solid two hours, conferring awards to citizens being honoured for meritorious service in all branches of British life. Her Majesty had a personal message for each one of us: to me she said how pleased she was to make the award and asked whether I had come to England especially to receive it. I had to say 'no', but added that I had stayed on in London for the occasion. At the end of the morning's proceedings, she showed no sign of fatigue, despite the demanding programme of acknowledging each recipient in person.

Because I am not a British subject, I am not entitled to be called Dame Helen. I have had the scroll framed and it has pride of place in my study at 'Blue Haze'. The medal is in the cupboard together with the scrolls of my honorary degrees and other memorabilia of my life as a public representative.

My last official visit to Parliament, on 11 February 1991, was to attend the small ceremony of acceptance of the recently commissioned portrait of myself. It was to hang in solitary splendour in the corridor that links the old House of Assembly with the new tri-cameral debating chamber, with a plaque beneath it inscribed, in English and Afrikaans, 'Helen Suzman, MP (Houghton) 1953– 1989' – the only 'commoner' to join the dour visages of former Governors-General, State Presidents, Prime Ministers, Speakers and Cabinet Ministers, hanging elsewhere in those hallowed premises.

To mark the occasion there was a small gathering of my former colleagues, the artist, Fleur Ferri and other friends including the British ambassador, Sir Robin Renwick and his wife Annie; the Right Honourable Lynda Chalker, Minister for Overseas Development (now Baroness Chalker), and my daughter Francie. Colin Eglin, on whose initiative the portrait had been commissioned, made an affectionate speech, and the Acting Speaker, Dr Helgard van Rensburg, a one-time vociferous opponent, described my parliamentary career in glowing terms. My own speech was less gracious for I could not resist reminding van Rensburg that when I opposed bills which were now being repealed in the interests of the 'New South Africa', he and his fellow Nationalist MPs had accused me of being unpatriotic, a sickly humanist and a dangerous subversive.

It is a moot point whether my portrait, or indeed the others, will survive in the New South Africa. They may well be relegated to the cellar.

It would leave a false impression to describe those thirty-six years in Parliament as one long dreary slog. During the sessions, on weekends when I was in Cape Town, I played golf or went to the beach. I gave up golf only about four years ago, as by then my game had deteriorated to a frustrating extent. The winning ethic drummed into me by Sister Columba so many years ago persisted – I hated losing. The magnificent Muizenberg beach at False Bay was a regular destination for me and Francie's in-laws, Emily and Jack Jowell. I swam in the warm sea and we all walked for miles along the golden sands. And a game of bridge in the evening usually rounded off those weekends.

Naturally Cape Town during the parliamentary sessions was much taken up with diplomatic functions. All the foreign embassies migrated from Pretoria, the administrative capital, to Cape

Town, the legislative capital. Most did so happily, despite the nuisance of having to keep up two households and to move family, staff and pets back and forth, because Cape Town's natural beauty – its superb beaches, magnificent Table Mountain and lovely inland wine country – offers a great deal of enjoyment during leisure time. Diplomatic dinners occupied many an evening – some very enjoyable, others boring, and many simply an extension of the day's work as my hosts lobbed questions at me, hoping (often in vain) to extract information worth sending home in their diplomatic bags.

The spin-off was the lasting friendships that resulted from so many encounters over the years with the ever-changing occupants of the embassies belonging to the different countries. Apart from Robin Renwick, South Africa was fortunate indeed to have the guidance of two other outstanding ambassadors during the last few traumatic years of transition – Bill Swing, the American ambassador and Immo Stabreit, the German ambassador. On my overseas visits I always renewed my links with former ambassadors and their staff with whom I had had a close relationship during their South African tours of duty.

Whenever possible, I went trout fishing at the lovely stretch of river or in one of the dams at the farm Hiddendale at Dullstroom in the eastern Transvaal, owned by Max Borkum and his partner, Henry Hare. I thought up some of my best *bon mots* for speeches as I walked along the banks – only to find I'd forgotten them when I got back to the cottage. But those excursions kept me sane and I shall be forever grateful to the generous owners of Hiddendale, and also for the end of year visits to their magnificent farm on the borders of the Kruger Game Park. How many people have had the pleasure of seeing seventeen giraffe, in a semi-circle not fifty yards away, blinking their long lashes, as I did on one such visit?

Retirement has not relegated me to the rocking chair. Perhaps now that I am no longer an MP, people think I need occupational therapy, for certainly the number of requests to address organisations and prize-givings or to attend conferences are as numerous as ever. I am frequently asked, both at home and abroad, to give my views on the bewildering political scene of 'the new South Africa'.

Since leaving Parliament I have received eight more honorary degrees – six from British universities and two from the United States, bringing the total to twenty-two. In September 1992 I was presented with a Dor 'L Dor award by the B'Nai B'Rith International (the highly regarded Jewish service organisation) in Washington (introduced by Don McHenry), and later I delivered the Wallenberg Address at the University of Michigan (commemorating Raoul Wallenberg, the heroic Swedish diplomat who saved the lives of thousands of Hungarian Jews during the Nazi onslaught).

I have been the president of the South African Institute for Race Relations since July 1990, more than forty-five years after preparing evidence for the Fagan Commission on behalf of the Institute – the project which launched me into politics, thus bringing my career full circle.

Epilogue

When I look at the future of South Africa, my crystal ball is clouded.

The euphoria that engulfed me (and all other liberals) in February 1990 when State President de Klerk made his commitment 'to create a new South Africa, free of oppression and discrimination' was heightened by the positive steps he took early that year. Nelson Mandela and his fellow prisoners were released; organisations and individuals were unbanned and the state of emergency was lifted. During the next two sessions, laws which had been the foundation stones of apartheid – the Separate Amenities Act, the Land Acts, the Group Areas Act and the Population Registration Act – were repealed. Significant amendments to the Internal Security Act were introduced.

A promising start was made by the Convention for a Democratic South Africa (CODESA) at its first meeting in December 1991. Codesa was sponsored by the Government and attended by delegates from nineteen organisations across the political spectrum, with the exception of the far-right Conservative Party and the PAC and Azanian People's Organisation (AZAPO).

I attended Codesa I as a delegate of the Democratic Party. I was outraged to see how few women delegates were there – about ten out of 228 – and I persuaded the co-chairmen, Judges Ismail Mahomed and Pieter Schabort, to allow me to address the gathering on this example of gender discrimination. Nevertheless, I was also able to say how pleased I was to witness what I had never anticipated I would live to see: a genuine non-racial gathering discussing a genuine non-racial future for South Africa, and empowered to translate its proposals into reality. It was indeed remarkable to observe men who only a few months before had been in prison or in exile chatting amiably with the men responsible for putting them there.

The felicitous Declaration of Intent was signed by all the participants of Codesa I except for Inkatha. There was, alas, no follow-through and the spirit of optimism was shortlived.

After losing two parliamentary by-elections, the government held a referendum (on 17 March 1992) among the White electorate which was asked whether it supported the continuation of the reform process aimed at a new constitution through negotiation. The answer was a resounding 'Yes', with 68.7 per cent in favour, due, some cynics say, to the fear that the South African cricket team would not have been allowed to continue to compete in the World Cup in Australia had the answer been 'No'.

Codesa II then took place, in May 1992. Several important principles were accepted: universal franchise on a Common Voters' Roll; an electoral system incorporating proportional representation; an independent judiciary and a justiciable Bill of Rights. But Codesa II ended in stalemate because no agreement could be reached on a number of constitutional proposals, particularly those relating to regional powers.

A month later, the terrible massacre at Boipatong, a Black township south of Johannesburg, took place. Hostel dwellers attacked township residents. Forty-two people were killed and many more injured. The ANC announced it was withdrawing from Codesa, cancelled all previous agreements it had made there, and stated it would not participate in further negotiations until the government met certain demands. The ANC organised a massive stayaway of two days' duration.

A debate was held at the United Nations on the South African situation; Cyrus Vance and a team of observers were sent out as its representatives.

However, the widespread violence in the Black townships continues, despite Peace Accords and the valiant efforts of the

Goldstone Commission appointed to inquire into public violence and intimidation. The residents there continue to live under the unremitting threat of violence from one quarter or another.

The alarming escalation of ordinary criminal violence is the cause of much anxiety about personal safety. Firms supplying security services in the White suburbs have mushroomed in South Africa – one of the few growth industries in the economy, providing guards, remote-control gates, high walls and rott-weilers. Farmers and their families have been subjected to murderous attacks; every day the press carries reports of armed robbery, murder and the hijacking of vehicles. All this has resulted in a disturbing escalation of right wing activities. The formation of the Volksfront (Peoples' Front) – led by the retired head of the South African Defence Force, General Constand Viljoen (the attentive officer in charge of my Angolan expedition in 1984), together with three other generals, in alliance with the Conservative Party and other organisations, is one manifestation of this development. Fears of a military coup have been expressed, but I believe this to be unlikely.

Contradictory statements issued by the ANC leadership on economic policy, for example on nationalisation, have compounded uncertainty. Another disquieting aspect of ANC policy has been its insistence that sanctions be maintained and investment from overseas discouraged until an interim govern-ment is established. The ANC's strong links with the Communist Party and its threats of mass action have added to the suspension of confidence in the future stability of South Africa.

The end of communist control throughout the USSR and Eastern Europe was interpreted differently in South Africa by the Nationalist government and by its critics from the far left. The Nationalists accepted that they could no longer use the threat of the 'total onslaught' of communism against which the Republic of South Africa stood as a bulwark; Black activists and others refused to accept the failure of communism as a reason for favouring a free-market economy. They proclaimed that the Soviet leaders had made mistakes which they, the Blacks, would not make in a socialist South Africa. And given the fact that relatively few Blacks have gleaned a fair share of the fruits of the capitalist system as it operates in South Africa, it is not surprising that the heady promises of a new economic order, with redistribution of wealth and property would arouse expectations, especially among young Blacks, to astronomical heights. When one takes into consideration the fact that about 50 per cent of Blacks are under the age of twenty-five, it bodes ill for any new government to ignore such expectations.

What is desperately needed is action which will jump-start the stalled economy, and stability and investment are essential for that to happen. We need jobs to take up the slack of all those young and not-so-young unemployed. Without stability, investment and jobs, whoever inherits this country, be it an ANC government or any other, will inherit an ungovernable country inhabited by a generation of undisciplined youths who accept no guidance from parents or teachers.

One thing is certain: negotiations towards a new constitution must proceed, for there is no alternative. The government is on an irreversible track; it cannot reimpose apartheid legislation, states of emergency, detention without trial. And the ANC cannot overthrow the government. It may cause the government to pause and reconsider, but it cannot overthrow the government either by armed struggle or by mass action. Indeed talk of armed struggle is mere rhetoric; Umkhonto we Sizwe (the armed wing of the ANC) is not an army which could defeat the South African Defence Force. Mass action is a potent weapon, but the ultimate damage is a high price to pay, and it is paid not only by government and industry, but also by the workers themselves. The last thing South Africa needs at this juncture is for industry to be turned into a battleground.

Fortunately, 1993 seems to have been accompanied by a more reasonable attitude by the major players. Meetings have taken place between Mandela and de Klerk, Inkatha and ANC, and groups who previously boycotted negotiations are now participating in multi-party talks. The first non-racial election based on universal franchise for a government of national unity is expected to be held in April 1994.

Much remains to be done, however, over and above resolution of constitutional issues. Perhaps above all, South Africa has to develop a culture of democracy. Educating an electorate which has had no experience of free and fair elections is a priority. Only belief that the ballot is secret will counter the intimidation which could jeopardise the impartial outcome of the elections.[1] The ravages of forty years of apartheid have to be dealt with. What to do with those thousands of officials, presently employed in the vast civil service of South Africa, programmed to administer a system based on gross discrimination?

Change also entails rehabilitating a generation of young Blacks who in the aftermath of the Soweto unrest in 1976 refused to attend school. Adherence to the slogan 'Liberation before Education' was enforced ruthlessly by intimidation, 'necklacing' and other brutal measures, and as a result there are hundreds of thousands of functionally illiterate youths, unemployable except in low-paid, unskilled jobs. Adult education and vast state-sponsored employment schemes are suggested, but it will be a long time before positive results emerge.

Providing shelter for the homeless is another overwhelming problem created by the government's refusal over forty years to accept the permanent urbanisation of the Black population. The Urban Foundation estimates that seven million people are living in informal settlements – a euphemism for squatter camps, garages and backyard shacks. A monumental effort is required to cope with this problem and the government have placed huge sums at the disposal of the Independent Development Trust. Provision of land and infrastructure for site and service schemes,[2] and one-off grants to purchase building materials for low-income housing have made a start on the problem. The NIMBY (not in my back yard) syndrome is well in evidence, and settled communities object strongly to any proposal that Black squatters be located in their vicinity.

Overshadowing everything is the widespread poverty and unemployment among Blacks, which will decrease only when the economy produces a growth rate of at least five per cent a year. That depends on a massive injection of investment capital from local sources and from abroad, and that in turn depends on confidence in the stability of the country.

Given all these imponderables and all these seemingly insuperable problems, why do I believe there is hope for a peaceful and prosperous South Africa?

The answer is that South Africa has a solid base of developed infrastructure: roads, railways, airports, ports and communications are excellent. Though not the treasure house the world thinks, South Africa does have valuable mineral resources, sophisticated financial institutions and well-run industrial sectors. It has good agricultural areas (when not ruined by drought) and, best of all, it has many remarkably innovative citizens. Despite all the handicaps imposed by the apartheid regime, there has been, in the words of John Kane-Berman, director of the South African Institute of Race Relations, a 'Silent Revolution' among the Black population which has resulted in the emergence of a significant informal economy of self-employed people. Moreover, I have no doubt that the vast majority of citizens of all races in South Africa want the same things: a better standard of living, good education for their children and equal opportunities for gainful employment, and they want to live in a stable society free of intimidation and violence.

There is good reason to believe that, finally released from the shackles of apartheid, South Africa will become the workshop of the African continent. At peace with itself and its neighbours, it will assume a position of respectability in the comity of nations, able to enhance and enrich not only its own geographic region but the world at large.

Nearly thirty years ago at my Report-Back meeting, I told my constituents that the task of all of us who believed in multiracism in South Africa was to survive. I said: 'Quite inevitably, time is on our side. I am not one of those who think that great changes are around the corner. But I am absolutely certain that we cannot maintain our isolation indefinitely and that sooner or later a settlement will have to be reached between moderates of all races. Apart from external and internal pressures, economics alone will compel this. The immediate present belongs to the extremists, but the future belongs to the moderates.'

A few years ago a former editor of a Nationalist newspaper said: 'We had to try apartheid to show that it would not work.'

Whatever the obstacles, we now have to try democracy to show that it will work.

Acknowledgments

I owe a great debt of gratitude to many people: to my colleagues who advised me when I was the lone Prog; to Jackie Beck my research assistant; to Barbara Mouat who was my secretary at that time, and to Judith Briggs and Louie Kenyon who became my secretaries later. To the secretaries and other members of the parliamentary staff who assisted me in coping with the intricacies of procedure; to the many experts who were ever willing to study Bills and to suggest points for me to use in debate – Professors John Dugard, David Welsh and June Sinclair; and to Professor Nic Olivier and James Selfe of the Progressive Federal Party's research department. Also Ann Bernstein, Geoff Budlender, Raymond Tucker and the ardent women in the Black Sash, to name some of the people whose advice I sought. To Peter Soal, DP MP for Johannesburg North, who never failed to respond to my calls for help in countless situations. And to the late Andrew Savage MP and Lindy Pagden whose support buoyed me up over the years.

To the men and women in the Press Gallery who gave me invaluable coverage over the years, and to the editors such as Laurie Gandar, Raymond Louw and Allister Sparks of the *Rand Daily Mail*, Tony Heard of the *Cape Times*, Ian Wyllie, John O'Malley, John Patten and Harvey Tyson of the Argus Group, Ken Owen of *Business Day*, now editor of the Johannesburg *Sunday Times,* Richard Steyn of the *Natal Witness* (now editor of the *Star*) and Donald Woods of the East London *Daily Dispatch*, Peter Sullivan and David Braun of the *Star*, and Brian Pottinger of the *Sunday Times*, without all of whose support the Progressive Party and I would not have survived.

To the foreign correspondents, such as Joe Lelyveld and Christopher Wren of the *New York Times*, Michael Hornsby of *The Times*, Graham Leach and James Robbins of the BBC, John Carlin of the *Independent*, Vicki Butler and Mallory Selsen of Voice of America, Bruce Nelan of *Time*, Ned Temko of the *Christian Science Monitor*, Robin Wright, Caryl Murphy and Glenn Frankel of the *Washington Post*, Andrew Torchia of Associated Press, Richard Sergay of ABC, and many other friends in the media whose coverage ensured a warm welcome for me abroad.

To Max Borkum, without whom my career would have ended in 1961.

To my other election campaign manager, Irene Menell; to the canvassers who braved the growling rottweilers in Houghton; to my constituents who returned me at election after election; to the provincial councillors and the city councillors in Houghton who looked after local government so efficiently; and to the enthusiastic staff at my constituency office at 38 Ivy Road. And finally to my long suffering family – Mosie and the girls, who had to put up with so much.

In writing this book I was greatly assisted by my ever-patient and competent secretary, Mary Meyer, and by Phyllis Lewsen's painstaking checking of the manuscript. I am also grateful to Professors David Welsh and G.H. le May, and to Joel Mervis who read earlier drafts. My grandson Daniel Jowell contributed the fresh and critical eye of the younger generation. My thanks go too to my zealous editors, Jonathan Segal and Kevin Bourke of Knopf in New York, Jonathan Ball in Johannesburg and Roger Cazalet of Sinclair-Stevenson in London, and especially to Penelope Hoare who spent many hours revising the manuscript with me; and to my unofficial editor, my daughter Francie, whose criticism and advice have been invaluable.

Notes

Foreword

1. So-named because the accused were arrested at the African National Congress's underground headquarters in Rivonia, a suburb north of Johannesburg. Eight of the defendants (six black, one white and one Indian) including Nelson Mandela, were found guilty of sabotage and conspiracy and sentenced to life imprisonment after a seven month trial, which ended in June 1964. Two accused were found not guilty and discharged. Another agreed to give evidence for the state but skipped the country to avoid doing so. (Two others had made a spectacular escape before the trial began.)

1. The Background and Beyond

1. The Pass Laws, which existed long before the Nationalist government came to power, required South African Black men to produce on demand official documents (reference books) which permitted them to be in urban areas. Under the Nationalist government these laws became increasingly restrictive and were extended to Black women.
2. Hansard Vol. 27, col. 8348, 17 June 1969.

3. Opposition Politics – United Party Style

1. Hansard Vol. 83, col. 3576, 17 September 1953.
2. Hansard Vol. 83, col. 3585, 17 September 1953.
3. Hansard Vol. 86, col. 5854, 31 May 1954.
4. Hansard Vol. 101, col. 7364, 5 June 1959.
5. Hansard Vol. 101, col. 6237, 20 May 1959.

4. The Birth of the Progressive Party and Keeping It Alive

1. Hansard Vol. 22, col. 1654, 5 March 1968.

5. Confronting Verwoerd, Vorster and Botha

1. Hansard Vol. 96, col. 150, 23 January 1958.
2. Hansard Vol. 5, col. 2389, 7 March 1963.
3. Hansard Vol. 5, col. 2390, 7 March 1963.
4. Based on the Westminster principle that 'redress of grievance precedes supply' (of money) each Minister gives Parliament the opportunity of criticising his management of his portfolio.
5. Hansard Vol. 107, col. 3616, 24 March 1961.
6. Hansard Vol. 9, col. 139 *et seq.*, 22 January 1964.
7. Hansard Vol. 32, col. 227, 3 February 1971.
8. Hansard Vol. 32, col. 228, 3 February 1971.
9. Hansard Vol. 27, col. 6511 *et seq.*, 23 May 1969.
10. Hansard Vol. 27, col. 6517/18, 23 May 1969.
11. Hansard Vol. 52, col. 5601–3, 16 October 1974.
12. After de Klerk assumed the Presidency, Parliament passed a law which converted to Black all terminology referring to Native or Bantu.
13. Hansard Vol. 15, col. 6243, 18 May 1965.
14. Hansard Vol. 38, col. 5807, 26 April 1972.
15. Hansard Vol. 38, cols 5828 and 5830, 26 April 1972.
16. Hansard Vol. 39, cols 7988–90, 24 May 1972.
17. Hansard Vol. 78, col. 519, 8 December 1978.

6. The Years Alone, 1961–74, I

1. Pejorative Yiddish for Gentile, used by a frequent anonymous correspondent who I gathered had been employed by a Jew.
2. An Afrikaner Nazi sympathiser dropped off the coast of South Africa by a German submarine to sabotage the war effort and assassinate General Smuts. He was captured, sentenced to death, reprieved by Smuts, sentenced to life imprisonment, and released soon after the Nationalist regime took power.
3. Hansard Vol. 5, col. 109, 23 January 1963.
4. Hansard Vol. 5, col. 110, 23 January 1963.
5. Hansard Vol. 6, col. 4672, 24 April 1963.
6. Hansard Vol. 6, col. 4675, 24 April 1963.
7. Hansard Vol. 6, col. 4680, 24 April 1963.
8. Yiddish for non-Jews.
9. Hansard Vol. 8, col. 8195 *et seq.*, 18 June 1963.
10. Hansard Vol. 9, col. 2640, 6 March 1964.
11. Hansard Vol. 9, col. 2642 *et seq.*, 6 March 1964.
12. Hansard Vol. 21, col. 7052, 1 June 1967.
13. Hansard Vol. 21, col. 7114, 2 June 1967.
14. Hansard Vol. 21, col. 7255, 6 June 1967.

The Years Alone, 1961–74, II

1. Hansard Vol. 2, col. 1477, 23 February 1962.
2. Hansard Vol. 103, col. 323, 9 March 1982.
3. Hansard Vol. 13, col. 1077, 12 May 1989.
4. Hansard Vol. 9, col. 1952, 25 February 1964.
5. Hansard Vol. 9, col. 1953–4, 25 February 1964.
6. Hansard Vol. 14, col. 3840, 1 April 1965.
7. Hansard Vol. 14, col. 3841, 1 April 1965.
8. Hansard Vol. 104, col. 3732, 21 March 1960.
9. Hansard Vol. 28, col. 205 *et seq.*, 4 February 1970.
10. In 1990 amendments were introduced which gave full discretion to the courts, previously applicable only if there were extenuating circumstances, and an automatic right of appeal. In 1991 when a moratorium on the death penalty was declared, some 310 people were on death row.
11. Hansard Vol. 73, col. 5481, 24 April 1978.
12. Hansard Vol. 30, col. 3433, 4 September 1970.

7. In and Out of the House: 1961–74

1. Phyllis Lewsen's title for her edition of my speeches in those years. *Helen Suzman's Solo Years*, Johannesburg, 1991.
2. In Lewsen, op. cit., p. 193.
3. Hansard Vol. 27, col. 7114, 2 June 1969.
4. Hansard Vol. 39, col. 6222, 1 May 1972.
5. Hansard Vol. 39, col. 6223, 1 May 1972.
6. Hansard Vol. 44, col. 7339, 23 May 1973.

8. Prisons and Prisoners

1. Breyten Breytenbach, *The True Confessions of an Albino Terrorist*, p. 182 *et seq.*, Taurus, Emmerentia, South Africa, 1984. The book was banned in South Africa shortly after publication.

9. Robben Island – University for Leaders

1. The UDF was a conglomeration of some four hundred organisations formed some years after the ANC and the PAC were banned. Its leaders were mainly Black, Coloured and Indian activists who used it as their major outlet for mass protest and trade union activities.
2. On 2 June 1993, the Appeal Court confirmed Winnie Mandela's conviction on four counts of kidnapping four young black men, but set aside her five-year prison sentence and substituted a R15,000 fine. She was also ordered to pay a total of R15,000 in compensation to the victims. Her conviction and one-year prison sentence on four charges of being an accessory to assault were overturned.

10. Back in Business: Opposition Politics – Prog Style, 1975–7

1. Thelma Henderson, a close friend and Prog colleague, the wife of the Professor of Applied Mathematics; Professor John Dugard of the Law faculty, and Professor Phillip Tobias of the Medical faculty. They, as well as three prominent members of the University Council – Sid Newman, Pinky Hill and Isie Maisels – signed the nomination form.

11. Opposition to Apartheid in and out of Parliament: 1977–87

1. Hansard Vol. 85, col. 86, 4 February 1980.
2. Hansard Vol. 85, col. 240, 6 February 1980.
3. Hansard Vol. 85, col. 833, 14 February 1980.
4. Hansard Vol. 63, col. 10102, 22 June 1976.
5. Hansard Vol. 94, col. 1921 *et seq.*, 25 August 1981.
6. Now Executive Director, Development Strategy and Policy Unit at the Urban Foundation, established by the business community after the 1976 Soweto unrest to improve the quality of life of urban Blacks.
7. Dr Ramphele went to Cape Town when her banning orders were lifted. She is now Deputy Vice-Chancellor, Student Affairs, at the University of Cape Town.
8. The conversions from rands to pounds reflect the deteriorating value of the rand vis-à-vis the pound and are based on averages over the years. Thus while in 1965 the rand was worth 10/-, by 1991 it was worth only 20 pence. The falling value of the rand clearly mirrors the adverse international image of South Africa.
9. Hansard Vol. 105, col. 853 *et seq.*, 11 February 1983.
10. Hansard Vol. 2, col. 1421, 26 February 1985.
11. Hansard Vol. 2, col. 1422, 26 February 1985.

12. Three Martyrs: Sobukwe; Biko; Aggett

1. Hansard Vol. 6, col. 4652, 24 April 1963.
2. Hansard Vol. 72, col. 116 *et seq.*, 31 January 1978.
3. Hansard Vol. 72, col. 117 *et seq.*, 31 January 1978.
4. Hansard Vol. 72, col. 6804 *et seq.*, 12–17 May 1978.
5. Dr Ivor Lang was appointed Chief District Surgeon in Port Elizabeth in 1985. In an interview in the Johannesburg *Sunday Times* on 6 June 1993 he stated that he has ensured that everyone in prison or in police custody in the area under his authority is protected against police maltreatment. He said his system could be an example to the rest of the country. His colleagues endorse his claims.
6. Hansard Vol. 99, col. 233, 3 February 1982.
7. Hansard Vol. 99, col. 336, 4 February 1982.
8. Hansard Vol. 99, col. 994 *et seq.*, 16 February 1982.

9. Hansard Vol. 99, col. 1040 *et seq.*, 16 February 1982.
10. Hansard Vol. 99, col. 1021, 16 February 1982.

13. The Tri–cameral Parliament – A Flawed Constitution and its Wake

1. Hansard Vol. 3, col. 2828 *et seq.*, 27 March 1985.
2. Hansard Vol. 3, col. 2833 *et seq.*, 27 March 1985.
3. Hansard Vol. 3, col. 4434, 29 April 1985.
4. Hansard Vol. 2, col. 2283, 14 March 1985.
5. Hansard Vol. 10, col. 8423, 16 June 1986.
6. Hansard Vol. 55, col. 659, 12 February 1975.
7. Hansard Vol. 55, col. 482, 10 February 1975.
8. Hansard Vol. 55, col. 508 10 February 1975.
9. Hansard Vol. 55, col. 606, 12 February 1975.

14. Sanctions: Pressure from Without

1. Hansard Vol. 73, col. 3821 *et seq.*, 3 April 1978.
2. The Sullivan code was initiated by a Philadelphian minister of religion to ensure that United States companies investing in South Africa adhered to social responsibility programmes and acceptable labour practices.

15. The End of My Parliamentary Career

1. Hansard Vol. 9, cols 3 and 7, 3 February 1989.
2. P. W. Botha was referred to, pejoratively, as die groot Krokodil [the Big Crocodile]. This was declared unparliamentary by the Speaker.
3. Hansard Vol. 12, col. 9626, 18 May 1989.
4. Hansard Vol. 12, col. 10013 *et seq.*, 23 May 1989.
5. Hansard Vol. 12, col. 10021, 23 May 1989.
6. The contributors were Neville Alexander, Ann Bernstein, John Dugard, Sheena Duncan, Colin Eglin, Laurence Gandar, Nadine Gordimer, E. J. Kahn junior, Ellen Kuzwayo, Joe Latakgomo, Phyllis Lewsen, Irene Menell, Nic Olivier, Harry Oppenheimer, Robin Renwick, June Sinclair, Jan Steyn, David Welsh.

Epilogue

1. Recent research based on the 1985 census figures (adjusted to 1992) estimates that of a total population of 39 million there are about 21 million people in South Africa eligible to vote, i.e. over the age of eighteen) of whom 14 million are black, 4 million are white, 2 million are Coloured and 600,000 are Asian. Ninety per cent of Whites, Coloured and Asian people are urbanised; 45 per cent of Blacks are urbanised. (Figures from J. M. Calitz, Centre of Information Analysis at the Development Bank of Southern Africa, and Reuben Sive, former MP and Democratic Party delimitation expert.)
2. Where land and basic services such as roads, reticulated water and sewerage disposal are provided.

Index